The Politics of Race, Gender
and Sexuality in *The Walking Dead*

CONTRIBUTIONS TO ZOMBIE STUDIES

White Zombie: *Anatomy of a Horror Film.* Gary D. Rhodes. 2001

The Zombie Movie Encyclopedia. Peter Dendle. 2001

American Zombie Gothic: The Rise and Fall (and Rise) of the Walking Dead in Popular Culture. Kyle William Bishop. 2010

Back from the Dead: Remakes of the Romero Zombie Films as Markers of Their Times. Kevin J. Wetmore, Jr. 2011

Generation Zombie: Essays on the Living Dead in Modern Culture. Edited by Stephanie Boluk and Wylie Lenz. 2011

Race, Oppression and the Zombie: Essays on Cross-Cultural Appropriations of the Caribbean Tradition. Edited by Christopher M. Moreman and Cory James Rushton. 2011

Zombies Are Us: Essays on the Humanity of the Walking Dead. Edited by Christopher M. Moreman and Cory James Rushton. 2011

The Zombie Movie Encyclopedia, Volume 2: 2000–2010. Peter Dendle. 2012

Great Zombies in History. Edited by Joe Sergi. 2013 (graphic novel)

Unraveling Resident Evil: *Essays on the Complex Universe of the Games and Films.* Edited by Nadine Farghaly. 2014

"We're All Infected": Essays on AMC's The Walking Dead *and the Fate of the Human.* Edited by Dawn Keetley. 2014

Zombies and Sexuality: Essays on Desire and the Living Dead. Edited by Shaka McGlotten and Steve Jones. 2014

...But If a Zombie Apocalypse Did *Occur: Essays on Medical, Military, Governmental, Ethical, Economic and Other Implications.* Edited by Amy L. Thompson and Antonio S. Thompson. 2015

How Zombies Conquered Popular Culture: The Multifarious Walking Dead in the 21st Century. Kyle William Bishop. 2015

Zombifying a Nation: Race, Gender and the Haitian Loas on Screen. Toni Pressley-Sanon. 2016

Living with Zombies: Society in Apocalypse in Film, Literature and Other Media. Chase Pielak and Alexander H. Cohen. 2017

Romancing the Zombie: Essays on the Undead as Significant "Other." Edited by Ashley Szanter and Jessica K. Richards. 2017

The Written Dead: Essays on the Literary Zombie. Edited by Kyle William Bishop and Angela Tenga. 2017

The Collected Sonnets of William Shakespeare, Zombie. William Shakespeare and Chase Pielak. 2018

Dharma of the Dead: Zombies, Mortality and Buddhist Philosophy. Christopher M. Moreman. 2018

The Politics of Race, Gender and Sexuality in The Walking Dead: *Essays on the Television Series and Comics.* Edited by Elizabeth L. Erwin and Dawn Keetley. 2018

The Subversive Zombie: Social Protest and Gender in Undead Cinema and Television. Elizabeth Aiossa. 2018

The Politics of Race, Gender and Sexuality in *The Walking Dead*

Essays on the Television Series and Comics

Edited By ELIZABETH ERWIN
and DAWN KEETLEY

CONTRIBUTIONS TO ZOMBIE STUDIES
Kyle William Bishop, series editor

McFarland & Company, Inc., Publishers
Jefferson, North Carolina

LIBRARY OF CONGRESS CATALOGUING-IN-PUBLICATION DATA

Names: Erwin, Elizabeth L., 1976– editor. | Keetley, Dawn, 1965– editor.
Title: The politics of race, gender and sexuality in The walking dead : essays on the television series and comics / edited by Elizabeth L. Erwin and Dawn Keetley.
Description: Jefferson, North Carolina : McFarland & Company, Inc., 2018 | Includes bibliographical references and index.
Identifiers: LCCN 2018032819 | ISBN 9781476668499 (softcover : acid free paper) ♾
Subjects: LCSH: Walking dead (Television program) | Walking dead (Comic book) | Race on television. | Gender identity on television. | Sex on television.
Classification: LCC PN1992.77.W25 P65 2018 | DDC 791.45/72—dc23
LC record available at https://lccn.loc.gov/2018032819

BRITISH LIBRARY CATALOGUING DATA ARE AVAILABLE

ISBN (print) 978-1-4766-6849-9
ISBN (ebook) 978-1-4766-3476-0

© 2018 Elizabeth L. Erwin and Dawn Keetley. All rights reserved

No part of this book may be reproduced or transmitted in any form or by any means, electronic or mechanical, including photocopying or recording, or by any information storage and retrieval system, without permission in writing from the publisher.

Front cover image © 2018 iStock

Printed in the United States of America

McFarland & Company, Inc., Publishers
  Box 611, Jefferson, North Carolina 28640
    www.mcfarlandpub.com

Table of Contents

Introduction: Identity Politics in The Walking Dead
    DAWN KEETLEY   1

Arête of Violence: Hypermasculinity as Power Currency in the Post-Apocalyptic Political Economy
    DUSTIN DUNAWAY   11

The Curious Case of T-Dog: A Magical Negro?
    ELEXUS JIONDE   21

The Hyperreal Hillbilly: Horror, Melodrama and Backwoods White Protagonists
    KOM KUNYOSYING *and* CARTER SOLES   31

"There's no niggers anymore… There's us and the dead": Masculinity in a Post-Racial, Post-Apocalyptic America
    BROOKE BENNETT   43

Becoming Glenn: Asian American Masculinity
    HELEN K. HO   54

"Look at the flowers": Meme Culture and the (Re)Centering of Hegemonic Masculinities Through Women Characters
    TIFFANY A. CHRISTIAN   65

A Woman's Work Is Never Done: Mothering and Marriage
    ELIZABETH ERWIN   78

"We ain't ashes": Daryl, Carol and the Burning Away of Traditional Gender Roles
    CATHERINE PUGH   93

Table of Contents

The Beauty of Beth Greene DEBORAH KENNEDY	107
The Sexualized Heroics of Rick and Michonne EMILY ZARKA	119
Rules for Surviving Rape Culture NATALIE WILSON	129
"We can't just ignore the rules": Queer Heterosexualities JOHN R. ZIEGLER	142
Afterword: From Identity Politics to Tribalism DAWN KEETLEY	155
Episode List	165
Bibliography	173
About the Contributors	183
Index	185

Introduction
Identity Politics in The Walking Dead

DAWN KEETLEY

There is an important moment early in the first season of AMC's *The Walking Dead* (2010–present) in which Rick Grimes (who is white) confronts Merle Dixon (who is white) as he is terrorizing his fellow survivors on a rooftop in Atlanta where the group has gone to get supplies. Merle is hurling racial epithets and ends up assaulting T-Dog (who is African American). Rick intervenes, punching Merle and handcuffing him to the roof, telling him, "Things are different now. There are no niggers anymore. No dumb-as-shit, inbred white-trash fools either. Only dark meat and white meat. There's us and the dead. We survive this by pulling together, not apart" ("Guts"). In this scene, the series marks its aim to move beyond the conventional politics of identity that shape pre-apocalyptic America—the politics, that is, of race, class, gender, and sexuality. As Rick articulates it, black and white become "dark meat and white meat," a displacement of race onto a common fate as meat. The characters are caught in the stark binaries of predator and prey, of living and (un)dead—the only differences that matter now. This moment represents the agenda of the series: to represent those differences that drive the politics of identity as increasingly irrelevant in a post-apocalyptic world that pits (all) humans against the hungry dead and in which (all) humans are just different kinds of food.

Despite its reduction of humans to meat, Rick's declaration can be seen as a utopian one—a clarion call for humanity to work together across multiple differences that used to keep people apart. This is how he surely intended it. On the other hand, his claim articulates a rigid division of beings into two (and only two) defining categories. Rick overgeneralizes; he literally carves the world into black and white ("dark meat and white meat"). And the "us" that Rick pits against the dead (the utopian goal of a collective humanity) not surprisingly fails at every moment to hold. "Us" is an infinitely shifting set of traits, alliances, and deadly internecine battles; indeed, it is in this very variety, in its mutable identities and affiliations, that the strength of *The Walking Dead* lies. The series is not without its artistic and narrative failures, certainly. But in a binarized nation, as the U.S. has increasingly become during the run of the series, *The Walking Dead* frequently escapes bifurcated politics, offering representations and points of identification for multiple positions. As the essays in this collection together make clear, *The Walking Dead* is not easy to categorize politically.

This collection joins the robust academic and popular media conversations about the representation of race, sexuality, and gender in both Robert Kirkman's comics (2003–present) and AMC's television series. The tendency in these conversations has been to argue that, for the most part, identity politics in *The Walking Dead* has veered toward the conservative, offering up relatively traditional understandings of masculinity, femininity, heterosexuality, and racial hierarchy. Ashley Barkman, for instance, argues that *The Walking Dead* supports a gendered division of labor rooted in biology, concluding approvingly that the series reinforces as "natural" the idea that "leadership remain in the hands of good men." Abby Graves similarly reads the series as perpetuating "the hierarchical structure of genders known as hegemonic masculinity," but is much more critical of this tendency. Still more harshly, writing of *The Walking Dead*'s "sexist woman problem," Megan Kearns insists that, no, the series is not commenting on "patriarchy and sexist gender tropes" but is instead "a defense of hypermasculinity."[1] Other critics have taken up ways in which the series increasingly idealizes the heterosexual reproductive family, foreclosing alternatives in a world structured by the exigencies of mere survival. Andrea Dulanto, for instance, laments the failure to develop the relationship between Andrea and Michonne, claiming that the series instead "brought us back into the closet."[2] Indeed, later in the season, Andrea appeared to abandon her friendship with Michonne entirely in order to begin a sexual relationship with the Governor. Race in *The Walking Dead* has caused even more controversy, and fans and critics alike have protested what one blogger aptly calls the series' "Black Man Problem"—i.e., "a repeated inability to depict more than one ass-kicking Black man at a time."[3] Despite the increased number of characters of color in later seasons after severe fan backlash against their early sparsity, critics argue that somehow the mantle of leadership (both of the group and in terms of characters' screen time) still seems perennially bestowed on whites.[4]

While critics have discussed the series' undeniable evolution toward less traditional gender and race relations,[5] there is still much more to be said. *The Walking Dead* depicts an encompassing and evolving post-apocalyptic world—and its relations of race, gender, and sexuality (as well as class) are complex and mutable. All of the essays in our collection explore how relationships among the survivors (particularly those based in identity politics) change over the course of time, adapting to the conditions of the new world in ways that still (and always) serve as commentary on our present world. The essays in this collection sometimes agree with the criticism that has been leveled against *The Walking Dead* for its representations of identity politics, but they also challenge that criticism; in either case, they provide alternative ways of understanding relations of gender, race, class, and sexuality, and their inevitably complex intersections in both the TV series and the comics.

In "Arête of Violence: Hypermasculinity as Power Currency in the Post-Apocalyptic Political Economy," Dustin Dunaway uses social exchange theory to explore the nearly seamless power of a hegemonic white masculinity in *The Walking Dead*. Social exchange theory is an economic, social, and behavioral concept that attempts to explain human behavior as a series of exchanges: individuals will make and maintain relationships with other individuals who provide more benefits than they do costs. In the post-apocalyptic world of AMC's *The Walking Dead*, the collapse of a fiat economy (money) shifts the value away from symbolic currency to the direct delivery of goods and services: one's worth is based on what one can directly contribute to his or her social group. When coupled with the existential threat of the walkers, social exchange theory forms the basis for a new political economy in which the ability and willingness *to commit violent acts* is the new, most valuable currency. Because violence equates with manliness, the resulting social structure in *The Walking Dead* becomes a hypermasculine fantasy in which the most violent and masculine characters (even when they are women) are rewarded with leadership positions.

In "The Curious Case of T-Dog: A Magical Negro?" Elexus Jionde also takes up the profound dominance of white hegemonic masculinity in AMC's *The Walking Dead* by looking at one of its casualties: Theodore Douglas, better known as T-Dog. Jionde argues that T-Dog, a black man who exists to aid a white man, is a striking example of the cinematic stereotype of the "magical negro," a stereotype that directly serves the white power structure. While T-Dog epitomizes this stereotype, other black characters (mostly comic originals) do manage to transcend it, suggesting that the "magical negro" trope might be particularly entrenched in film and television. Jionde's essay ends by discussing *The Walking Dead*'s evolution in depicting black people, an evolution in part enabled by T-Dog and his enthusiastic fans.

In "The Hyperreal Hillbilly: Horror, Melodrama and Backwoods White Protagonists," Kom Kunyosying and Carter Soles continue Dunaway's and Jionde's exploration of white masculinity in AMC's series. They argue that, despite making strides toward representing well-rounded characters of color and women, *The Walking Dead* has consistently foregrounded the suffering

4   Introduction

of its white male backwoods protagonists, thus reifying dominant hierarchies and a focus on a beleaguered white masculinity. Daryl Dixon in particular functions as what Kunyosying and Soles call a "hyperreal hillbilly," whose brutal childhood implicitly enhances his survival skills, while those negative attributes stereotypically associated with such an upbringing (such as bigotry) are muted: he is, for instance, egalitarian toward people of color and queers.[6] Daryl's traumas, Kunyosying and Soles point out, are notably highlighted, mainly in terms of the internal turmoil he endures as he performs noble acts for his group. Daryl is thus to be understood through the melodramatic mode in which suffering equals virtue and moral superiority. A poor, rural, culturally maligned white identity thus becomes morally sympathetic within the diegesis of the show. Furthermore, *The Walking Dead* shapes people of color differently than it does the show's white leads. Korean American Glenn Rhee specializes in scurrying around undetected, embodying stereotypes about Asian Americans. And African American protagonists Michonne and Morgan acquire fantastical martial arts abilities disconnected from real-world potency outside of genre films. (As Jionde does, Kunyosying and Soles point out *The Walking Dead*'s unfortunate reliance on the "magical negro" stereotype.) As the show's multiseason arc unfolds, it increasingly foregrounds backwoods white masculinity, giving to Daryl storylines and time that, in the comics, are given to people of color.

In "There's no niggers anymore… There's us and the dead": Masculinity in a Post-Racial, Post-Apocalyptic America," Brooke Bennett, like Jionde and Kunyosying and Soles, explores the fundamentally racialized representations of masculinity in *The Walking Dead*. Bennett contextualizes the importance of Rick Grimes' characterization within the show by focusing on alternative forms of masculinities—namely those of Glenn, Tyreese, and Morgan—which Bennett finds to be more empowered than do Kunyosying and Soles. Her approach takes into consideration "hegemonic masculinity" as outlined by R.W. Connell and James W. Messerschmidt (2005), ultimately turning to Amanda Lotz's (2014) work on male representation within contemporary cable television, which argues that every narrative universe contains its own unique hegemonic masculinity that stands in opposition to the show's subordinated (nonhegemonic) versions of masculinity. Following Lotz, Bennett argues that *The Walking Dead* embodies the narrative's hegemonic white masculinity not through the trope of the "hyperreal hillbilly," as Kunyosying and Soles argue, but through Rick Grimes' "protective paternalism," which legitimates his ever-increasing violence. By analyzing the subordinated masculinities of men of color within the series, namely those of Tyreese, Glenn, and Morgan, Bennett demonstrates that challenges to Rick's way of running things often lead to symbolic punishment. Through those same characters, however, as well as through the increasingly evident flaws of Rick's hegemonic white leadership, some space, however tenuous, is opened up for alternative forms of masculinity embodied by men of color.

Helen K. Ho finds perhaps the greatest space for non-hegemonic, racially-diverse masculinities in AMC's *The Walking Dead*. In "Becoming Glenn: Asian American Masculinity," Ho ultimately argues (like Bennett) that the masculinity of the show's white "heroes" or leaders (Rick Grimes, the Governor, etc.) is demonstrably unsustainable. Their failures allow for a racialized masculinity like Glenn Rhee's to succeed and bring more flexibility to the malleable social, racial, and gender relations of the zombie post-apocalypse. Ho briefly discusses the role of the model minority stereotype in shaping Glenn as an Asian American character on screen, but then she analyzes Glenn as a fighter, lover, and leader in his own right, arguing that Glenn challenges the rigid frameworks imposed by white masculinity and presents an alternative formulation of manhood that is an "exemplar of adaptability." While Glenn's death in season seven ultimately, and troublingly, serves white hegemonic masculinity, his character provided hope that Asian American characters could surpass stereotypes.

For several contributors to this collection (for example, Jionde, Bennett, and Ho), fan culture is an important part of *The Walking Dead* world, and the show's very vocal fans—sometimes through their enthusiasm, sometimes through their anger and outrage—have put significant pressure on the producers as they shape their continuing narrative. In "'Look at the flowers': Meme Culture and the (Re)Centering of Hegemonic Masculinities Through Women Characters," Tiffany A. Christian directly takes up fan culture, specifically the "memes" that circulate around loved (or hated) characters. The meme—usually a still or promotional shot from the show, overlaid with text—provides another layer of commentary on characters and plot developments. In examining meme culture, certain patterns emerge that reflect the ways in which fans relate to characters with regard to gender: fans routinely masculinize central female characters, Christian argues, in ways that perpetuate the dominance of hegemonic masculinities. Many popular memes generated for Michonne and Carol, in particular, connect their continued survival to their masculinity, even hypermasculinity. Feminine-coded character traits and behaviors are relegated to the background or even mocked in memes (as Lori Grimes often is). So, while *The Walking Dead* pays lip service to the idea of a future where one's gender has no bearing on survival, meme creations by fans often work completely un-ironically to re-center hegemonic masculinities.

In "A Woman's Work Is Never Done: Mothering and Marriage," Elizabeth Erwin shifts the attention of the collection to femininity. Erwin takes aim at the criticism that *The Walking Dead* purveys the "female in distress" trope popularized in the horror genre: indeed, women do seem to be pushed into

6 Introduction

conventional feminine roles, thus propelling the overwhelming emphasis on hegemonic masculinity that earlier essays in this collection have described. Erwin argues, however, that far from fitting its characters into conventional feminine roles, AMC's *The Walking Dead* actually offers a subversive depiction of the limitations imposed by the two most traditional roles of women: marriage and motherhood. Examining first the arcs of *The Walking Dead's* three original, visible female characters, Andrea, Lori and Carol, Erwin argues that each character goes through a divestment period in which she steps outside her prescribed (feminine) role in order to achieve independence. Yet, her ability to survive the apocalypse as a contributing member of the community is ultimately dependent upon whether she willingly returns to the role of wife and mother. Those who do return to their conventional roles perish, while those who do not live to fight another day. This narrative is extended in the ongoing stories of Michonne and Maggie. Both characters are beginning to suggest that even though conventional femininity still seems fatal, women may not need to be (hyper)masculine to survive, thus posing an alternative to those contributors (e.g., Dunaway and Christian) who argue that women in *The Walking Dead* become masculinized as the price of survival.

Like Erwin, in "'We ain't ashes': Daryl, Carol and the Burning Away of Traditional Gender Roles," Catherine Pugh examines the characters of Carol Peletier and Daryl Dixon, mapping how, through a series of intense traumas, they each experience a phoenix-like transformation of gender identity that is supported by imagery of fire and wild nature. Pugh's essay suggests that the transgressive politics and topography of the post-apocalyptic landscape sets the stage for a transformation of identity, despite (or because of) repeated suffering. Daryl and Carol are phoenixes, "burning away" (as Carol puts it) their old identities as their roles progress through eight seasons (to date). Carol's transformation progresses through a series of cycles whereby the traditional female roles she is assigned (wife, mother, nurse, teacher/mentor and so on) are systematically destroyed. Daryl's narrative arc, on the other hand, transforms him from rough, hypermasculine "redneck" to a hero who is flexibly able to incorporate traits often seen as feminine (and in this way, Pugh's essay stands as a counterpoint to Kunyosying and Soles' essay, who read Daryl's evolution more negatively in terms of class and race). Daryl and Carol mirror each other as they shape new gendered identities, their relationship catalyzing as well as reflecting the changes they undergo.

In "The Beauty of Beth Greene," Deborah Kennedy offers a quite different view from the other essays in this collection, which all tend to argue that women are to some degree or another masculinized by the exigencies of the post-apocalyptic world. For Kennedy, the character of Beth Greene, unique to the televised version of *The Walking Dead*, brings into focus particular aspects of female identity that offer a veritable counterforce to the violent world in which the characters live. Beth has a gentle and nurturing presence—indeed, Kennedy argues that her character reaches back to the heroines of the eighteenth-century gothic novels of Ann Radcliffe, novels that offer a valuable framework for viewing the AMC series. Beth is known for her love of music, for song, for the imagination, and for her enduring belief in the ability of these aspects of humanity to serve as means of uplift within the harsh realities of the world. Although Beth must learn to fight in a post-apocalyptic and masculinist world of constant warfare, her artistic and spiritual beauty offers an alternative form of female heroism. Kennedy's essay values not only art and music, then, but Beth's distinctive kind of feminine heroism, one that draws its strength from a female *difference* not from the show's otherwise pervasive masculinity.

In the end, though, gentleness and beauty do not fare well in *The Walking Dead* universe. In "The Sexualized Heroics of Rick and Michonne," Emily Zarka takes up the more brutal and exploitative side of sexual difference. Zarka explores the development of Michonne's sexuality in Robert Kirkman's comics, focusing on her consensual sexual encounters as well as her brutal rape by the Governor and her even more brutal retaliation. Zarka reads the representation of Michonne's sexuality against not only the representation of sex, more generally, in the comics but, more specifically, against the sexuality of protagonist Rick Grimes. Rick emerges as a foil accentuating the dominance of white men in the narrative not only in terms of leadership but also in terms of their sexuality—what is shown, what is sanctioned, what is condemned. By addressing the split that emerges in the representations of Rick and Michonne, it becomes obvious, Zarka, claims, that the fear of a liberated woman (especially a liberated black woman), even in the apocalypse, is too much of a threat to what remains of patriarchal society.

The Michonne storyline in the comics is not the only instance of rape or sexual assault in *The Walking Dead* world. In "Rules for Surviving Rape Culture," Natalie Wilson argues that while AMC's *The Walking Dead* has a marked emphasis on sexual violence and rape culture (like many twenty-first century zombie texts), it does not, contrary to what some of its critics claim, exploit the topic. Defining rape culture to mean not only rape, but also the swathe of acts that violate other bodies or groups of bodies in non-consensual, damaging, and manipulative ways, Wilson argues that the series emphasizes that sexual violence is a *result* of a patriarchal society. From its representations of domestic violence and sexual assault in season one to its later focus on torture, cannibalism, sexual slavery, and gang rape, the series depicts a world in which rape culture is itself one of the things threatening humanity. Further, by representing survivors of domestic abuse, people of color, and children as in *more* danger than powerful white males, the series echoes the realities of our current world—and, like much horror, it offers a certain level of catharsis, allowing similarly precarious audience members to process trauma and fear on the one hand and to imagine themselves as sword-wielding, zombie-killing warriors on the other. Arguing that the series represents a pervasive rape culture as a form of zombie-ism—as similarly unstoppable and infectious—Wilson contends that the show does important critical work in terms of its exploration of all bodies as equally deserving of bodily integrity and freedom from assault.

If AMC's *The Walking Dead* is critical of a patriarchal rape culture, Kirkman's comics, at least, are not so critical of an underlying heteronormativity. In his "'We can't just ignore the rules': Queer Heterosexualities," John R. Ziegler points out that while the structures and strictures of human society have collapsed to the extent that acts of deadly violence, for example, are always partly excused by circumstances, such radical transfiguration appears not to extend to conceptualizing the family. If the rules are different now, that difference only holds in some arenas. Indeed, the radical refashioning of social practices makes it all the more striking how tightly the protagonists of *The Walking Dead* cling to the traditional nuclear family. (Erwin's essay poses something of an alternative to this view; she argues that, in AMC's series, clinging to the traditional family is fatal.) Ziegler cites Lee Edelman, who, in *No Future*, positions queerness in opposition to reproductive futurism, an ideology in which the central figure of the Child symbolizes the continued existence of individual and collective futures and sharply constrains political possibilities. This political foreclosure in Kirkman's *The Walking Dead*, Ziegler argues, results in the continued dominance of the reproductive, heteronormative nuclear family. In the comics, for example, Carol's proposal of a polyamorous marriage meets with aggressive rejection and signals her mental instability. Similar conflict arises from a patriarchal rivalry over Lori's unborn baby. Further, the zombies themselves constitute queer antagonists to reproductive futurism. Zombies threateningly reproduce without heterosexual sex, removing the Child from primacy, and they act merely to satisfy their unrestricted drives toward consumption and death. Consequently, families such as Hershel's and the Governor's that attempt to incorporate zombies, especially zombie children, must be purged. In whatever form they take in *The Walking Dead*, queer family arrangements do not merely fail to materialize; they are, in fact, actively rejected and even destroyed.

Notes

1. Barkman, "Women in a Zombie Apocalypse," 98, 106; Graves, "There's a New Sheriff," 131; Kearns, "Nothing Can Save." For other articles that argue that *The Walking Dead* reproduces traditional gender roles, see, for example, Pye and O'Sullivan, "Dead Man's Party"; Lavin and Lowe, "Cops and Zombies"; and Kistler and San Juan, "Masculinity Narratives."

2. Dulanto, "Stranger Than Zombies." For a critique of the representation of queer characters in the TV series, see Erwin, "The Function of Queerness." For a discussion of the fate of the heteronormative family, see Berger, "Propagation and Procreation."

3. Jenn, "The Walking Dead's Ongoing Black Man Problem."
4. For a discussion of the predominant white masculinist supremacy in the series, see Lavin and Lowe, "Cops and Zombies," and Beech and Guy, "Rick Grimes."
5. For a discussion of how *The Walking Dead* breaks (to some degree at least) from the thrall of traditional race and gender roles in later seasons, see, for example, Ho, "The Model Minority," and Cardona and Taylor, "Diversity and Strength."
6. Kuniak and Blink discuss Daryl Dixon's journey from "Hillbilly" to "Hero" using Joseph Campbell's discussion of the hero's journey. In many ways, their discussion provides exactly the kind of view of Daryl as "Hyperreal Hillbilly" that Kunyosying and Soles (in this volume) critique. See Kuniak and Blink, "Hillbilly to Hero," 234–45.

Arête of Violence

Hypermasculinity as Power Currency in the Post-Apocalyptic Political Economy

DUSTIN DUNAWAY

> "Arête simply means the act of offering all actions as of sacrament to excellence, of devoting one's life to finding excellence, identifying it when it offers itself, and achieving it in your own life."
> —Odysseus[1]

Since the birth of the social contract, humanity has been obsessed by the concept of its own destruction. The majority of the world's major religions, most notably the Abrahamic religions, prophesize the events of "the end times" in varied eschatological degree. Christian dispensationalist "end times," for example, portend the total disassembly of the social fabric. Indeed, what most post-apocalyptic canonical texts—from The Bible to Stephen King to Mad Max—share is the question of what happens to those left behind after the social order has been shredded. In what ways do those who survived the apocalypse begin to rebuild a semblance of society (or do they)? How do they parcel out resources? With whom does political power lie? The answers to these questions often reveal more about the philosophy of the author and the ideologies of the culture from which it came (at least, when that work successfully resonates with audiences). Barbara Gurr notes "post-apocalyptic narratives ask us to consider what it means to be truly human ... by testing not only our physical survival skills, but also our values, our morals, and our beliefs."[2] One way in which they do this is through the distribution of "power currencies" to its cast of characters. *The Walking Dead* explores all power currencies and ultimately settles on reinforcing the dominant violent hypermasculine narrative as a reluctant inevitability in a dangerous post-apocalyptic society.

12   The Politics of Race, Gender and Sexuality in *The Walking Dead*

Zombie apocalypse narratives like AMC's *The Walking Dead* are hardly exclusive to American media, which means that their politics are malleable, even if their plot points are often similar. Most notably, the late 1970s saw an explosion of Italian cannibal and zombie apocalypse films. Horror author and scholar Stephen King speculates that this may be a reflection of the political and social upheaval found in that country.[3] In many cases, these post-apocalyptic narratives open the door for white, heterosexual, able-bodied men to establish (or, in the case of American narratives, retain) a white, heterosexual, able-bodied Western future.[4] As with other eschatological narratives produced in the United States, *The Walking Dead* attempts to answer the central questions about political power and social capital through the multiple lenses of race, religion, gender, and class. Because these questions are answered through exchanges of capital, the post-apocalyptic political economy can best be understood through social exchange theory.

Social exchange theory continues the social and psychological traditions of utilitarianism and behaviorism.[5] Exchange theory postulates that most exchanges of power currencies can explain most human interactions. "Currency" is the generalized term for anything of value that an individual can exchange on the political economy marketplace in order to control people or events. Typically, five power currencies manifest in interpersonal relationships: resource currency, expertise currency, social network currency, personal currency, and intimacy currency.[6] How the authors of the text allocate power currencies to the characters reinforces a dominant narrative, proposes an oppositional narrative, or offers a hybrid of both dominant and oppositional narratives. Often, in the realm of post-apocalyptic narratives, the battle is over resource currency (a safe house, fresh water source, food, fuel, weapons), and the competing currencies in the exchange involve belonging to the largest, most powerful group (social network currency) or the ability and willingness to engage in violence (expertise currency). Individuals can either provide value to the group through protection or be superior at making themselves safe. In both cases, the individual's level of hypermasculinity dictates how much currency they possess.

Because gender is a performative act, those who engage in hypermasculinity in daily life (primarily men already in leadership positions) find themselves more capable and valued in the post-apocalyptic political economy.[7] What we see, then, is a recursive loop of re-masculinization in both media and culture. Post-apocalyptic zombie fiction often operates on the same male-fantasy level, wiping out all the social progress that the authors see as "superfluous" in favor of a "hard reboot" of society. The apocalypse *necessitates* a return to the "natural order of things" where traits men already have are most valued. In these media texts, including *The Walking Dead*, hypermasculinity—specifically, the ability and willingness to commit violent acts—

becomes a subset of expertise currency due to the circumstances of the constant threat of death.

Hypermasculinity is a psychological term for the exaggerated behaviors of stereotypical male behavior, specifically physical strength, aggression, and sexuality. According to Mosher and Sirkin, hypermasculinity is marked by callous attitudes toward women, the belief that violence is manly, and the experience of danger as exciting.[8] These attitudes and beliefs often correlate with violence and aggression as well as emotional stoicism.[9] The hypermasculine protagonist has become a staple in Western media. Every trope from the hard-nosed cop who plays by his own rules to the one-horse-town sheriff to the captain of the rag-tag underdog football team engages in hypermasculine behavior. The hypermasculine hero is so prevalent some estimates show the trope shows up in 90 percent of magazine advertisements.[10]

Barring the asynchronous cold-open, in the first line of the opening episode of *The Walking Dead*, sheriff's deputy Rick Grimes asks "What's the difference between men and women?" gendering the show from the first exchange ("Days Gone Bye"). His best friend and partner Shane answers with a misogynistic tangent on light switches, a response Shane admits he does not repeat in polite company. Shane solicits Rick's thoughts on his relationship with Lori, and Rick intimates he fears sharing his feelings with his wife because she seems upset by them. Rick says women are crueler because Lori questioned his love for the family in front of their son Carl. Shane comes by misogyny naturally in his first lines, but Rick seems desperately to want to share his emotions openly without reprisal. When Rick vents to Shane, Shane simply reassures him "that's just shit couples go through." Shane's attitude about the problems of couples is naturally cavalier. Rick struggles with the emotions involved in his earlier exchange with Lori, which positions him as more complex and more feminized. This exchange sets up the friendship between Rick and Shane as one based on compulsory hypermasculinity and an "us versus them" mentality about the sexes. The first scene of the show sets up the dichotomy of the two men while positioning women as "the other." Shane embraces hypermasculinity as a way of life. Rick feels like hypermasculinity is something he has been told he *has* to engage in because of the various roles he occupies. As Leonard Pierce describes them: "Shane is all cocky certainty and Rick unsure nobility."[11]

Shane and Rick's hypermasculine demarcation becomes further pronounced in the following scene in which they engage in a shootout. Dispatch has already informed Rick and Shane that the fugitives have fired at police. Shane jokes that it would be "kinda cool" to appear on one of those "world's craziest police chases" shows. Rick, however, focuses on safety and survival. Shane is not only clearly demonstrating the third tenet of hypermasculinity—the experience of danger as exciting—but he is set up as oppositional to

Rick, who is concerned about the real possibility of being shot. This concern turns out to be valid when one of the suspects shoots Rick in the side. Shane shoots the final suspect before trying to stabilize Rick and save his life. Shane's reaction to danger is more at home with James Bond or *Die Hard*'s John McClane than a real-life shootout, but many in the audience find comfort in that surety and lack of nuance. Indeed, what we see over the next five episodes is Rick Grimes taking on more hypermasculine traits. If he was uncomfortable with the hypermasculine expectations of manhood, husbandry, fatherhood, and law enforcement before, his path in a post-humanity world is helpfully spelled out for him: hypermasculinity or death. Once he has regained his bearings after waking up in a hospital bed, Rick is soon situated as the quintessential Western sheriff. He is emblazoned with the sheriff's six-point star on his hat. He wears the official uniform, even after the police department has crumbled and has no enforcement authority. At one point, he even mounts a horse to ride through the deserted streets. All of the symbols recall the cultural representations of the Old West.[12] Darabont and company have wiped the slate clean and it is up to the Rick Grimeses of the world to put together the new world order. This reframes the post-apocalyptic landscape as a new opportunity to re-masculinize the world.

Feminism is not even an option in this environment because those who engage in feminized behavior or possess feminized traits do not survive or are relegated to submissive positions in the group. The Old West iconography serves to reassure the audience that Rick is just the man (with emphasis on the "man") you would want in this situation. Although he is out of his element and stumbling through survival early on, by the end of the first episode, he is the living embodiment of the American west and its can-do spirit. The filmmakers assure the audience of Rick's expertise capital through association with American masculine icons like John Wayne, Gary Cooper, and Jimmy Stewart. What he trades in exchange for this resurgence in control is his depth of emotion and willingness to accept nuance. Over the course of the next dozen episodes, Rick finds himself making moral compromise after moral compromise until his world becomes black-and-white—the only morality measured in an arête of violence.

While hypermasculinity is ubiquitous in media, it also manifests in society through media's role in public pedagogy.[13] Patriarchal societies enculturate men and young boys to engage in hypermasculine behaviors in order to receive any of the five power currencies. Women are encouraged to fulfill submissive and subservient roles and to position themselves as receivers of violence and sexual callousness.[14] In exchange for subservience and submission, women receive protection, intimacy, and resource currency. Rick does eventually find his wife and child with Shane and a small group of survivors. Immediately, Rick finds that the social order is out of balance in more ways than just a countryside full of walkers. Shane has usurped his position of authority, his relationship with Lori, and (to some extent) his relationship with Carl. Shane, largely through force of will, has become the de facto leader of the group of survivors. He has also been having sex with Lori. This relationship between Shane and Lori displays a telling difference in how remasculinized societies view men and women. The others automatically look to Shane as a leader for his expertise in law enforcement and his perceived strength of character.

His heroic (in his eyes) rescue of Lori and Carl creates a sense of entitlement in Shane. At various points over the first few episodes of the second season, Shane claims that he saved Lori and Carl and, therefore, she *has* to love him. Lori, on the other hand, displays conflicted emotions about her actions. When Rick returns, she intimates that she was sleeping with Shane out of grief (an exchange of sexual personal currency for intimacy currency) and as a form of self-preservation (an exchange of sexual personal currency for expertise currency). This exchange implies that Lori lacks (or believes she lacks) the requisite skills for survival on her own. That this relationship continued even after Shane, Lori, and Carl joined with the other survivors, indicates that Lori's fear was that she could not live without a male figure in her life. "You don't think I can keep Lori or Carl safe," Rick presses Shane in "18 Miles Out." "You can't just be the good guy and expect to live," Shane responds. The implication is that, in order to be a protector and leader, one must be quick to violence and remove even the hint of a threat. Rick's willingness to commit violent acts is tested in "Pretty Much Dead Already." Shane discovers that Hershel has been keeping walkers in the barn at the farm where they have been staying. Shane unleashes the walkers, revealing that Carol's missing daughter Sophia is among them. While the rest of the group is too stunned to do anything about it, Rick finally shoots her in the head—a turning point for Rick.

For the first seven episodes of season two, Rick was willing to accommodate Hershel's point-of-view that the walkers were merely sick and eventually a cure would be found. It was this view of the walkers that kept Rick from engaging in wholesale violence. Shooting Sophia represented a loss of hope and empathy for walkers that never returns. Rick's turning point did not go unnoticed by fans and critics. "Finally, here was Rick stepping up and doing something effective, logical, and meaningful as the leader of the group. Finally, here was Rick showing some balls," *Collider's* Scott Wampler wrote. Wampler continues, "He just stepped up, hoisted the gun, and fired. In that moment, much of the ill-will I've felt towards Rick receded, and I finally started thinking that I might be brought around on considering him a 'leader.'"[15] "[Rick demonstrated] he will put safety first," *The Washington Post's* Jen Chaney writes.[16] Alan Sepinwall of *Hitfix* stated that Rick had "re-established his leadership bonafides" after his initial questionable decision to show mercy.[17] In the reaction to Rick's killing of Sophia, we see the hegemonic structures of the hypermasculine view of leadership take shape. Feminine characteristics of nurture and compassion are incompatible with leadership in the harsh reality of deadly external threats. As a culture, we give social currency to those who are willing to do violence, and we take it away from those who refuse.

Rick's journey to fan acceptance of his leadership contrasts somewhat with fan-favorite Daryl Dixon's ascent. The show positions Daryl and his brother Merle as oppositional everymen to Rick and Shane's clean-cut establishment characters. Rick, especially in early episodes, is still the stalwart lawman even in a post-law society. The Dixons are never portrayed as law-abiding, even though Daryl does have his own personal code of ethical conduct that unfolds over the first four seasons. The oppositional nature of the Dixons is apparent in Merle's first interaction with Rick in the episode "Guts." Rick refers to Merle's pre-apocalypse identity as a "dumb-as-shit, inbred white-trash fool," and when he threatens to shoot Merle, Merle responds that Rick would never do something like that because he is a cop.

Sarah Mulvey notes that the recent pop-culture trend of splitting heroes along class lines has given people who feel "othered" a relatable avatar in the narrative.[18] The dramatic tension in this episode is the characters' various realizations that the old distinctions of race and class have become meaningless in the new social order. Wealth in *The Walking Dead* is measured in direct resource currency, not fiat, and, as Rick states about race, "[There is] only dark meat and white meat. There's us and the dead." This new order benefits the Dixons to some extent. Although their pasts are mostly obscured, they were clearly on the wrong side of the law before society collapsed and this makes them quicker to adapt to the lawless nature of their surroundings. As Mosher and Sirkin point out, the tenets of hypermasculinity correlate highly with criminal behavior.[19] The Dixons, being criminals prior to the collapse, find their social capital rise considerably in a post-apocalyptic environment.

Masculinity scholar David Buchbinder notes that the apocalypse creates a shift in the value of the performative act of masculinity.[20] Daryl exemplifies this shift routinely throughout the show. Compared to his brother, Daryl's masculinity is non-toxic, more measured. In "Tell it to the Frogs," Daryl angrily turns on the group when he learns Merle has been left behind, but he is resistant to killing anyone, even T-Dog, who was responsible for Merle's predicament.

The complexity of Daryl Dixon's moral conflict between big brother Merle's hypermasculinity and his own desire to show caring and allegiance to the group is one component of what made the character so popular with fans. Later, in "Chupacabra," after getting bucked off a horse, Daryl hallucinates an emotionally abusive Merle who berates him for not being man enough to stand up to Rick. This exchange serves to fill in Daryl's relationship with his brother, most of which was told, not explicitly shown. Rather than demonstrating the close fraternal ties of brotherhood, Daryl's vision of Merle is of a hypermasculine bully. The taunting becomes a reconciliation of Daryl's dialectic between his hypermasculine self and a neo-masculine self that sees the need for caring, loyalty, and socialization. This is not to say that Daryl does not achieve social capital diegetically and with fandom through his traditional masculinity. In fact, his willingness to do violence makes him a go-to character when chaos breaks out. However, as the seasons wear on and Daryl becomes more emotionally invested in individual group members, his usefulness as an ally increases. In instances involving Sophia, Hershel, Beth, and Glenn, Daryl is ineffective in saving them, or his emotional decision-making indirectly leads to their deaths. The emotional stoicism exhibited by Rick and associated with masculinity is what elevates him above Daryl as the leader.

While examining male characters' gender role performance is important, it is also important to explore the masculine/feminine role expectations in the female characters. The sex-for-protection/intimacy exchange is not limited to Lori, and the comparable arcs are considerably more regressive. Andrea was a successful civil rights attorney prior to the fall of society. Because Lori's pregnancy limits her ability to travel outside of the group, Andrea becomes the de facto female lead. Andrea's story is more complex than most of the women on the show. She grieves for her younger sister to the point where she makes the decision to commit suicide. This leads to a philosophical clash with Dale, the moral center of the group and allows her a high level of agency. In the second season, moreover, Andrea makes herself valuable to the group by becoming a sharpshooter. In fact, she becomes the group's best sniper. "I contribute. I help keep this place safe," Andrea tells Lori in "18 Miles Out." Lori tells her that the men can handle it on their own, and they do not need her help. In this moment, Lori and Andrea summarize the complexities of belonging to a co-cultural group that has historically been denied expertise capital. Lori moves that they return to clearly defined gender roles where there is an unambiguous "men's work" of protection, violence, and providing for family, and "women's work," which includes all domestic roles. Andrea, however, has adopted a strategy of transformative assimilation, taking on skills and traits that are valuable to the dominant group in order to elevate her individual standing. In this scene, Lori also provides a defense for feminine traits and non-violent activities. "We are trying to make a life worth living," she explains.

This contested space between those who prefer the status quo and those who seek transformative resistance is a common one within co-cultural communities. Advocates of cohesive group identity, as Lori is in this scene, often label nonconformists as "sellouts." The result of this in-group dissension is a diminishment of the value of expertise capital for the nonconformist. In Lori's world, Andrea's expertise at killing is not valuable because it is not a skill that she is *supposed* to have. Within the group, Andrea's currency has been wiped out to the point that she arguably becomes an out-grouper. This, too, is common among people who find themselves caught between co-culture and dominant culture. They will never truly belong to the dominant group due to racial, gendered, or sexual orientation traits, but they also do not conform to the identity traits in the co-cultural group. Despite this, Andrea finds a unique identity in her value to the group, an identity and skill that gives her agency. She even initiates sex with Shane to satisfy her own desires. Andrea violates traditional gender norms by seeking expertise in violence and being willing to be the sexual aggressor.

Season three of *The Walking Dead* sees a sharp turn in Andrea's characterization. At the end of season two, a walker attack separates Andrea from the group and she ends up in Woodbury, a walled-in township under control of the Governor. Perhaps in order to introduce contrast with newly-introduced masculine character Michonne, Andrea's character becomes more docile. Again, Andrea finds herself in conflict with another woman, but this time Andrea adopts the hegemonic point-of-view.[21] She forms a sexual relationship with the Governor, in part out of a sense of obligation for his having saved her and in part because he is the most powerful man in Woodbury. Contrary to the empowered Andrea we saw in season two, this iteration of Andrea walks through most of the season reacting to events. In Woodbury, Andrea's acquired skill set from season two is moot. The Governor's guard has already filled the role Andrea previously occupied. This has the dual consequence of erasing Andrea's expertise currency while she resides in Woodbury and pushes her into relying on her personal currency. Ultimately, her entwinement with the Governor leads to her demise. Michonne, who adopts the traits of the masculine samurai figure on which much of our Old West iconography is based, actually joins with Rick's group and quickly rises as a leader. Viewing these actions in terms of social exchange shows that characters, even women, who engage in masculine behaviors are more likely to thrive.

Perhaps most salient is the way in which the show deals with Carl Grimes. Carl, son of Rick and Lori, is the most prominent child when the series begins. Shane adopts Carl as his own, teaching him survival techniques while Rick is still in the hospital. In the first few seasons, Carl is little more than a pawn between Rick, Shane, and Lori. Once Shane is killed at the end of season two, Carl begins to achieve more agency. How Carl develops becomes incredibly important to the political economy in *The Walking Dead*. In the third season's most pivotal moment, Carl shoots his own mother rather than see her turn into a walker. When paired with the flashback in which Rick discusses hard choices with him, Carl's shooting of his mother is presented as a dark coming-of-age moment: Carl is now a "real man." Like his father, he had to jettison a naïve hold on hope and empathy to do "what a man has to do." Later, when Carl and Rick are isolated after the prison assault, Rick is incapacitated. Carl erupts emotionally at his father, primarily for the death of Lori. In this moment of emotional upheaval for Carl, he expresses his view of the duty and responsibility of men, specifically his father, as leaders. In both the internal narrative and the explicit pedagogy, the message that the "burden of leadership" belongs to the masculine is apparent.

Examining *The Walking Dead*, and other post-apocalyptic narratives like it, through the exchanges of power currency is valuable to us because we see a microcosm of the political economy in the real world. End-of-the-world fantasies potentially represent a *tabula rasa* in which the characters are not encumbered with the social and moral baggage of the social contract. How they choose to exist offers the audience several forms of political economy to choose from—whether it is the naïve pacifism of Hershel's farm, the isolationist police state of Woodbury, the kill-or-be-killed cannibalistic xenophobia of Terminus, or the sadistic colonization of the Saviors. When the authors and audience collaborate on which character is right and which character is wrong, that process builds cultural values. The producers of *The Walking Dead* draw stark lines between the traditional binary genders represented in the first two seasons. Lori, Andrea, Shane, Rick and, later, Michonne all represent different points-of-view about men's and women's roles in the economy. Which skills should receive the most emphasis? What truly defines humanity? Are the humans worse than the walkers? The dialogues that emerge around these questions can reinforce, critique, or create value systems. Therefore, examining how the representation of masculine and feminine traits are valued and rewarded in popular culture becomes critical in defining how we will transmit these values to others.

NOTES

1. Simmons, *Ilium*, 467.
2. Gurr, *Race, Gender, and Sexuality*, 8.
3. King, *Danse Macabre*, 139.
4. Gurr, *Race, Gender, and Sexuality*, 13.
5. Cook and Rice, *Handbook*, 61–62.
6. Emerson, "Social Exchange Theory," 335–62.
7. Butler, "Performative Acts," 519–31.
8. Mosher and Sirkin, "Measuring a Macho Personality," 150–63.
9. Ben-Zeev et al., "Hypermasculinity in the Media," 53–61.
10. Krans, "Hypermasculinity in Advertising."
11. Pierce, "The Walking Dead."

12. See Young, "Walking Tall or Walking Dead?" 56–67.
13. Ben-Zeev et al., "Hypermasculinity in the Media," 61
14. Scheff, "Hypermasculinity and Violence."
15. Wampler, "The Walking Dead."
16. Chaney, "'Walking Dead'"
17. Sepinwall, "'The Walking Dead'"
18. Mulvey, "The Zen of Daryl," 8.
19. Mosher and Sirkin, "Measuring a Macho Personality," 161
20. Buchbinder, *Studying Men and Masculinities,* 50–53.
21. Thomas-Hunt and Phillips, "When What You Know," 1585–89. Andrea is hardly alone in losing her efficacy as her masculine traits are diminished. Thomas-Hunt and Phillips find that, in matters of non-quantitative capital, the value of a woman's currency is diminished by both men and women. Women in traditionally male fields find that they must acquire more capital (especially expertise capital) in order to maintain the same exchange power. Women who are conventionally attractive find their currency amplified, but only if their primary purpose is titillation. See Heldman, "The Hunger Games."

The Curious Case of T-Dog
A Magical Negro?

ELEXUS JIONDE

Despite the monotonous stream of zombies tinted in varying shades of vomit green and pallid gray that has tormented the protagonists for seven seasons, the bevy of hardened post-apocalyptic survivors on AMC's *The Walking Dead* come in a variety of races and ethnicities. And they operate in a multitude of capacities, ranging from dangerous antagonists to friendly protagonists. The show is filled with characters who represent an arguably realistic view of how the world might be after an apocalypse—which is why the case of character Theodore Douglas, better known as T-Dog, is so curious. While other minority characters exist in *The Walking Dead* world (and many have occupied more of the narrative), there is still much to be said about T-Dog. As the token black survivor of Rick Grimes's original group, T-Dog embodies traditional "magical negro" qualities, an historical stereotype that represented the type of black people white America would tolerate during the 1950s, made famous by actors like Sidney Poitier. T-Dog's mostly silent stint on the show outraged the character's unexpected fans and led many to accuse the showrunners of sly racism. T-Dog was the only character of his kind in the series and fans definitely took notice. As the show, now in its seventh season, contains a multitude of black characters, one might surmise that T-Dogs fans paved the way.

Because T-Dog was created strictly for the television series, had little group input or character development, and embodied the classical negro trope at every turn, one can surmise that he was meant to be Hollywood's symbol of the desirable black male … not only in the post-apocalyptic world but the real one as well. "African American characters are now more than stereotypes of 'mammies,' 'coons,' and 'bucks,' as they currently portray lawyers, doctors, saints, and gods, [but] they seem welcome only if they observe certain limits imposed upon them by mainstream, normative conventions."[1] These normative conventions involve constraining black characters to the sole purpose of helping white characters—conventions T-Dog seems to embody. He is muscular, quiet, and docile. For most of his time on the show, he is uncomplicated, patient, and strong. T-Dog's qualities are reminiscent of the *magical negro* and *ebony saint* character archetypes, aiding him in his short-lived post-apocalyptic mission of protecting everyone around him—and the overwhelming majority of these people are white.[2] Is this just a happy accident, or is perpetuating stereotypes the price of an appearance in mainstream U.S. media?

T-Dog's introduction to the TV series shows that contemporary racial attitudes didn't just go away because of the apocalypse. When we first meet T-Dog in the season one episode "Guts," he is one of several characters the protagonist Rick Grimes encounters in a zombie-filled Atlanta after waking from a coma. His storyline involves a heated and tense moment infused with racism as Merle Dixon calls him a nigger before beating him to a bloody pulp. Rick, who begins as a moral compass in the series, subdues Merle. He then tells him that "Things are different now. There are no niggers anymore. No dumb-as-shit-inbred-white-trash-fools either. Only dark meat and white meat." As Rick triumphs over the racist redneck and cuffs him to a pipe, the viewers can feel comforted by the fact that the main character is not a racist. It is in this moment that both Rick Grimes and the writers declare that racism will not be tolerated in the post-apocalyptic world. But the showrunners' treatment of T-Dog tells a different story.

After Rick Grimes gives him the key to Merle Dixon's handcuffs and lets him choose whether or not to let him go, T-Dog accidentally drops the key down a drain when returning to the roof to free him. We gather that he is a man with a conscience, as he later volunteers to return to Atlanta to rescue Merle, despite their violent altercation on the rooftop. We are minimally introduced to T-Dog over the next few episodes. One thing that we do learn is that he is hesitant to kill humans. In "Vatos," Rick Grimes, Daryl Dixon, and T-Dog must trade a hostage for their own group member, Glenn. T-Dog is put on sniper duty, and his reluctance to kill is made clear. As he aims the gun at an enemy from a rooftop, he nervously whispers, "C'mon man, make the trade. Please." In the first season, T-Dog is just one of three black characters, and little information is given about him. His cohorts are not on screen nearly as long as he, with Morgan Jones briefly appearing in the series premiere and exiting until season three, and background character Jacqui committing suicide in the sixth episode after herself getting very little screen time. (It should be noted that Morgan Jones is an original comic book character and Jacqui is original to the television adaptation.) Before long,

T-Dog is the only recurring black character on the show, but it never becomes a role of substance. He is repeatedly seen slaying zombies, flanking Rick during group missions, providing muscle, doing heavy lifting, and little else.

The exception to the sparse screen time given to developing T-Dog as a dynamic character is a brief moment in the season two episode "Bloodletting," in which he nearly succumbs to blood poisoning and has a brief existential crisis. In this moment he questions his role in the group in a sickened daze, puffing on a cigarette. T-Dog discusses his social status with fear and some annoyance, ultimately suggesting to Dale (who is white, but older) that they should both leave the group in an attempt to survive. "I'm the one black guy. You realize how precarious that makes my situation," he muses to a bewildered Dale. "What in the hell are you talking about?" asks Dale incredulously. "I'm talking about two good old boy cowboy sheriffs and a redneck whose brother cut off his own hand because I dropped a key. Who in that scenario do you think is gonna be the first to get lynched?" T-Dog replies. Dale, mirroring the same disbelief of a modern day white person who believes America is truly postracial, gives T-Dog a look of pure skepticism. "You've gone off the deep end," Dale reasons. It is eerily similar to real life race conversations where black people are accused of imagining the persistent racial hierarchy in this country, or are told that their concerns are not worth deeper analysis. The only difference is that T-Dog actually has gone crazy, thanks to blood poisoning. In this meta-moment of clarity, the black character who seldom steps outside of his role to offer criticisms only does so because he is momentarily mentally unstable. T-Dog even apologizes for the temporary break from reality, before being relegated to the background of the show for the remainder of the season. In the next episode, after T-Dog is given drugs to temper his blood poisoning symptoms, he introduces himself to Maggie Greene by saying he and Glenn are there to help and offers his labor. How Hollywood.

The Walking Dead is an adaptation of the wildly popular comics by Robert Kirkman and Tony Moore, brought to life by filmmaker Frank Darabont. Before *The Walking Dead*, Darabont was the celebrated director of *The Shawshank Redemption* (1994) and *The Green Mile* (1999). Both films have a few things in common: a prison setting, a white man down on his luck, and a black man there to aid the white man in a journey to self-redemption. While both films garnered critical acclaim, they were also criticized for their blatantly stereotypical representations of black people. Notable among the critics was filmmaker Spike Lee, who said of *The Green Mile*, "Michael Clarke Duncan tongue-kisses cancer out of a white woman and cures her. And in the end Tom Hanks offers to set him free, but guess what? He refuses to leave Death Row. He'd rather die with Hanks looking on.... That's old grateful slave shit."[3] Upon closer examination, one can agree with Matthew Hughey's declaration that "these films draw upon the idea that black folks are, underneath all the politically correct discourse, simple and unsophisticated people that desire an uncomplicated life of servitude."[4] This is a common theme in depictions of not only the magical negro character but also the other Hollywood stereotypes of black people that preceded it.

According to a recent study, three quarters of white people in America don't have any black friends.[5] The term "aversive racism" has been coined for white people who try to avoid interracial interactions with black people without considering themselves racists.[6] Therefore, it isn't a far-fetched idea that white people get their ideas of race and racial relations from mainstream media. Their ideas about black behavior, interactions, and values are packaged up for them and presented by Hollywood, which has historically depicted black characters as negative troublemakers, service characters, or divine beings who exist solely to aid the main character. This is problematic. "When black actors are constantly cast as angels, spirits, gods, and other incarnate supernatural forces, they displace the realities of history into more viewer-friendly narratives. That is, the various filmmakers create scenes of trouble-free and uncomplicated black/white reconciliation."[7] Blacks are cast in magical protector roles because it provides a non-threatening and more appealing view of race relations. These roles of angels, spirits, and gods can be literal or abstract, but they usually encompass many of the same qualities.

There are several clear indicators of the magical negro. "Most films begin with the sudden and rapid integration of the magical negro character into a white man's personal life, and conclude with the magical negro's sacrifice, and disappearance, for the betterment of white men."[8] They are harmless and temporary characters who rarely stick around for an entire movie or TV series, and they are usually of a low economic or social status, thus demonstrating how race intersects with class. The magical negro, moreover, displays no sexual desires. They have enormous patience with the character they are guiding, rarely defying them or putting their own needs first. They have little to no backstory, which keeps them uncomplicated and entirely focused on their ward.[9] This character is an evolution of two stereotypes before it—the ebony saint and the Uncle Tom. The Uncle Tom character originated in 1852 in Harriet Beecher Stowe's classic novel *Uncle Tom's Cabin*. In the novel, Uncle Tom offers selfless assistance with a strong dose of religious conviction to the white characters. He is loyal and good-natured despite his lot in life as a slave. This character has since evolved into a stereotype and epithet signifying a docile black person who loves and protects his oppressors. It also serves as a foundation for the magical negro, who is likewise loyal to his white "superiors" and remains good natured through life trials that non-magical humans struggle against.

As race relations progressed in America for the better, Hollywood began to make a few changes. "Today, media exercises no less an influence in promulgating and protecting de facto racism through the patterned combination of white normativity and anti-black stereotypes under the guise of progressive black-white friendships that supposedly indicate improving race relations."[10] While black characters could not remain blatantly "coonish" in their adoration of white people, small adjustments could be made to feign progress, offering the illusion of destroying old stereotypes while actually keeping them alive. Blithely different from notions of the black brute popularized by films like 1915's *Birth of a Nation*, Sidney Poitier and his regular portrayal of ebony saint characters became Hollywood's new normal in the 1950s. "Poitier ... championed the cause of assimilation through the repeated portrayal of a friendly, desexualized black man that was little more than a nonthreatening confidant to virginal white women."[11] The ebony saint existed to help the white people around him live better lives, promoting a sterilized ideal of black goodness for the benefit of white people everywhere. The black saint was the type of black man that didn't scare white people, and was therefore acceptable to mainstream society.

So let us return to T-Dog. T-Dog is not an original comic book character. He is a creation of Frank Darabont, strictly added to the adaptation of *The Walking Dead* for mainstream television. T-Dog has no backstory, except for a brief line delivered after his death by Asian-American character Glenn, who remarks that T-Dog was a church volunteer who drove around to the homes of elderly people after the zombie outbreak to try to save them. This bit of religiosity and selflessness adds to the mounting evidence of his assigned stereotype. He has no sexual interests, despite the availability of women around him. Rick relies on his physical strength and often yells T-Dog's name when he needs assistance. His sole critique of his role as expendable savior is only brought about by intense medical duress, implying that, when in his right mind, T-Dog would never question his role, and further signifying that he is in his rightful place as a glorified extra.

In season two, T-Dog's status in the show diminished greatly, even though the survivor group had gotten much smaller after the season one finale. T-Dog had approximately four minutes and fifty seconds of speaking time in season two, even though it was comprised of thirteen episodes all averaging forty-two minutes apiece (for an approximate total of 546 minutes). T-Dog spends most of this time appearing in background shots, being told to do something, and getting completely ignored when it comes to group decisions. The few lines he has often reinforce his identity as the token black guy. In "Secrets," the group is having shooting practice and one of the survivors cocks his gun to the side, prompting T-Dog to tell him not to "give [him] any of that gangster shit." The sole line he is given in this episode is loaded with an ebonic term for comedic effect, strengthening his role as "the black guy" in the group. In "Beside the Dying Fire," as walkers attack the farm and the group becomes fractured, T-Dog's role is that of protector, as he wheels Lori Grimes and Beth Greene away from danger. He has numerous lines in this episode, but they are only extended to him because the task he has been given—protecting these two particular white women—is crucial to the show's plot. As noted by IBN critic Eric Goldman, "T-Dog stands out as being the only Season 1 character who really didn't have, well, anything to do in Season 2."[12] T-Dog's absence in the second season was noticed by plenty of other critics, who lamented at the end of season two that they forgot T-Dog was around.

A quick search of "T-Dog" on Google with time parameters set between 2010 and 2012 reveals a slew of memes, discussion boards, and blog reviews regarding the character's existence and fate. Before the beginning of season three, the majority of these articles, memes, and chat groups discussed why T-Dog had so few lines during season two. "Oh hey, T-Dog is on this show! I forgot about him, much as the writers apparently did," wrote AV Club's Zack Handlen.[13] These sentiments were echoed by many other essayists and fans, who thought that T-Dog's role in the group was serving a racist Hollywood agenda. In short, the fans weren't happy. IronE Singleton attempted to quell fans' dissatisfaction with his character's treatment, saying before the premiere of the third season that "People will be really excited by what they get from T-Dog this season."[14]

The Walking Dead writers obviously took note of fan discontent, as T-Dog's speaking time increased immensely during his short time in the third season. He's still "just 'the black guy with that name,' but at least he's getting more lines," commented Handlen during his review of the season three episode "Sick."[15] Perhaps sensing that there would be fan outrage at T-Dog's death in the fourth episode of season three, showrunners prepared to fight accusations of racism by introducing four minority characters who weren't the katana-wielding comic book original Michonne. Show-runners even attempted to give T-Dog more power in the group, as evidenced by the moment in "Sick" when his opinion is sought out by Rick when they are deciding what to do with the survivors found in the prison. This was a complete 180 degrees from the season two episode "Judge, Jury, Executioner," in which T-Dog is left completely out of the decision about whether or not to kill the prisoner, Randall. By the end of the next episode featuring Rick and company at the prison, however, T-Dog is dead. His death was heroic, as he sacrificed himself not once but twice for the sake of his fellow characters in "Killer Within." After being bitten by a zombie when volunteering for a risky mission to secure prison gates, he uses his last moments of clarity and life to help fellow survivor Carol find a safe place to hide from the horde of zombies. Dying of fever from the bite, he asserts that God has revealed to him his purpose in aiding Carol to safety—and he allows himself to be eaten alive by walkers as Carol escapes. To him, his life and death—both entrenched in servitude—are God's will. Making his death even more notable is the fact that it happened in prison, especially in a time when the mass incarceration of black men has become a more prominent topic of discussion, with books like Michelle Alexander's *The New Jim Crow* (2012) and films like *13th* (Ava DuVernay, 2016).

While T-Dog fits many characteristics of the magical negro stereotype, the other central black characters transcend them. Katana- and sword-wielding Michonne spent her introductory episodes carrying around a sickly white character who slowed her down, Tyreese spent multiple episodes being the caretaker of three white children, and Morgan risked his safety and resources to take care of Rick Grimes, but each received a backstory and a lot of character development. These characters were fixtures in the comic book series, and their importance translated to the screen adaptation. All of which raises the question: since black characters in the comics are strong and multi-faceted, why did Frank Darabont create a character for the TV adaptation that spent virtually his whole existence serving his white cohorts? In a word, comfort.

The magical negro stereotype is useful for white people who want to extend the promise of equality to good black people and justify why others aren't eligible for such kindness. "The *magical negro* is an acceptable identity in mainstream Hollywood films because it rests upon a racial salvation and redemption motif of the American myth that, in the end, reinstalls the centrality of whiteness and leaves it unchallenged."[16] Essentially, non-threatening black characters are a selling point of anti-racism because they don't make white people feel guilty (the good-natured black people *want* to be subservient to you) and also because it represents a positive alternative to harmful black stereotypes, elevating Hollywood in the eyes of those who champion racial equality. Aversive racists are white people who are well intentioned in their actions and support racial equality but who also harbor negative attitudes about blacks. "Despite their conscious good intentions, aversive racists unconsciously harbor feelings of uneasiness towards blacks and thus try to avoid interracial interaction."[17] Because aversive racism is the result of dominant racism becoming more socially unacceptable, showing positive and uncomplicated depictions of blacks with little discussion of race makes aversive racists more at ease. "Instead of hostility or hatred, [aversive racism] manifests as discomfort, uneasiness, disgust, and sometimes fear."[18]

The absence of race in social interactions and media is meant to erase guilt associated with past racial relations, which may explain why race is often glossed over, for instance, in science fiction. "In numerous science fiction films, black people are missing, or if they are present, they are so extremely marginalized and irrelevant to the narrative that they are, for all intents and purposes, invisible."[19] Perhaps T-Dog's race isn't designated as important in the social order of the show, but it ends up being so anyway. Aversive racism is not addressed in *The Walking Dead*, but it's there. In addition to his name reeking of a generic ebonic marinade, T-Dog's most prominent story line involved him being called "nigger" on a roof and then risking his life to save the man who used the epithet on him. So even after Rick Grimes cuffed Merle Dixon to the roof and symbolically declared racism a pre-apocalypse scourge, T-Dog's fate as the token black character had been set for the series permanently. He was a *black* character and it was ingrained into his identity as a survivor in the post-apocalyptic world. Characters who were born in the pre-apocalypse did not simply discard their racial ideas when the apocalypse began. They were just pushed to the back of the mind. Later as the world grew darker, bleaker, and less populated, these racial stereotypes and beliefs faded ... eventually. In the season three episode "The Suicide King," Tyreese comments that he's the first black man to break into prison. Recall that many white people do not interact with non-white people regularly. Despite this, the joke is obvious to the audience, as they are likely to be familiar with the stereotype of the incarcerated black thug. But race jokes become rarer as the series continues, perhaps explaining why later black characters like Michonne and Tyreese develop much more depth and nuance and built greater relationships with the white protagonists. But T-Dog was around when there was still some hope in the survivors of *The Walking Dead*, before he and Lori died and Rick descended into a more primal version of himself. In the first two seasons there were glimpses of human capacity for evil with Merle and Shane, but season three was really when humans showed how vicious they could be. T-Dog was around before a new tone of hopelessness was ushered in along with the Governor and when chaos due to humans, not just walkers, became the norm. The new hopelessness made it clear that there was no returning to the old ways of society—a society where there were not only social rules but also a racial hierarchy, one where T-Dog was comfortably out of sight unless a task needed to be performed. One where T-Dog could be a good magical negro.

T-Dog began the show as a stereotype, berated on a roof by an overtly racist white person and reacting violently to a racial slur. T-Dog continued his life in the series as a stereotype, serving as a flat, one-dimensional submissive character for a cast of whites constantly in need of his labor and protection. Finally, T-Dog went out as a stereotype, dutifully sacrificing his life for others with a few droplets of religious conviction to allow viewers a shame-free acceptance of his fate. Among all of the characters on *The Walking Dead*, all of various races, T-Dog stands out like a zombie in a pack of humans. Though he was created strictly for the TV adaptation, had little character development, and was the main subject of less than three storylines, he's nonetheless more important than one might think. If T-Dog had not saved Carol after he was bitten, she never would have been able to save the group from hungry cannibals at Terminus in season five. Ultimately this stereotypical and silent character emerges—perhaps accidentally—as a vital reason for the survival of the other characters. Like cotton-picking antebellum-era slaves, who offered southern whites economic security with little representation or fanfare, so T-Dog protected his white co-survivors.

The imagining of the social and racial order in a fictional post-apocalyptic world reveals a lot about contemporary race relations. It can be chalked up to pure coincidence that the sole recurring black character for the show's first two seasons existed as a hardworking quasi-golem who rarely spoke or received much attention. To those who recognize the patterns that dictate how black people are depicted in film and TV, however, it is not at all surprising. It is also a mirror of how blacks today are valued and respected. Since whites are more likely not to have black friends, and many get their sole glimpses of blacks by way of the media, their views on racial relations are likely to be skewed in a way that makes a black person possessing magical negro traits a prerequisite for their respect. When black people don't fit neatly into the box of white acceptability by way of cheerful life assistance and unquestioning role fulfillment, new racists will claim that any repercussions they face as a result are based on their own shortcomings, not on racial status. Basically, when a black person does not seek to fill his Hollywood-allotted role in society as a docile and subservient being, he is troublesome or undeserving of being extended the promise of equality.

The Walking Dead is currently in its eighth season, and has no plans to stop anytime soon. In the most recent episodes of the series, black characters operate as active protagonists and antagonists, with depth and quality storylines. The bulk of these characters are adaptations of the comic, but, apart from Morgan, they were all preceded by T-Dog. His unexpected fan support is perhaps the only thing that caused showrunners to boost T-Dog's character during the third season. Created just for the TV adaptation and given little story to garner emotional attachment or too much fan importance, he was always supposed to die at the right moment. He was created specifically to fill the role of the group's submissive character and to ease viewers into an unfamiliar world with familiar themes of desirable race relations. The comics don't include a magical negro character, but Hollywood obviously felt like something was missing. Dragged through the first two seasons like a dying pet that an owner refuses to part with until the forced bitter end, T-Dog was Hollywood's symbol of the desirable black male … not only in the post-apocalyptic world, but the real one as well.

Notes

1. Hughey, "Cinethetic Racism," 544.
2. *Ibid.*, 545.
3. *Ibid.*, 556.
4. *Ibid.*, 556.
5. Ingraham, "Three Quarters of Whites."
6. Dovidio and Gaertner, "Aversive Racism," 4.
7. Hughey, "Cinethetic Racism," 550.
8. *Ibid.*, 559.
9. Glenn and Cunningham, "The Power of Black Magic," 137–38.
10. Hughey, "Cinethetic Racism," 544.
11. *Ibid.*, 545.
12. Goldman, "The Walking Dead."
13. Handlen, "The Walking Dead: 'Pretty Much Dead Already.'"
14. Eldredge, "Oh, HELL No!"
15. Handlen, "The Walking Dead: 'Sick.'"
16. Hughey, "Cinethetic Racism," 561.
17. Dovidio and Gaertner, "Aversive Racism," 8.
18. *Ibid.*, 4.
19. Nama, *Black Space*, 10–41.

The Hyperreal Hillbilly
Horror, Melodrama and Backwoods White Protagonists

Kom Kunyosying *and* Carter Soles

In the anti-intellectual cultural climate of the contemporary United States, the figure of the undereducated hillbilly holds a specific appeal. Paralleling the rise of the pop-cultural geek, and often produced by the same creators, the hillbilly is prevalent in twenty-first-century media, from feature films (*Talladega Nights, Tucker and Dale vs. Evil, Winter's Bone, The Hunger Games*) to television sitcoms and dramas (*Eastbound and Down, The Walking Dead*), to reality TV (*Duck Dynasty, Here Comes Honey Boo Boo*). Anthony Harkins argues that the hillbilly stereotype has been "consistently used by middle-class economic interests to denigrate working-class southern whites" and to promote "the benefits of advanced civilization through negative counterexample." Yet Harkins also notes that the "hillbilly" moniker has been taken up at various points "by thousands of Americans within and outside the southern mountains to both uphold and challenge the dominant trends of twentieth-century American life—urbanization, the growing centrality of technology, and the resulting routinization of American life."[1] As with the reclamation of "queer" as a term of defiant, coalition-building identification for LGBTQ activists in the 1980s and '90s, the hillbilly has been reappropriated as an umbrella figure for all manner of rural whites longing for cultural validation.

As we have argued elsewhere, postmodernity requires its protagonists to take on authenticating features in order to garner audience sympathy in an increasingly diverse mediascape.[2] As marginalized groups such as women, LGBTQ individuals, and persons of color slowly gain access to the pop-cultural spotlight, white males seek ways to foreground their own suffering and social marginalization in order to stay centralized in the mainstream media's melodramatic imagination. As Linda Williams writes, American popular culture operates in a fundamentally melodramatic mode that "move[s] us to pathos for protagonists beset by forces more powerful than they and who are perceived as victims."[3] The suffering of these victim-heroes renders their moral value emotionally legible to us, staging their virtue and innocence via contrast to the irredeemably villainous forces that beset them.[4] As our culture becomes increasingly aware of the privileged position of white males, it is correspondingly difficult for white, male protagonists to elicit melodramatic sympathy; hence, such protagonists seek a simulated victimhood and even simulated ethnicity to justify their centrality. In contemporary media, an authenticating victimhood is necessary to remain viable as a protagonist.

Rural, poor, white people, here called hillbillies, possess this authenticating quality via their economic disenfranchisement and social marginalization *vis-à-vis* middle and upper-class whites. Harkins writes that "despite their poverty, ignorance, primitiveness, and isolation, 'hillbillies' [are] 'one hundred percent' Protestant Americans," a group that mainstream white audiences perceive "as a fascinating and exotic 'other' akin to Native Americans or Blacks" while simultaneously finding them sympathetic as "poorer and less modern versions of themselves."[5] Thus, the rural hillbilly functions as a new kind of white male protagonist who is uniquely positioned to take advantage of his melodramatic cachet due to his real-life and imagined abject socioeconomic status.

The hillbilly's whiteness is key to his appeal because it allows his image "to serve as a seemingly apolitical site for often highly charged political struggles over the definition of race, class, [and] gender norms and roles."[6] His disenfranchised, not-quite-whiteness allows mainstream audiences to identify with him while simultaneously taking pleasure in the more grotesque elements of his marginalized *milieu*. It also allows media producers to "portray images of poverty, ignorance, and backwardness without raising cries of bigotry and racism from civil rights advocates and the black and minority communities."[7] This ambiguity contributes to contemporary hillbilly media's ideological insidiousness: it allows its audiences to vicariously align themselves with retrograde sexist and racist ideological positions.[8]

Hit AMC TV series *The Walking Dead* (2010–present) is one of the most successful contemporary hillbilly-centered texts. We examine images and narratives from the series and the long-running source comic (2003–present) to expose how both versions foreground the suffering of their white male backwoods protagonists, reifying dominant patriarchal hierarchies. We pay particular attention to the hillbilly Dixon brothers, who exist only in the show, since Daryl Dixon is one of the series' most popular characters and the

Dixon storylines often eliminate the stories of non-white characters who appear in the comics.

AMC's *The Walking Dead* recentralizes its hillbilly leads' ethnicized white maleness, moving characters of color into the background. Even Glenn Rhee, who gets more screen time than any other character of color on the show, has his death in the season seven opener reduced to an afterthought caused by Daryl's impulsiveness. Glenn's death transpires in order to create melodramatic suffering for his white cast-mate, setting up a "darker Daryl" according to Reedus.[9] Furthermore, Glenn utters his last line to Maggie as an abject, googly-eyed monster, his melodramatic sendoff compromised by B-movie special effects. Meanwhile Abe gives a final, silent peace sign to Sasha, the type of emotionally overdetermined gesture that signals the ennobling presence of the melodramatic mode ("The Day Will Come When You Won't Be").

Protagonist Rick, a Southern sheriff's deputy, and second lead Daryl both embody folksy masculine values. Rick's mainstream appearance allows for viewer identification while his Southern roots give him the authenticity of hillbilly ethnicity. As a popular meme points out, Woody the Cowboy of *Toy Story* and Rick Grimes have a lot in common in appearance and leadership dynamics. The comics version of Rick and Woody are great examples of generic faces upon which to project audience identification.[10] They are the viewers' entry points into their respective stories. Woody and Rick are the relatable leaders of a less relatable, diverse gang of misfits.

Audience favorite Daryl functions as a "hyperreal hillbilly" whose brutal childhood implicitly enhances his survival skills while negative attributes stereotypically associated with such an upbringing, such as bigotry, are muted. The hyperreal, according to Jean Baudrillard, is "the generation by models of a real without origin or reality." The hyperreal offers "all the signs of the real" while eliding "all its vicissitudes."[11] Daryl is generally egalitarian towards people of color and queers, functioning as manifestation of the sign "hillbilly" stripped of its vicissitudes, racism, and homophobia. The long-term effects of Daryl's traumas are emphasized mainly in terms of internal turmoil he endures.

Daryl's hyperreal hillbilly qualities are established from his first introduction in "Tell It to the Frogs." Group members patrolling their camp's perimeter discover a walker feeding on a deer carcass. Arrows stuck in the carcass foreshadow Daryl's appearance: as the patrollers talk among themselves, Daryl appears silently out of the woods, alone. "That's my deer!" he shouts. Daryl angrily kicks the walker that infected his kill, yells at Dale, and then shoots the still-sputtering walker in the head: "It's gotta be the brain." Not only is Daryl an expert backwoodsman, but he has to lecture the other group members about how to properly dispatch walkers. Upon returning to the camp and hearing of the rooftop abandonment of his brother Merle, Daryl flies into a violent rage. Despite his smaller stature, it takes both Shane and Rick to subdue him. Like the murderous hillbillies of rural slashers like *The Texas Chain Saw Massacre* (1974), Daryl possesses superhuman strength and endurance.

While Daryl lacks conscious racism, he is regularly placed in brief, verbally aggressive confrontations with black men. For example, he complains when T-Dog volunteers to join the city-bound rescue party in "Tell It to the Frogs" and harshly interrogates Bob in the opening vignette of "Alone." These confrontations never become physical nor lead to Daryl's using racial slurs, but this restraint is precisely what makes Daryl hyperreal. The visuals and underlying anger suggest the racial tensions that have been muted in Daryl's upbringing and cultural circumstances to make him a more powerful point of identification within the show.

Merle Dixon's death in "This Sorrowful Life" is especially pertinent to *The Walking Dead*'s elicitation of sympathy for Daryl and for white male hillbilly characters in general. Despite his role as an on-again, off-again villain, Merle is given one of the most noble and meaningful deaths in the series. Rather than simply being taken out, Merle chooses the manner of his death, nobly sacrificing himself in an attempt to get close to and kill the villainous Governor. Merle reappears as a walker and is, of course, dispatched by a sobbing, heartbroken Daryl. As Williams argues, exaggerated tears and suffering of this kind ennoble our victim-hero—and "mute pathos entitles action."[12]

Daryl is long-suffering and occasionally tearful, yet always stoic and effective. Unlike Glenn and Tyreese, Daryl is given a backstory involving abuse by his hillbilly father. The markings from his father's lashings are put on display in "Home." Particularly because it involves whipping, Daryl's personal victimization is meant to equal or surpass Tyreese's victimization as an African American. If, according to the logic of the melodramatic mode, suffering equals virtue and moral superiority, then the virtue of a marked identity type can be reduced to how much one suffers for it.

Daryl expresses real pain while squatting in his former family home in the season four episode, "Still." The setting alone emphasizes his anger's origins in family trauma. Enraged after Beth asks about his troubled past, Daryl calls himself "some redneck asshole with an even bigger asshole for a brother." He evinces awareness of the cycle of patriarchal violence that created him, bolstering his sympathetic status as a victim-hero and reassuring us that he is not really like that—he is hyperreal, not an actual, poor rural white. This clear articulation of Daryl's victimhood at the site of his childhood abuse gains him "an empathy that is equated with moral virtue" through ongoing travail. His explosive rant, like burning his arm with a cigarette in "Them," conveys the prolonged dimension of his agony while simultaneously turning his "virtuous suffering into action."[13] In the deadly world of *The Walking Dead*, Daryl's upbringing, whatever its traumas, proves a benefit when action is called for: his backwoods skills and resourcefulness make him the perfect protagonist for the zombie wasteland. In the denouement of "Still," Beth tells Daryl "you were made for how things are now," concluding that he will be "the last man standing."

Daryl's biggest action moments as victim-hero include the funeral home sequence in "Alone," during which he loses Beth to mysterious, car-equipped kidnappers. The funeral home where Daryl and Beth hole up, play house, and experience increasing sexual tension is the "space of innocence" where melodrama always begins and where it longs (but often fails) to end.[14] Following melodramatic convention, this idyllic space is invaded by villainous forces greater than our victim-heroes, in this case the relentless walker hordes. Daryl opens the front door confidently, assuming the noise he hears outside is the small dog who visited earlier that day. His soft spot for the dog shows his heart of gold and his tenderness toward those weaker than himself: "I'm gonna give that mutt one more chance," he says, as he heads to the front hall with food. Once he opens the door, a mob of walkers swiftly invades the home. Beth tosses Daryl his crossbow and he orders her to flee out the window, telling her he will meet her at the nearby road. We see one additional cutaway shot of Beth, and then we do not see her again for the remaining ninety seconds of the sequence. Meanwhile, Daryl bravely fights his way out, killing numerous walkers, with several shots depicted from Daryl's direct point of view. It is his sequence, his heroic action moment. Yet in true melodramatic fashion, where "too late" is the rule, his efforts are not enough. The sequence culminates with a long tracking shot following Daryl as he runs out to the nighttime road, just in the "nick of time" to see a car taking Beth away but "too late" to do anything about it.[15] Much like Leatherface at the end of *The Texas Chain Saw Massacre*, Daryl fails because he doesn't have motorized transport: his backwoods hillbilly powers are temporarily trumped by his urban counterparts and their technology.

This tragic loss of the space of innocence represented by his and Beth's time at the funeral home is only the prelude to a much greater loss: she dies when Daryl tries to rescue her midway through season five ("Coda"). Epitomizing high melodrama, he carries her dead body out of the hospital like Mary carrying Jesus in Michelangelo's *Pietà* (1499). Even Daryl's most personally tragic moment of sadness and suffering is hyperreal as his loss of Beth is depicted in hyperbolic, intertextual terms. It is a moment of extreme melodrama and artifice—only a grand-scale excess of pathos-laden music and mise-en-scène (the wasted city) proving capable of conveying the emotions on display.

Similarly melodramatic are the opening episodes introducing series protagonist Rick Grimes. Unlike Daryl, who comes from a broken home and is a social outsider, Rick is initially easier to identify with because of his middle-class traits. Daryl and his brother Merle are already wild and therefore more prepared for an apocalyptic situation. Unlike Rick, they don't live on the grid and they do not rely as much on the collective institutions of modern society. While the show sets Daryl up as the expert on survival, Rick possesses some of the same survival skills by virtue of his more conventional training as a police officer and upbringing in a rural family. As a result, Rick's transition to living without society is a more dramatic one than Daryl's.

After escaping an Atlanta hospital where he has been left for dead, Rick is reunited with his wife and son in a pathos-laden scene in the third episode of the first season ("Tell It to the Frogs") in which he takes over leadership of the group from Shane. Here, as throughout the first few seasons, Rick is a restrained, handsome, clean-cut leader. *The Walking Dead* creator Robert Kirkman's choice to make a straight-laced sheriff's deputy a capable horror-genre hero is an unusual one, given the genre's long history of incompetent law enforcement officers stretching from *Psycho* to *Night of the Living Dead* to *Halloween* and beyond. George A. Romero's *Night of the Living Dead*, *The Walking Dead*'s most direct antecedent, features the worst sheriff of all, a callous, unfeeling man who kills the surviving protagonist at the film's conclusion.[16] Interestingly, Kirkman acknowledges his debt to Romero, highlighting his tendency to humanize and melodramatize Romero's material—"Stephanie Meyer is to Bram Stoker as Robert Kirkman is to George Romero" he proclaims in a 2016 interview—yet he does not explicitly discuss the ideological implications of choosing a white, male sheriff as his main character.[17] In foregrounding Rick, Kirkman's comic and the TV series re-gender and re-race the typical horror protagonist: instead of the slasher film's "Final Girl" or Romero's first two "living dead" films' black male protagonists, *The Walking Dead* gives us white male survivor-heroes in leading roles.[18]

Rick's white maleness and iconic good looks invite easy viewer identification for a majority of viewers and allow him to transform from sensitive, law-abiding family man to violent, unhinged wild man over the course of the first four seasons without being deposed as group leader. As Susan Jeffords argues, white male characters like Rick transform and change at will without affecting their privileged status in patriarchal culture; their shifts in character remain in the realm of the personal, never the structural.[19] Rick starts going backwoods by growing his beard at the prison early in season four, and by "Us," late in the season, he has become full-on wild man, with long stringy hair and beard.

Rick's accompanying wild violent streak emerges in "A," when Joe's gang of abject hillbillies threaten to rape Carl, evoking *Deliverance*. Taken by surprise at night, Rick, Michonne, and Carl are held at gunpoint. Joe tells Rick that he and his men intend to "have the girl, then the boy, then I'm gonna shoot you." Rick escapes Joe's grasp, and in the ensuing fight, bites Joe in the throat, an act which visually equates him to a walker, though he's no cannibal: he spits out the flesh. Moments later he brutally butchers Carl's attempted rapist at close range with a knife, at first depicted via handheld camera with Rick's blood-doused face in medium close-up. However, the second half of Rick's attack is portrayed in audio only while the camera slowly tracks into a close-up on Carl, reassuring us that Rick commits this bloody murder on his son's behalf yet simultaneously revealing Carl's horrified reaction to the deed.

Rick's murderous rage aligns him with sympathetic yet horrific hillbillies like *Texas Chain Saw*'s Leatherface family and *The Hills Have Eyes*' Papa Jupe clan.[20] Carol J. Clover notes the oscillation of viewer identification from the psychopathic killer to the heroic Final Girl in slasher films.[21] Building on her notion that viewers initially identify with the killer, then root for the Final Girl in the second half, Carter Soles has argued that certain rural slashers like *Texas Chain Saw* and *The Hills Have Eyes* prolong our identification with the cannibalistic hillbilly even after we would normally switch sides.[22] In this scene, *The Walking Dead* simplifies this horror formula by conflating the two figures into one: Rick is both our civilized protagonist *and* our bloodthirsty hillbilly killer. By the time he unleashes his lethal onslaught, the show has staged a near-rape scene, introducing completely irredeemable hillbillies to shift Rick into the relative position of avenging city dweller tapping into internal killer instincts to vanquish a despicable foe.

While Rick oscillates between civilized magnanimity and monstrous violence, displaying a range of characterizations that is facilitated by his whiteness, *The Walking Dead* portrays people of color more narrowly and stereotypically. The show's depiction of supporting characters of color reinforces the centrality and three-dimensionality of its white male protagonists. Korean-American Glenn is especially important in this regard since he is right-hand man to Rick from the second episode of the series. He consistently acts as a group mediator, bolstering the ultimate authority of the white leaders (Rick, Abe) to whom he plays second-in-command.

Glenn specializes in scurrying around undetected, reifying stereotypes about Asian Americans, historically depicted as shifty and vermin-like. Glenn is good at scavenging, yet he cowers in battle in early seasons of the show; for example, in the season two episode "Nebraska," Glenn freezes in a gunfight, forcing Rick to defend him and exemplifying the feminized, hyposexual Asian male. In fact, his first appearance is a visual play on another Asian icon, Short Round from *Indiana Jones and the Temple of Doom*. Glenn is twenty-two in the comic but visually infantilized, sporting a backpack and baseball cap, while Rick, his Indiana Jones, towers over him, rangy and lined, juxtaposing Glenn's youthful energy with world-weary reserve (issue 2). Daryl confirms this reading, calling Glenn "Short Round" on the show ("What Lies Ahead"). Thus Rick's position as a hillbilly leader relies upon people of color being willing to act as his followers. The social hierarchy within the group reaffirms white, male authority, simultaneously appeasing liberal viewers with the inclusive multiculturalism of Rick's group while assuring more conservative viewers that people of color still know their place in the hierarchy.

This is why Glenn, no matter how his fortunes might rise in the show—dating Maggie, co-leading a small splinter group of survivors in season four, etc.—will never be a true leader in a hierarchy that includes Rick or Daryl. Even Daryl's miscreant brother Merle, in his first appearance, singlehandedly overcomes both Glenn and his companion T-Dog, violently beating the latter ("Guts"). Merle further establishes dominance over Glenn in "Hounded" when he captures Glenn and his girlfriend Maggie despite both of them having guns trained on Merle. Their capture directly leads to Maggie's sexual humiliation at the hands of Merle's boss, the Governor, further emasculating Glenn ("When the Dead Come Knocking").

Since comics employ shorthand in depictions of all physical characteristics including racial ones, when an artist draws a cartoon of a person of color, the specific, iconic characteristics they select reveals their perspective vis-à-vis their subject's status as a visual other. In the comic, Tyreese is hypermasculine, a stereotypical African American male. He prefers a hammer to more modern technologies. In his appearances in the comic, Tyreese is drawn particularly *not* to evoke audience identification, based on the generic face that Scott McCloud theorizes allows for such identification. Tyreese is repeatedly shown in black silhouette with few facial details visible, including his introduction (issue 7). In the show, he is arguably split into two characters, the relatively inert T-Dog, who shows up in the series at the same point as Tyreese in the comic, and the more substantive Tyreese, who is feminized, defanged, and rendered marginal and ineffective by season four.

Despite high levels of screen time and moments of character depth, *The Walking Dead*'s black characters most often prop up white centrality and power, many of them functioning as "magical negroes." The magical negro is a persistent pop-cultural stereotype Audrey Colombe describes as having "no history": his "vaguely defined" magical powers cannot be explained except via his "other worldly" origins. The magical negro "has a threatening aspect" at least when he first appears: "there is initial danger, which makes the White people nervous in some way." Yet ultimately, "his sole purpose in the story is to selflessly use [his] powers to help a White man."[23]

African American protagonists Morgan, Michonne, and Ezekiel all function as magical negroes. Morgan acquires a disproportionate amount of fighting ability with insufficient explanation, for instance. Captured by a pacifist psychiatrist who practices Aikido ("Here's Not Here"), Morgan is trained by the aptly named Eastman over some months (two minutes of montage-laden screen time) and, as a result, he is able to singlehandedly defeat multiple groups of armed attackers in seasons five and six.

Ezekiel's powers similarly veer toward the magical. The comic portrays Ezekiel's tiger companion, Shiva, defending him to the death against walkers, ostensibly because he was her zookeeper pre-apocalypse, yet the level of loyalty Ezekiel must instill to cause the animal to abandon all survival instincts is beyond the realm of any ordinary zookeeper (issue 118). Ezekiel makes his first appearance in AMC's series in the second episode of season seven, "The Well," where he explains Shiva's loyalty: he saved her life when her leg was injured after she fell in a moat. However, we still read Shiva's presence as an aspect of Ezekiel's magical negritude because, like Morgan's brief period of training, it is not sufficient to explain Ezekiel's ability to keep Shiva on a chain by his side with no fear of her attacking him or the many other people who come into her range.

Though still farfetched, Michonne's backstory is nonetheless a little more believable than Morgan's or Ezekiel's. On the show, she is given relatively little history, but in the comic Michonne was a lawyer who practiced fencing, which translated into her mastery of the katana in the apocalypse. In "Beside the Dying Fire," the season two finale, Michonne, who has no last name, comes from nowhere, surviving the apocalypse with only her katana and two seemingly magically controlled walkers (though it's later explained how she does this without magic). Her very presence creates a cliffhanger, a mystery, suggesting her enigmatic other-worldly origins. This mimics her striking first appearance in the comics (issue 19).

Despite the real-world origins proffered for these characters' skills, their origin stories are flimsy and fantastical compared to the clear connections to personal history with which Daryl is afforded. Michonne, Morgan, and Ezekiel are role-playing game character types projected onto black characters. They are the samurai, monk, and beastmaster. The inclusivity of casting African Americans is commendable, but the connection between their abilities and identities is weak at best. In contrast, Daryl's abilities emerge organically from his backwoods identity, upbringing, and life experiences, making them much more authentic and believable.

Not only are their backstories less realistic, but characters of color in *The Walking Dead* frequently serve either as rescue bait for the white characters or as sacrifices to legitimate their rage. In the comic, for example, Michonne is captured and tortured by the evil Governor. In the show, Glenn takes her place in the storyline. Both are like Tonto, captured and beaten up in countless episodes of *The Lone Ranger* so that the Lone Ranger can rescue him. Glenn's and Tyreese's deaths are particularly telling. In different storylines, in the comic, they are restrained and executed in front of Rick by major villains, transformed into plot devices to motivate Rick's vengeance and producing the suffering that melodramatically justifies his actions. It requires four slashes of a katana to chop off Tyreese's head, moreover, evoking the armor-like skin of black superheroes such as Luke Cage and its connection to racist ideas, born in slavery, about tough black skin.[24]

Glenn frequently acts as a deferential mediator who must appeal to white male authority to get anything accomplished. He is always positioned as a sidekick to white males like Rick and Abe who are more masculine than he is. He mediates between Rick and Abe in the season four episode "Four Walls and a Roof," insisting the group not split up. His intervention prevents hillbilly hero, Rick, from having to go toe-to-toe with Abe, and ultimately reaffirms Rick as the true leader of the group. Similarly, in "Us," Glenn talks Abe into pressing on to find Maggie, technically a group discussion but with Abe as final arbiter: Glenn appeals to Abe's authority to make his "deal." And again in "Self Help," Glenn acknowledges that Abe is "calling this thing" but simply wants to know that the sergeant is "good," thereby mitigating the driven ex-soldier's intensity and giving the other, feminized group members (Eugene, Maggie, Tara, Rosita) a chance to weigh in on their next steps. Yet there is no doubt that Abe, the hypermasculine, white military man, is in charge.

In sum, *The Walking Dead*'s focus on the sufferings of white males and their superiority as survivors and leaders has retrograde cultural implications. In the current cultural moment, real-life police are viewed as melodramatic victim-heroes in the face of Black Lives Matter protesters, despite being heavily armed and getting away with killing people of color with minimal consequences. Furthermore, in light of president-elect Donald Trump's gleeful comments during his campaign about Second Amendment supporters possibly assassinating his opponent, Rick's (and the show's) pro-gun stance is poignantly troubling.[25] Rick is a pro-gun, military style leader: the first thing he says when he takes over the group is "What you really need here is more guns." Additionally, the opening of "Coda" features a *Dirty Harry* homage with Rick in the Harry Callahan role, gloating over a fallen, injured Hispanic man before fatally shooting him. In this context, it is noteworthy that Rick's group is most often pitted against matriarchal societies such as Terminus, Grady Memorial Hospital, Alexandria, and even Woodbury, whose psychotic Governor has a secret serial-killer room and who is queered via his closeness to Milton and symbolically castrated via his missing eye.

Robert Kirkman is heavily involved in both the comic and the TV series as creator, executive producer, and writer. In 2013, Kirkman was interviewed on financial news channel CNBC, speculating that *The Walking Dead* was the reason AMC's stock rose 25 percent that year. He further supposed that *The Walking Dead* was thriving on the U.S.'s weak economy: "People now are, you know, worrying about how to pay their mortgage and worrying about how they're going to afford groceries and it's nice to sit down on the couch and watch a simpler time."[26] Along with clinging to guns, the concept of post-apocalyptic "simpler times" allows Rick's wife Lori, in the comic, to chastise a skeptical feminist companion who has been relegated to laundry duty: "This isn't about Women's Rights. It's about being realistic and getting things done" (issue 3). The line is changed in the show to, "How did we get stuck doing all the Hattie McDaniel work? The world ended. Didn't you get the memo?" ("Tell It to the Frogs"). Nevertheless, *The Walking Dead* has incredibly broad mainstream appeal especially in the prized 18–49 year-old bracket.[27] The show synergized with *Mad Men* and *Breaking Bad* to create a reputation for AMC as a premier source for buzzworthy dramas. The comic benefits from this prestige as well, being reissued for its new readers.

The prestige and wide appeal of the series and comic are disturbing given their insidious racial ideologies. The adoption of imagined hillbillyness is driven by the idea that racism is natural to hillbillies. If one suffers enough, as a poor white person does, then racism is almost allowable. According to melodramatic logic, suffering equals justification. This is why the imagined hillbilly is a valuable model for postmodern protagonists. Merle calls T-Dog a "nigger" in season one. Daryl calls Glenn "Short Round." Audiences accept this as an organic component of the hillbilly's ethnic identity. Hillbillies are also imagined to be the only racist white people, scapegoats for a bigotry and prejudice that is actually practiced across economic classes in the U.S., comforting *The Walking Dead*'s audience that if they're not poor white people, then they cannot be racist. Kirkman's reference to "simpler times" is a loaded one. Ultimately there is a politics to gritty realism and to his brand in particular.

NOTES

1. Harkins, *Hillbilly*, 4.
2. Kunyosying and Soles, "Postmodern Geekdom."
3. Williams, "Melodrama Revised," 42.
4. *Ibid.*, 77, 59.
5. Harkins, *Hillbilly*, 7.
6. *Ibid.*, 8.
7. *Ibid.*
8. The hillbilly has experienced historic marginalization and continues to be marginalized. We differentiate between actual rural backwoods Americans and what is imagined about the hillbilly by media creators. We ultimately side with the backwoods American and are interested in the critique of how their qualities are imagined and appropriated to create authentic protagonists in a postmodern milieu. The actual backwoods American does not benefit from this appropriation. Reality shows are a good example of this. When the hillbilly protagonist is extended into reality television such as *Here Comes Honey Boo Boo* and *Swamp People*, he or she is mostly laughed at as a spectacle. It is the imagined characteristics of the hillbilly when tacked onto a fictional postmodern protagonist that allows for audience sympathy.

9. Baxter, "The Walking Dead."
10. McCloud, *Understanding Comics*, 36.
11. Baudrillard, *Simulacra and Simulation*, 1–2.
12. Williams, "Melodrama Revised," 71.
13. *Ibid.*, 66.
14. *Ibid.*, 65.
15. *Ibid.*, 69.
16. Dillard, "*Night of the Living Dead*," 27.
17. Fear, "Robert Kirkman."
18. Clover, *Men, Women, and Chain Saws*, 35–41.
19. Jeffords, "The Big Switch," 206–7.
20. Soles, "Sympathy," 237.
21. Clover, *Men, Women, and Chain Saws*, 45–6, 60.
22. Soles, "Sympathy," 242–3, 245–7.
23. Colombe, "White Hollywood's New Black Boogeyman."
24. Plous and Williams, "Racial Stereotypes," 796.
25. Corasaniti and Habermanaug, "Donald Trump Suggests."
26. Huntington, "Robert [Kirkman]."
27. St. John, "The Most Watched Hour Ever."

"There's no niggers anymore... There's us and the dead"
Masculinity in a Post-Racial, Post-Apocalyptic America

BROOKE BENNETT

In terms of gender representation in AMC's *The Walking Dead*, most existing scholarship analyzes only women, giving short shrift to the various facets of masculinity the series has to offer. To fully understand the significance of gender within any text, critics must dissect representations of women alongside those of men, as they are highly interdependent.[1] In this essay, I emphasize the contextual relationship between popular television texts and the contemporary postfeminist and post-racial (i.e., colorblind) politics within popular culture.

Most important to understanding gender representations, hegemonic masculinity is a theory reflective of an underlying power structure woven into social life, culture, and politics, ultimately upholding the ruling class's ideologies and norms.[2] There is an ideal version of masculinity and manhood—as seen via cultural artifacts such as television—which encapsulates the favored social behaviors and physical characteristics of a specific time period and culture. R.W. Connell and James Messerschmidt state that one "fundamental feature of the concept remains the communication of the plurality of masculinities and the hierarchy of masculinity."[3] Masculinities are, moreover, built upon an intersectional interaction of gender, race, sexuality, class, and able-bodiedness. Most importantly, Connell and Messerschmidt determine that "patterns of masculinity are socially defined in contradistinction from some model (whether real or imaginary) of femininity."[4] As a social construction, gender is defined by binary categories wherein the definition of one—femininity—reflects upon the definition of the other—masculinity; one cannot exist without the other.

Elaborating hegemonic masculinity, Amanda Lotz states that, overall, "television storytelling has ... performed significant ideological work by consistently supporting some behaviors, traits, and beliefs among the male characters it constructs as heroic or admirable, while denigrating others," thus recalling the hierarchical nature of how hegemonic masculinity functions.[5] Like famous athletes, whom men and boys are made to admire, television constructs masculinity. Over the range of television programming, as in real life, Lotz explains, the "[e]mbodiment of purely patriarchal or feminist masculinities is undoubtedly rare and fairly unimaginable. Rather, characters embody a variety of attributes that can be tied to both patriarchal power structures and feminist endeavors that seek to dismantle them."[6] Labeling texts as simply morally "good" or "bad" in terms of gendered representation is thus counterproductive since doing so ignores a more holistic examination of intersectional politics within the media.[7] Overall, each television series embodies its own form of idealized masculinity, and that represented in *The Walking Dead* is entwined, most significantly, with racial politics. The contemporary politics surrounding postfeminism and post-racial ideologies are crucial to understanding the masculinities within *The Walking Dead* since the series is highly reflective of these contemporary hegemonic discourses.

First of all, postfeminism both invokes and revokes feminism, providing an ironic distance from which to critique the progress made in equality for women. On the other hand, Geraldine Harris defines the term "postmasculinism" as a recurring motif in television, arguing that it describes an ambivalent relationship to feminism which has seemingly worked toward "the de-centering and de-naturalisation of the normative, white masculine subject."[8] Though reiterations of traditional white masculinity can easily be seen in *The Walking Dead*, I argue that the series' masculinities have become much more entangled with other races in recent seasons. At points, these masculinities can be seen as reiterating traditional hegemonic masculinity, symbolically punishing men of color, yet some narrative points seem to challenge the superiority of this ideal, de-centering the "normative, white masculine subject."[9] There does, though, appear to be an implicit invocation and repudiation of feminism among representations of masculinity, one of the main characteristics of postfeminism. One important typology of postfeminist masculinity that has been consistently found within popular culture, and is at play within *The Walking Dead* via Rick, is fatherhood. As an ideal of masculinity, the ideology surrounding postfeminist fatherhood "'simultaneously evokes and rejects' feminism."[10] Overall, I argue that the various types of fatherhood representative of postfeminism, such as "protective paternalism," "paternal payback," and the "widowed single father" (which I will detail in full later), are reflected within *The Walking Dead*.[11]

Important to my emphasis on relating masculinity to an intersectional approach to identity, Michael L. Wayne found, by applying the idea of "post-masculinism" (another way of articulating postfeminist masculinity), that race is inexplicably tied to the creation of an ironic distance between masculinity's recognition and repudiation of feminist progress within television narratives. In short, race becomes intertwined with idealized white males in order to shape a morally superior and idealized postfeminist masculinity.[12] Furthermore, Hannah Hamad states that the "white hegemony of postfeminist fatherhood makes clear the continuing need to see and address race."[13] Finally, as Ralina L. Joseph points out, "discourses of post-race are undeniably gendered, and discourses of post-feminism are undeniably raced."[14] To examine one, we must examine the other; identities are always intersectional, continually interacting, as opposed to existing in a vacuum.

Protecting the Family and Postfeminist Masculinity

Martina Baldwin and Mark McCarthy state that *The Walking Dead* "privilege[s] a notion of citizenship that is overwhelmingly white, male, and heterosexual, where women and people of color are valued only in so much as they are useful. These survivor narratives, then, are predicated on non-whites as plot devices to support the white characters."[15] This is important to understand because there are clearly other groups of survivors, yet the series chooses to focus on a predominantly white group led by a white male, thus supporting the idea that these types of individuals are most successful within the post-apocalyptic world.[16] Our principal group of survivors have encountered many other formed groups: in the first season episode, "Vatos," for example, Rick, Daryl, T-Dog, and Glenn encounter a group of Latino men who have found refuge in a nursing home, caring for the elderly who were left behind. Nonetheless, the series' creators choose to foreground Rick's particular band of survivors, deliberately positioning a predominantly white narrative as the access point for an (ideal) audience to identify with in this post-apocalyptic world.

At the beginning of the series, Rick assumes the position of leadership over the group, replacing Shane and remaining unquestioned in the process. Coming into the group of survivors wearing his sheriff deputy's uniform and hat, Rick represents hope for the law and order that structured the pre-apocalyptic world.[17] As long as Rick clings to this past embodiment of traditional masculinity—which the group seems invested in as well—the ability for *The Walking Dead* to become a revolutionary text, in terms of gender and racial politics, remains low. The disappearance of this symbolic uniform and its correspondent political ideologies is crucial in the move toward a more radical universe in which people of color and women move into leadership roles, increasing in power.

Rick Grimes is important in establishing the hegemonic order within the series in relation to the show's idealized masculinity.[18] Rick's masculinity is largely defined in relation to his status as a father and former sheriff's deputy, reflective of the "protective paternalism" archetype.[19] The subordinated masculinities exhibited in characters such as Glenn, Tyreese, and Daryl open spaces of leadership in opposition to Rick's. As the series progresses, Rick's leadership abilities are brought into question, thus enabling alternative masculinities the opportunity for critiquing and/or challenging *The Walking Dead*'s hegemonic masculinity. The postfeminist archetype of "protective paternalism" is a large aspect of Rick's identity, particularly emphasizing the notion of providing for his family, as Rick continually tries to protect Carl and Lori (who eventually becomes pregnant and gives birth to Judith) by any means possible: his prime motivation in episode one involved finding his family, and that prime motivation (family) has not diminished.[20] This type of masculinity within the show is also found in Hershel Greene, who wishes to protect his family and who embodies more traditional ideologies as well. Hershel is also respected by everyone and gives advice to Rick, thus lending more support to the argument that Rick's masculinity is highly idealized. Additionally, Morgan Jones also desires to protect his son, Duane, at all costs. As Rick is wondering where Carl is, we are introduced to Morgan and Duane as they explain to post-coma Rick what has happened since he has been in a coma. In this way, the narrative strength of protective paternalism crosses racial lines as well, demonstrating how crucial it is to the formulation of *The Walking Dead*'s masculinity.

The rhetoric of protective paternalism and the post–9/11 environment are highly intertwined; we—as a society—need a male protector and vigilante to safeguard our women, children, and families.[21] Via the seemingly harmless idea of fatherhood, this form of "post–9/11 protectorate masculinity negotiates violent vigilantism and rampaging violence/protectiveness as culturally viable when enacted in the name of fatherhood."[22] Rather than bringing back the pre-feminist ideologies of traditional manhood, the post–9/11 environment—via fatherhood—enables the ability of men to enact these anachronistic traditions of masculinity through atrocious acts of violence in ways that appear not to push back against the new formulations of masculinity brought on by the feminist movement of the 1970s. Yet this discourse is dependent upon continual female vulnerability and victimhood: women thus become in need of constant protection from men.[23]

Rick's motivation for violence involves the reunion of the patriarchal family—he begins killing the undead as part of his mission to locate Lori and Carl. The fact that he succeeds both marks narrative sanctification of the nuclear family and reinforces the idea that this protective paternalism is justified and affectively rewarded—the Grimes' family reunion is a highly emotional scene.[24] Later on in the series, in season four, in an intense display of protective paternalism, Rick uses his teeth to rip out the throat of a bandit who was threatening to rape and kill Carl ("A"). Here Carl takes on the ultimate feminized role—that of an object threatened by sexual violence and bodily violation. This scene thus becomes an extreme example of defending women and children from outsiders. Additionally, this scene exemplifies one of the tropes associated with protective paternalism, that of "paternal payback," in which "bereaved or aggrieved fatherhood" sanctions a character to "do anything necessary" as payback for a death or to "effect the safe return of his imperiled child."[25] Thus, Rick is morally justified in taking vengeance upon those threatening Carl because it is a state of exception embedded within his status as a father.

Rick is also able to perform egregious violence because he is a widowed, single father after Lori's death in season three. This archetypal image serves as an affective appeal to gain sympathy for lost male power, while simultaneously tapping into "a feminist espoused masculine ideal" that masks its antifeminist implications.[26] Rick's status as a widowed single father supplies him with sympathy from the audience, ultimately overshadowing the antifeminist politics at play in killing off the mother.[27] The seemingly feminist ideal of masculinity, in which domestic fatherhood becomes a central role for men to aspire to, is thus achieved in these texts via the marginalization and literal killing of the mother. Significantly, in Lori's death scene, Carl emulates his father's protective paternalism as he volunteers to shoot his mother to prevent her from coming back as a zombie, protecting his newborn sister. As the mother dies, the son emulates the postfeminist masculinity embodied in his father.

From a Post-Racial World to a Critique of Violent White Masculinity

Although Rick is morally permitted a large degree of violence in the name of protective paternalism, the development of his character, especially during season five, questions his ability to be an effective leader. This critique of the white male as the inevitable group leader is concurrent with the progression of the series away from the negative politics associated with color-blind post-racial ideology. Season five especially brings into the narrative challenges to white masculinity and to Rick's leadership and morality as well as to the denigration of people of color within the series. *The Walking Dead* has consistently been critiqued as dismissing people of color, as seemingly all of the nonwhite characters are killed off, leading to the assumption that the show is incapable of having more than one character of color at a time.

Ashley Doane defines colorblindness, or "the claim that race no longer 'matters' in American society," as, the idea that racism is "no longer embedded in the U.S. social structure," and that if there is still racism it is because of "minority group members."[28] Similarly, Jennifer Esposito claims that post-racism occurs when categories of race no longer have significance.[29] Additionally, Sean Brayton argues that science fiction narratives often contain post-racial ideologies via the "alien "other," which is used to deemphasize the racialized binary dividing the human characters.[30] In the case of *The Walking Dead*, this "alien other" becomes the zombie. Dawn Keetley has also made this connection, arguing that *The Walking Dead* is undeniably a post-racial text established by Rick's argument with Merle in the season one episode, "Guts," which culminates in Rick stating that the world they live in now has become one of "us against them"—there is no longer "white" or "black," just "dead" or "undead."[31] Subsequently, Keetley tells us that "Rick's banishing of all racial difference (shaping his post-apocalyptic world as 'post-racial') allows it to creep back in unrecognized."[32] One important aspect of post-racial discourse in popular culture is the idea of multiculturalism. As Catherine R. Squires argues, a "way of conveying post-racial illusions in the media is through a 'celebration' of differences," a seemingly progressive move evidenced by the selection of many actors of color for a given television show.[33] Just because *The Walking Dead* has a diverse cast in later seasons, however, does not mean it opens spaces for people of color; in fact, many characters of color die rather quickly, leaving room for the white protagonists to continue to survive and maintain charge of the group.

In an issue promoting season six of *The Walking Dead*, *Entertainment Weekly* brought together characters that have died up to this point in the show (before the beginning of season six), taking a picture of them with their eyes shut.[34] Strikingly, five out of the eleven present are people of color, a ratio disproportionate to the number of living characters of color in the show. All of the people of color, moreover, played important characters (Jacqui, Tyreese, Noah, T-Dog, and Bob) who had much more potential than was actually utilized before they were prematurely discarded from the series. In this instance, the argument claiming that characters of color become props to serve the white characters' narrative development would seem to hold up.[35]

The series consistently writes off not only characters of color but also serious discussion of race while simultaneously upholding whiteness, an important aspect of post-racial ideology.[36] Rick and Merle's confrontation on the rooftop in Atlanta, for instance, stunts the interrogation of racial politics, reflecting the trend in television narratives in which a "white anti-hero with ambivalent attitudes regarding racial equality [is] superior to an unambiguously racist white character(s) who more blatantly violate[s] 'the decorum of the white racial order.'"[37] Merle's never-ending verbal abuse, calling others in the group "taco bender," "nigger," and "rug muncher," presents him as an obvious bad guy. Via his "white trash" persona, Merle seemingly provides evidence for the myth that only "those kinds of people" are racist, while at the same time becoming a vehicle through which racist attitudes persist in the narrative.[38] Additionally, Merle's verbal abuse serves to belittle the existence of structural racism by reducing racism itself to the level of individual injustices, reflective of post-racial ideology.[39] Merle's actions here depoliticize systemic and institutional racism, demonstrating how the "ignorant" redneck Merle is simply an anomaly in modern society. As such, Merle's blatant display of racism uplifts Rick's actions, connecting them to his superior masculinity.

In these ways, Rick's white masculinity becomes the morally superior hegemonic form within the narrative. Yet, as seen throughout season five of *The Walking Dead*, Rick's ability to lead the community and the morality of his decisions become increasingly questionable—protective paternalism serves as a viable option to other characters only within certain ethical boundaries, which will be discussed below. In *The Walking Dead* it seems that "men must protect helpless women from monsters while not becoming too monstrous themselves."[40] Rick's becoming more monstrous is most easily seen in his emotionally-fueled altercation with Pete in the season five episode, "Try." In the name of protective paternalism, Rick uses violence to protect Jessie from her abusive husband. Rick's decision-making is called into question not only because he ignored Deanna's order not to get involved in Jessie and Pete's marriage, but also because he got involved because of his own sexual attraction to Jessie. In this way, like many other postfeminist series focused on masculinity, *The Walking Dead* "raises questions about which immoral actions can be justified and under what conditions," and, importantly, "[t]he protagonists are mostly driven by motivations related to families—a need to provide for or to reconstitute them."[41]

The protective paternalism that consistently supports and motivates Rick's violent vigilantism is called into question as he is symbolically punished for his actions via a woman of color, Michonne, who proves herself a more logical and levelheaded leader than Rick. After Rick attacks Pete in "Try," and then turns his anger on Deanna, Michonne (significantly attired in her constable uniform) has to knock him unconscious, emerging as distinctly *not* a prop used to further a white character's narrative; she symbolically interrupts the white hegemony of Rick's masculinity and its tendency towards unnecessary and selfish violence. This moment ultimately opens up a critique of the show's colorblind, post-racial ideologies as well as providing space for a more relational masculinity as an alternative to Rick's. As Helen K. Ho argues in relation to Glenn, these shortcomings of white masculinity fixed on violence as a tool of power and control "suggest ... that an adaptable, relational masculinity reaps more rewards than Rick's stoic and traditional hegemonic masculinity."[42] The masculinity presented through the men of color within *The Walking Dead* embodies a more relational, thus feminized and subordinated, masculinity, which does actually become a crucial facet of leadership in the series' vision of the post-apocalypse. Nonwhite male characters within *The Walking Dead* expose the limitations of the narrative's own hegemonic masculinity and provide alternative paths to peaceful coexistence with others.[43]

Since Rick is not purely heroic, then, the men of color are given the opportunity to amass directly oppositional, yet morally superior, positions in relation to him. White male characters like Rick or the Governor consistently have to struggle to maintain their positions of power. Rick's morality and leadership capabilities decline and are challenged later on in the series, especially after his confrontation with Pete in which he takes the ideology of protective paternalism to such drastic lengths that other characters finally voice concerns about his behavior. Minority characters are thus enabled to step up to the idealized attributes of masculinity—namely, that men must serve and protect women and children in the fight against zombies. For example, Glenn's development—one in direct opposition to the violence displayed by Rick—emphasizes how a new hierarchy of masculinity is not only possible but more viable.[44] When Rick wakes up from being knocked out by Michonne, he tells some of the members of the original group that he will take Alexandria by force if necessary. Glenn challenges Rick's logic, arguing that they must work together with the Alexandrians to achieve what they all want: to make the community prepared and ready for battle. Yet these oppositional spaces exist within contradictory narrative circumstances. For example, when the group departs from Terminus, Glenn opposes Rick in his desire to go back to Terminus and kill each and every one of the cannibals. By not enacting the retributive violence Rick calls for, Glenn allows Gareth and the others from Terminus to kidnap Bob and eat his leg. Glenn is thus symbolically punished—through another character of color's trauma and death, moreover—for his challenge to Rick's authority.

Another type of masculinity that is opposed to Rick's and that is symbolically punished is embodied in Tyreese and specifically highlighted by his death. Prior to his death, Tyreese begins a complex metamorphosis in which he starts to question the violent actions and decision-making of Rick. In the season five episode, "What Happened and What's Going On," Tyreese is met by the Governor and Martin in his hallucinations. The two repeatedly remark on how Tyreese said he would "pay his way" in return for protection in Woodbury, implying that he was supposed to follow the Governor's violent orders without question, and Martin claims that Tyreese cannot live in this world because he is unable to be violent and murder others to protect himself and his loved ones. Standing in direct opposition to the Governor and Martin, Beth, Lizzie, and Mika materialize to tell Tyreese to just "let go," and that "it's better now" since they are at peace in death. In his questioning of the violent hegemonic masculinity that the white men of the series embody, however, Tyreese is symbolically punished by his death at the end of the episode.

Tyreese's death could also be read as the realization that in the white order of masculine leadership in his new world, men have to surrender themselves over to this hegemonic masculinity or die. As Tyreese was becoming more humanized by not killing humans, he was beginning to be pushed out of the violent universe in which Rick thinks he exists. In a world dominated by white men that remain in positions of leadership, can men of color—or some type of alternative form of approaching dilemmas—be given opportunities to form a more peaceful existence? Tyreese certainly wanted to do so, only he was killed off too early to see this potential narrative through. Since Morgan Jones reappears in season five (having been mostly absent since season one) with a new outlook on life—as he tells Daryl and Aaron, "all life is precious"—maybe the nonviolent approach to the world that Tyreese began to introduce to *The Walking Dead* will be realized to some extent in the following seasons.

The Uncertainty of the Violent (White) Order

The Walking Dead establishes its own hegemonic masculinity via the show's protagonist, Rick Grimes. He repeatedly illustrates idealized masculinity through protective paternalism: women and children must be guarded from the enemy by any means necessary. Yet Rick's approach to the new world order is not sustainable, and the serial collapse of his communities demonstrates the untenable nature of his violent approach to leadership. These flawed aspects of *The Walking Dead*'s hegemonic white masculinity enable an oppositional space that disrupts the narrative universe via men of color. Glenn, for example, becomes representative of the possibilities of a more relational form of masculinity, one not utterly focused on violence, that subsequently challenges, from a holistic perspective, Rick's ability to make complex decisions.[45] Overall, I have attempted to begin a conversation about the complexities of race and masculinity within AMC's *The Walking Dead*. The series cannot be portrayed as conservatively "bad" or progressively "good" but instead necessitates an analysis demonstrating the interwoven politics of representational issues and subjective identities within individual characters. Any analysis of identity within the series thus demands attention to particular identity politics that emphasize intersectionality rather than asserting generalizations based solely on the politics of a monolithic and divided "race" or "gender."

Notes

1. See Dow, "The Traffic in Men."
2. For an extensive explanation of hegemonic masculinity, see Connell and Messerschmidt, "Hegemonic Masculinity."
3. Connell and Messerschmidt, "Hegemonic Masculinity," 846.
4. Ibid., 848.
5. Lotz, *Cable Guys*, 9.
6. Ibid., 38.
7. See also Horbury, "Post-Feminist Impasses."
8. Harris, "A Return to Form?" 444.
9. Ibid.
10. Hamad, *Postfeminism and Paternity*, 11.
11. Ibid.
12. Wayne, "Ambivalent Anti-Heroes."
13. Hamad, *Postfeminism and Paternity*, 27.
14. Joseph, "'Tyra Banks Is Fat,'" 240.
15. Baldwin and McCarthy, "Same as It Ever Was," 75–6.
16. Greene, "The Walking (Gendered) Dead," 70.
17. Staton, "Mad Hatters," 89; Nurse, "Asserting Law and Order," 72.
18. See Lotz, *Cable Guys*.
19. See Hamad, *Postfeminism and Paternity*.
20. Ibid.
21. See Godfrey and Hamad, "Save the Cheerleader."
22. Godfrey and Hamad, "Save the Cheerleader," 165.
23. As Stabile argues, the "affective pull of female vulnerability" enables a scenario in which "men are heroes and women are victims, perpetually in need of protection." Stabile, "'Sweetheart,'" 87, 89.
24. See Cortiel, "Travels with Carl."
25. Hamad, *Postfeminism and Paternity*, 63–4.
26. Ibid., 26.
27. As Hamad further details, "[C]ommensurate with the circuitous cultural logic of postfeminist masculinity, and the affective share carried by the figure of the widowed single father, there is no place for motherhood in this reconstituted nuclear family." Hamad, *Postfeminism and Paternity*, 57.
28. Doane, "Shades of Colorblindness," 15.
29. Esposito, "What Does Race Have to Do with *Ugly Betty*?" 521.
30. Brayton, "The Racial Politics," 70.
31. See Keetley, "Introduction."
32. Keetley, "Introduction," 9.
33. Squires, *The Post-Racial Mystique*, 7. In the context of television series, see Warner, "The Racial Logic."
34. Ross et al., "WE SEE Dead People."
35. See Baldwin and McCarthy, "Same as It Ever Was."
36. See Wayne, "Ambivalent Anti-Heroes."
37. Wayne, "Ambivalent Anti-Heroes," 207.
38. Ibid., 211–2.

39. See Doane, "Shades of Colorblindness."
40. Gavaler, "Zombies Vs. Superheroes."
41. Lotz, *Cable Guys*, 63.
42. Ho, "The Model Minority," 70.
43. *Ibid.*, 71.
44. *Ibid.*
45. After this writing, Glenn was killed off from the series during the season seven premiere, "The Day Will Come When You Won't Be," which obviously seriously compromises the ideals he stood for in opposition to Rick.

Becoming Glenn

Asian American Masculinity

HELEN K. HO

Since its debut in 2010, viewers of AMC's *The Walking Dead* have followed a band of survivors attempting to establish a sense of home as they navigate an apocalyptic wilderness. While many of *The Walking Dead*'s original characters have met their demise, a handful of major characters from the first season remain alongside the show's main character, Rick Grimes. As season seven began, these included Rick's son, Carl; Daryl Dixon, a stoic redneck with a motorcycle and a crossbow; Carol Peletier, the last female survivor from the original group; Morgan Jones, the first survivor Rick met after waking from a coma; and Glenn Rhee. Despite creator Robert Kirkman's claim that the show's cast "accurately portray[s] the world as it is, i.e. not all white,"[1] the show has been criticized for its lack of diversity. In fact, until his death in the first episode of season seven, Glenn was the only racial minority (except Morgan Jones) who had survived from the beginning alongside *The Walking Dead*'s main white characters.

Glenn's continued presence and in-depth storyline through the first six seasons have garnered him special attention from fans and popular media (he was named one of *People* magazine's sexiest men of 2013). Glenn's popularity was particularly evident when the season six episode "Thank You" placed him in a seemingly no-win situation, trapped under another character's dead body in the midst of hungry zombies. With a close-up of ripped flesh and innards, *The Walking Dead* led fans to believe that Glenn had died, even going so far as to remove Yeun's name from the show's opening credits for two episodes. As evidence of his popularity, ratings rose 8 percent among *The Walking Dead*'s target demographic and *The Talking Dead* saw ratings rise 49 percent, as viewers tuned in to find out what had happened to Glenn.[2]

A major part of Glenn's appeal comes from his story arc. Actor interviews, AMC promotional materials and cultural critics note that he is one of the characters—if not *the* character—that grows the most from the start of the show. As each season progresses, Glenn not only changes his physical appearance to become more ruggedly masculine, but his romance with Maggie Greene develops from a fling to a stable and monogamous marriage. Yeun has claimed that the zombie apocalypse helped Glenn "becom[e] a man,"[3] and to grow emotionally and physically from "plucky kid" to "very hardened ... probably the man he never dreamed he could be."[4] A post on Internet blog *Angry Asian Man* offered, "Glenn was one of the most complex and beloved Asian American characters in all of pop culture, where complex and beloved Asian American characters are few and far between."[5] A consistent fan favorite, Glenn served as a symbol of hope as he evolved from season to season.

The Walking Dead provided a new model for masculinity with Glenn that was, in part, due to his status as an Asian American. Given his character arc and his presence on screen as a racial minority, Glenn served as a counterpoint to the show's one-dimensional portrayals of white masculinity. In earlier seasons, Glenn's marginal masculinity was feminized, as he filled the role of an Asian American "model minority." As he incorporated qualities of dominant masculinity into his character, however, a more fluid, relational masculinity emerged. Overall, Glenn's flexibility and adaptability—and his ultimate demise—highlight the limitations of rigid, white masculinity.

Hegemonic Masculinity Among the Walking Dead

In previous work, I have detailed the argument that zombie narratives reflect upon and reinforce white masculinity and patriarchy in the social order.[6] By far, the main focus of *The Walking Dead* has been the white deputy sheriff Rick Grimes, particularly as his social, physical and emotional strength is tested by villains like Philip "the Governor" Blake (seasons three and four) and the Saviors' Negan (seasons six and seven). Rick's adventure begins in "Days Gone Bye" when he wakes from a coma to find the world overrun by zombies. Rick eventually finds his wife and son with a group of survivors outside of Atlanta and, despite the presence of other dominating male figures in the camp, he quickly becomes the group's leader. Over the next six seasons, he gains a steadfast group of loyal followers, all of whom work to establish a sense of social order and stability wherever they can. The fierce loyalty is reciprocal, with Rick maiming, killing and exiling those who threaten the people and social order under his care.

Dedicated to his role as protector and lawman, Rick represents a specific white/cowboy masculinity that propels him to success in the early stages of the apocalypse. R.W. Connell describes hegemonic masculinity as the dominant form of masculinity—with its particular set of characteristics and behaviors—in a given society. Hegemonic masculinity works in the defense of patriarchy; it maintains the superiority of not only men over women, but also legitimizes "manly" men over other types of men who become feminized in comparison.[7] To be a hegemonic male is to inhabit and embody positions of power, juxtaposed with all things feminine and weak. Nick Trujillo's work on hegemonic masculinity lists five main features of masculine power, at least when it comes to men in U.S. media: "physical force and control"; "occupational achievement"; "familial patriarchy"; heterosexuality; and a dominant symbolization in "the daring, romantic frontiersman of yesteryear and of the present-day outdoorsman."[8] A white heterosexual deputy sheriff who protects those under his care by physically overpowering and outgunning threats, Rick Grimes is the embodiment of this hegemonic masculinity.

The racial framework in America, and particularly in the American South, links whiteness with dominance. This racial hierarchy holds true in *The Walking Dead*, as white men lead almost every band of survivors roving the post-apocalyptic landscape. In the first season, the Atlanta camp found a leader in Shane, Rick's partner in the sheriff's department, as well as the expert hunter and tracker Daryl. As Rick supplants Shane, he still relies on the camp's other white men for help, including Daryl and the camp's elder, Dale. In the second season, the Atlanta survivors meet the Greene family, led by stubborn patriarch Hershel. Season three has the group meeting the Governor, leader of the fortified Woodbury community. Gareth, the leader of Terminus, is introduced in season four, as is the hotheaded ex-military Abraham, who eventually joins forces with Rick. In seasons five and six, Rick's group fights vicious bands of survivors including the Wolves, led by a man named Owen, and the Saviors, led by the infamous villain, Negan. They also meet the survivors at Hilltop Colony, led by Gregory. Even in the few communities—Grady Memorial Hospital, Alexandria, and Oceanside—without men at the helm, the women in charge (Dawn, Deanna, and Natania, respectively) are white.

As Connell explains, hegemonic masculinity can be understood through gender relations, but is also complicated by "the interplay of gender with other structures such as class and race."[9] Negative racial stereotypes (e.g., the black rapist) can exist to maintain the institutional and sexual power of white masculinity, while positive racial stereotypes (e.g., the black athlete) become masculine exemplars only when authorized by whites. The success of some racial minorities "has no trickle-down effect; it does not yield social authority to [minority] men generally."[10] Of the zombie narrative, Gerry Canavan writes, "anyone outside the white patriarchal community ... is a potential threat."[11] Martina Baldwin and Mark McCarthy also note that the genre only values "women and people of color" in so far as they are "useful" as "plot devices to support the white characters."[12] This is certainly maintained in *The Walking Dead*. In the first season, Theodore "T-Dog" Douglas is the Atlanta camp's only black man. While he is of invaluable help to his compatriots, he is still acutely aware of his low social standing as the group's token minority: "Realize how precarious that makes my situation," he tells Dale in season two; "Who ... do you think is gonna be the first to get lynched?" ("Bloodletting"). While *The Walking Dead* has included several minority male characters in its storylines, the show's approach to putting black actors on screen has been widely criticized. There has been a lack of black bodies in either human or zombie form, exacerbated by the show's apparent practice of "T-Dogging": killing off the cast's one black male character in order to replace him with another black male character.[13] As such, black men in particular have been interchangeable in *The Walking Dead* and have never managed to reach Rick's trusted inner circle.

The only racial minority who manages to become a leader beside Rick is Glenn, lauded not only for his strategic thinking and physical swiftness but also his loyalty and devotion to his wife Maggie (and, later on, their unborn child). If, as Murali Balaji writes, "race is a subtext that emerges in how leaders are selected and how the living organize themselves and make sense of their new reality,"[14] Glenn Rhee deserves a closer look as the only successful minority man in *The Walking Dead*.

Asian American Men on TV

Historically, the Asian American man has had limited, stereotyped roles in American mainstream entertainment texts. He is seen as the martial arts expert or street racing Chinatown gangster; alternatively, he plays the dutiful and loyal sidekick ready to help the white protagonist (sometimes, the Asian American character is both; a dutiful martial arts master who aids the white hero on his mission). Asian American characters on TV can be assimilated and Westernized (Daniel Dae Kim in *Hawaii Five-O*), or they can be perpetually foreign (Matthew Moy in *Two Broke Girls*); almost always, their presence justifies the dominance and success of white lead characters.

Gary Okihiro places Asian Americans on a continuum that has long been understood as a tool to maintain whiteness as an ideal of hegemonic masculinity. On one end are foreign and threatening characters, from Sax Rohmer's Fu Manchu to modern day gangsters, and on the other end are assimilated and meek characters, from Earl Derr Biggers' detective Charlie

Chan to modern day lab technicians and police sidekicks.[15] In contrast to white masculinity, both character types on the continuum are asexual (at worst, unattractive; at best, boyishly charming; regardless, neither is rewarded with romance) and endowed with a "racial femininity."[16] Neither end of the continuum offers a desirable Asian American representation. The model minority character, for example, is identified as timid and subservient to the point of childishness, ultimately serving to elevate white men as the norm for sexual desire, power, and social dominance.

At first glance, Glenn Rhee is positioned as a model minority character, helping to maintain Rick's position as the white hero. Glenn is introduced at the end of *The Walking Dead*'s pilot episode when Rick hides from zombies in an abandoned tank. It's obvious that Glenn has fared better than Rick in the post-apocalyptic world, given the fact that he discovers Rick while on a supply run and can help him navigate Atlanta's streets. Contacting Rick through the tank's radio, Glenn helps him escape and eventually brings Rick to the camp where he can be reunited with Lori and Carl. From the onset, Glenn is no group leader, though. Despite his manifest survival skills, his role is to save and serve Rick. Glenn functions as the group's gofer, a fast mover with a tactical mindset, who fetches desired items and puts his life on the line when white characters decide it's necessary. When Rick asks Glenn to return to the city for supplies in "Tell It to the Frogs," Glenn retrieves a bag of weapons and the symbol of Rick's authority—his sheriff's hat; in "Cherokee Rose," Glenn gets lowered into a water well because Andrea decides that the zombie at the well's bottom needs "live bait." Maggie points out Glenn's marginal position in "Secrets": "You're smart. You're brave. You're a leader. But you don't know it, and your friends don't want to know it."

The white male figure is continually elevated to leadership status in *The Walking Dead*, but the changing social and power relations of the post-apocalypse begin to prove that white masculinities are limiting and ultimately untenable. While hegemonic masculinity is comprised of multiple traits, the white men on *The Walking Dead* devolve into one-dimensional personalities. For example, the emotionally distant Daryl has difficulty expressing affection and coping with the deaths of those close to him, often lashing out in response. He breaks down after Beth's death in "Coda," and after Denise is killed in "Twice as Far," Daryl leaves the safety of Alexandria to hunt down her murderer, which leads to his friends' capture at the hands of the Saviors. In fact, Daryl's inability to handle his emotions, as I will discuss below, is the action that directly precipitates Glenn's death. Maggie's father Hershel shows that he can be physically strong, but his desire to protect—as the Greene patriarch and eventually as the group's doctor—overrides all else when making decisions. Despite his position as a father figure and dedicated family man, Rick falls into a position as a fighter who charges into the fray without consideration for his loved ones.[17] He is described by AMC as a "wartime leader" who has "trouble transitioning to the more peaceful world of Alexandria."[18] Unable to adapt and with a growing mistrust of forming new relationships, Rick's leadership abilities and moral compass grow more dubious as the seasons progress.

Perhaps most telling of Rick's inflexibility is how his qualities are reflected in the Governor. The Governor obsesses over protecting his community members, is a father unhinged by the zombification of his daughter, and is hostile to those who threaten his leadership. Rick and the Governor are two sides of the same coin, offering a cautionary tale to those who refuse to change while the world around them does. Similarly, Hilltop's Gregory and the Saviors' Negan present the extremes of charismatic tyrants, with Gregory as the manipulative coward and Negan as the narcissistic maniac.

If the white men on *The Walking Dead* exemplify the failures of inflexibility, Glenn stands as an exemplar of a multi-faceted adaptability. Unlike other characters, Glenn's personality, relationships, and storyline grow as the seasons progress. As the show's white men struggle with their limited personality traits, Glenn's own masculinity is allowed to flourish and his character becomes more than a mere racial token. Viewers also noted this change, as *Angry Asian Man*'s Phil Yu explained in an interview for *The Nerds of Color* website:

> You look at the search terms [on my blog] from the first season to now, and I got a lot of traffic in the beginning from, "Chinaman *Walking Dead*." Honestly, it would be like, "Chink *Walking Dead*." People just want to know who the "chink" is, the yellow dude, on *The Walking Dead*. And then over time you'd see "Glenn *Walking Dead*"; "Steven Yeun girlfriend." He became a human being to people. He was humanized ... he stopped being the Oriental dude on *The Walking Dead* and *became Glenn*.[19]

Watching Glenn "become Glenn" was a groundbreaking experience for viewers used to seeing stereotyped portrayals of Asian American men in popular media. Glenn Rhee might be "the most beloved Asian American male in the U.S.," wrote Ken Fong on *Angry Asian Man*. Identifying Glenn as "resourceful, reliable, romantic, and responsible," Fong describes a masculinity that is well-rounded and multi-dimensional, far from the stoic or physical one-dimensionality of *The Walking Dead*'s other characters. As an Asian American character, Glenn is "heroic-without-being-a-badass-martial-artist" and is "one of the only Asian American male characters on any screen who has wooed and won a non–Asian American wife."[20] Over the course of six seasons, Glenn transitions from boyhood to manhood, challenging the notion that life—and the construct of masculinity—comes to a standstill in the apocalypse.

As one of the only racial minorities in *The Walking Dead*'s first season,

Glenn highlights Rick's whiteness: he is the "Chinaman" to Rick's "Clint Eastwood." When viewers first meet Glenn, his diminutive status is reinforced by his appearance, particularly in contrast to Rick's sheriff uniform. In a baggy baseball jersey and baseball cap, warning the dashing white hero of dangers and helping him escape perilous situations, the similarity to *Indiana Jones and the Temple of Doom*'s Short Round (Jonathan Ke Quan) could not be denied.[21] Even Yeun acknowledged the similarity when he first started on the show:

> They put me in these clothes that made me look like Short Round … and I didn't say anything because I was just like, "Oh, don't make a fuss, even though this is absurd and you look like Short Round." Nobody noticed until it aired, and then they all said, "What a minute, you look like Short Round." And I was like, "I know!"[22]

In fact, Google Trends shows that searches for "short round" and "Indiana Jones" increased 1,200 percent in 2013, and were the most frequent, related queries for users who had also searched for "Walking Dead Glenn." Despite the fact that Quan is twelve years older than Yeun and that the former is Vietnamese while the latter is Korean, the link between Glenn and Short Round serves to highlight the dearth of Asian American male characters in America's cultural imagination.

With his humorous quips and earnestness, Glenn began as *The Walking Dead*'s "plucky kid" in direct contrast to the alpha male types of the show's white men. His marginalization early on was furthered by his friendship with Dale, who was similarly on the periphery as the eccentric and elderly man in the group. Glenn's naïve optimism ("I'm a glass-half-full kind of guy," he tells Rick in "Guts") was designed to reflect his boyishness and immaturity, as was his job as a pizza delivery *boy* pre-apocalypse. As an inexperienced youth, Glenn is reduced to a stuttering mess in season two once he realizes he has feelings for Maggie. When Maggie declares she'll have sex with him in "Cherokee Rose," Glenn asks, "Why?" His question suggests boyish nervousness but, given the history of asexual Asian American masculinity in American media culture, also projects incredulity that an Asian man can be sexually desirable. Maggie's first step to physical intimacy with Glenn is to remove the baseball cap that implies youth. As their relationship grows, his cap appears with less frequency. By the end of his run, Glenn's baseball cap is long gone and he wears, instead, facial hair—the marker of a grown man.

As Glenn's relationship with Maggie develops, so do his characteristics of masculinity. Viewers witness him having sex, both impulsive and intimate, with Maggie; he becomes an outspoken and demonstrative leader; and he hones his hand-to-hand combat skills. Glenn reaches the pinnacle of manhood in the season three episode, "When the Dead Come Knocking," in which he and Maggie are captured and taken to Woodbury to be tortured for information about their group. Driven by an overwhelming desire to protect Maggie from being raped by the Governor and to protect his friends, this is the episode where Glenn becomes a hardened man: his tormentor Merle even claims, "I gotta hand it to you—you're a lot tougher than I remember." In this episode, viewers witness Glenn's rite of passage into manhood as he smashes the chair he's tied to against a wall in order to stake a hungry zombie through the skull. After this, Glenn is brought into the fold of hegemonic masculinity as a powerful leader and exemplar of strength, as a protector of white femininity and, perhaps most importantly, as a progenitor.

Despite his starting point as a marginalized racial minority, on the periphery of hegemonic masculinity, Glenn nevertheless comes to embody multiple characteristics of that masculinity. The process of "becoming Glenn" takes the once "feminized" characteristics of a racialized masculinity and incorporates them into a well-rounded portrayal that *also* includes the traditionally "masculine" characteristics of white manhood. Glenn, therefore, becomes one of the few Asian Americans on American television to become a successful minority character in his own right—a three-dimensional character who succeeds not only in physically surviving but in developing and maintaining relational, emotional, and mental well-being. By season six, Glenn is no longer in service to white men, but instead has incorporated the best qualities he can find in the white men that surround him. As he tells the young Enid in "No Way Out," people "[make] you who you are." Thanks to Dale, Glenn can impress Abraham in "The Distance" with knowledge of how to find a spare battery for an RV.

Following Rick's example, Glenn develops a ruthlessness when it comes to protecting those he loves. Unlike Rick, however, he is also more willing to trust outsiders and even forgive Alexandria's Nicholas, the hotheaded coward who not only got Glenn's friend killed but tried to kill Glenn as well. Pointing out how Glenn's trusting nature contrasts the hardened mistrust of the group's leaders, in the season six episode, "First Time Again," Maggie matter-of-factly claims, "Glenn saves people. Even people like that [Nicholas]." Like Daryl, Glenn can swallow his feelings and remain steadfast and stoic. At the same time, he is open about his vulnerabilities and fears. Having had Hershel as a father figure, Glenn finds it in him to try and build a future with Maggie, first proposing to her, and eventually deciding to have a baby. While he is protective of Maggie, he also acknowledges her right to make her own decisions in a true partnership; Glenn is also a tender and caring lover who relishes small, intimate moments with Maggie. Indeed, as a model for a new masculinity in *The Walking Dead*, Glenn's declaration in "East," the season six finale, seems apt: "The world's not what we thought it was ... it's bigger."

Post-Apocalypse Postscript

Glenn's growth as a man suggested that the ever-blurrier social dynamics of *The Walking Dead* held no place for the limitations of traditional, white masculinity. With each passing season, Glenn added characteristics of that dominant masculinity to his once-marginalized identity, ultimately crafting a more fluid expression of manhood that addressed the challenges of the post-apocalypse more successfully than his white counterparts. Yet, while Glenn went from being a boy to becoming a man, he could still never be a *white* man. *The Walking Dead* ultimately remains a zombie narrative privileging the struggles of white patriarchy, and the show's focus continues to be on the struggles of traditional American (white) heroes. Perhaps, then, this is why Glenn "needed" to die in season seven.

The Walking Dead's season six cliffhanger ending centered on Negan choosing which of the remaining survivors in Rick's group he should kill with "Lucille," his barbed-wire-wrapped baseball bat. That episode, "Last Day on Earth," ended with the characters' screams as Negan beat one of them to death. The months that followed spawned a litany of tweets, blog posts, YouTube videos and more, as fans offered their theories about the identity of Negan's victim. Many expected Glenn to die at some point—Glenn had, in fact, died early on in episode 100 of Kirkman's comic, in this exact scene with Negan—but many held out hope given Glenn's fake death earlier in season six, as well as the fact that he had survived much longer on the TV show and was, ultimately, one of the show's more beloved characters.

The Walking Dead's promise to reveal Negan's victim worked to provide the show with a sizeable ratings bump: the season seven premiere drew approximately seventeen million viewers.[23] That episode, "The Day Will Come When You Won't Be," was widely criticized as gratuitously violent, even for a zombie drama, and as exploitative of fans' emotions and expectations. After a tense twenty minutes, viewers saw Negan impulsively choose Abraham as his victim, beating him in the head with Lucille. Overcome with rage, Daryl lunges at Negan, which provokes him to claim a second victim: Glenn. True to the comic, Glenn's death is not swift and is just as gruesome: "I just popped your skull so hard your eyeball just popped out … and it is gross as shit," crows Negan, as Rick's group watches in horror. The prolonged scene and its brutal violence, along with later moments in which Rick imagines—and viewers see—other members of the group beaten with Lucille, prompted *The Hollywood Reporter* to describe the episode as "nonstop traumatization and nonstop sadism … [and] nonstop torture porn … followed by 10 minutes of grief porn."[24]

Ultimately, Glenn's death serves the white masculine hegemony of *The Walking Dead* universe. Glenn's death was functional for the (white, male) showrunners, for one thing, as it supported a tidy narrative. Kirkman stated in an interview, "At the end of the day, we were like, pulling the thread on this sweater [keeping Glenn alive] just pulls too many things apart and it's too difficult to get back on that trajectory without that death."[25] Within the show itself, moreover, the graphic scene is less about Glenn and more about establishing Negan as an enemy and Rick's subsequent breakdown. In the episodes that follow, it becomes clear that Glenn's death is a narrative catalyst to add nuance and interest to the white masculinities that remain from season one: Carl steps into the role of vengeful action man as Rick turns into a simpering and broken submissive, and Daryl struggles with his grief, guilt, and rage.

As he embraced the best example of manhood he could—as a leader, fighter, lover, and father—Glenn juxtaposed the one-dimensional masculinities he lived beside. Glenn Rhee illuminates the struggle the white patriarchy faces to survive in a society where traditional frameworks of race and gender have broken down. Within *The Walking Dead*'s narrative, Glenn's strong relationships with Rick and Daryl instill in them an acute sense of loss that humbles them as men, reinvigorates their efforts to survive, and foregrounds their loved ones as priorities. Beyond *The Walking Dead*, Glenn's death also prompted an acute sense of loss among fans, particularly those in the Asian American community. However, this loss would not sting so much, be such a horror, if Glenn Rhee had not proven that an Asian American man can be present in a narrative as a desirable character, fighting alongside—and even rising above—the traditional white hero. Glenn Rhee's legacy proves that there is hope for an Asian American man to escape the label of "yellow dude" and instead "become Glenn," a full-fledged character in his own right.

Notes

1. Saria, "Into the Deep End."
2. Kissell, "'The Walking Dead.'"
3. "Who Is Glenn?"
4. Ross, "'Walking Dead' Star."
5. "So That Was the Worst Episode."
6. Ho, "The Model Minority," 57–76.
7. Connell, *Masculinities*, 77.
8. Trujillo, "Hegemonic Masculinity," 291–92. For a discussion of *The Walking Dead* in relation to Trujillo's definition of hegemonic masculinity, see Graves, "There's a New Sheriff."
9. Connell, *Masculinities*, 80–81.
10. Ibid.
11. Canavan, "'We *Are the* Walking Dead,'" 444.
12. Baldwin and McCarthy, "Same as It Ever Was," 76.
13. Moyer, "'The Walking Dead' Finale Recap." The lesser status of black men to white characters on the show might best be exemplified by the fact that one of the black men—Bob—gets literally *Eaten* by a white man turned cannibal in season five ("Strangers"). Ironically, in the same season three episode in which T-Dog tries to convince Rick to let the black prisoner Oscar join their group, he sacrifices himself to a mob of zombies so Carol can live

("Killer Within"). And in the later episode in which Oscar is shot by a Woodbury soldier, Tyreese and his sister Sasha join Rick's group at the prison ("Made to Suffer").

14. Balaji, "Thinking Dead," xii.
15. Okihiro, *Margins and Mainstreams*, 144.
16. Kim, *Writing Manhood*, 131.
17. Take, for example, Rick's return to the overridden streets of Atlanta immediately after reuniting with Lori and Carl; when Carl is shot in the eye, Rick leaves him in the infirmary to go on a zombie-killing rampage ("No Way Out").
18. "Rick Grimes."
19. "Zombies!"; emphasis added.
20. Fong, "Is Glenn Rhee?"
21. Google Trends shows that searches for "Short Round" and "Indiana Jones" increased 1,200 percent in 2013, and were the most frequent, related queries for users who had also searched for "Walking Dead Glenn."
22. "'Walking Dead' Star."
23. Schwindt, "'The Walking Dead.'"
24. Fienberg, "On 'The Walking Dead.'"
25. Ross, "'The Walking Dead.'"

"Look at the flowers"
Meme Culture and the (Re)Centering of Hegemonic Masculinities Through Women Characters

Tiffany A. Christian

During a panel discussion with the cast of *The Walking Dead* at the 2014 San Diego Comic-Con, actor Andrew Lincoln recited several lines of dialogue from the first season episode "Guts" in which his character, Rick Grimes, tells Merle Dixon that social differences within the show have essentially been erased thanks to the larger common threat of the zombie apocalypse: "There's just white meat and dark meat. There's just us and the dead. We survive this by pulling together, not apart." After delivering the lines from memory, Lincoln noted that he loves this "colorblind" aspect of the show: "This is it. We're in a colorblind ... genderless, classless ... apocalypse. And it's kind of the perfect place."[1]

It is difficult for some to imagine that *The Walking Dead* universe could be considered in any way "perfect." In this brutal post-apocalyptic landscape, characters manipulate one another, kill one another, and occasionally eat one another. But Lincoln's comment suggests that the show can be framed as utopian in that it can be viewed optimistically as ripe with potential for going back to "simpler times" or for "starting over"—the catch phrases of some contemporary survival narratives. In this case, the narrative provides a complete reset that will cure the ills of modern society—in particular, the domination of individual lives by commercial and state systems that operate to maintain its citizens as passive, dependent, and nameless laborers and consumers. In order for utopia to have a chance to emerge, however, it becomes necessary to first destroy the overly complex and diseased civilization—its corrupt institutions and "weak" individuals—in order to move forward by bringing everyone to a "base level." This narrative resonates strongly with the mythology of the American frontier, in which pioneers and trailblazers entered the "savage" wilderness of the so-called New World, endured the trials it offered, and were ultimately transformed into hardy, self-reliant Americans.

From its inception, this narrative of aggressive transformation in the wilderness has been associated with hegemonic masculinities. As environmental historian William Cronon explains, "The mythic frontier was almost always masculine in gender: here, in the wilderness, a man could be a real man, the rugged individual he was meant to be before civilization sapped his energy and threatened his masculinity."[2] In the realm of popular culture, strategic nostalgia in the rhetoric of "simpler times" and the mythic frontier have long been used to frame narratives that restabilize conventional gender norms and celebrate hegemonic masculinities in particular. The Western genre invokes a nostalgic simulacrum of the "Old West" as a simplistically savage setting where survival depends upon performances of aggressive, but usually moral, masculinity. As historian William Katerberg argues, "Part of the psychological power of Westerns is their emphasis on manliness, in the form of primitive masculinity that is undermined by modern comforts."[3] The masculine ideal embedded in the Western draws directly from the myth of the frontier in its celebration of particular forms of violence as a tool to reinvigorate manhood. The Western genre deserves mention because of its close relationship with science fiction and particularly the subgenre of post-apocalyptic speculative fiction. *The Walking Dead* has invoked the Western in various ways, from the visual imagery of the apocalyptic wasteland to the characterization of Rick Grimes as a small-town sheriff. The use of tropes, dialogue, settings, and motifs that reference frontier ideology simultaneously invoke hegemonic masculinities and proclaim them imperative for survival in the post-apocalyptic scenario.[4]

The destruction of civilization and the necessity for aggressively delving into the wilderness has, however, taken on some seemingly progressive features in recent decades. Granted, these features are in some ways a perceptual phenomenon. Scholars of sociology and anthropology, Tammy Garland, Nickie Phillips, and Scott Vollum, in their study of *The Walking Dead* comics, conclude that the source material does tend to rely on regressive notions of gender in portraying its female characters as dependent, often irrational, and happy to leave the leadership roles to men. And when women characters such as Michonne or Andrea flout conventional gender norms, they are often punished for it.[5] Katherine Sugg's study of the television show notes that while *The Walking Dead* grapples with large societal issues such as the "'crisis' of liberal individualism," that crisis centers on the particular issues faced by men in a twenty-first century neoliberal society. While the show is able to problematize its use of frontier discourse by calling attention to the "trap" that is the choice to be violent during a zombie apocalypse, the point remains that these issues and crises revolve more often around the male characters, and around Rick Grimes specifically.[6]

Still, the writers and producers of *The Walking Dead* seem cognizant of the need to showcase a diverse range of characters (and characterizations) in order to present a more "accurate" representation of a modern post-apocalypse. Female characters are not sexualized within the context of the show, for example, and many of them portray more nuanced values and behaviors than do their comic book counterparts. Not only that, but as Lincoln's quote about "the perfect place" seems to suggest, the "reset" that is embedded in the narrative hinges upon postfeminist and postracial rhetorics: the idea that gender and race no longer matter are seemingly taken to their logical conclusion. In this narrative, *anyone* is capable of the most barbaric and/or the most heroic acts. However, the celebration of this kind of aggression and the corresponding denigration (implied or otherwise) of behavior perceived as "weak" speaks to the ways in which the show cannot always escape the idea that masculine-coded behaviors are the most valuable in apocalyptic narratives. The presence of the ravenous undead, similar to the presence of the "savage Indian" of frontier mythology, helps to justify the valuing of traditional masculine ideals because the violence is deemed necessary.

Much of the current scholarship on *The Walking Dead* focuses on textual analyses of both the comics and the show, leaving unanswered questions about how audiences respond to and build upon the narratives provided. As my research shows, however often the show's writers and producers might attempt to complicate its characters and storylines, fan reception has a tendency to fixate on celebrating the masculinity, even hypermasculinity, of characters while simultaneously belittling their femininity.

"Hypermasculinity" refers to performances of stereotypically masculine-coded behaviors that are highly exaggerated. Qualities such as independence, physical strength, aggression, hierarchical ranking, and competition are emphasized, while feminine-coded cultural traits are devalued, neglected, or erased completely.[7] Although hypermasculinity is generally associated with characters who are identified as male, female characters can also portray these traits. While *The Walking Dead*'s tendency to celebrate the hypermasculinity of all its characters is somewhat mitigated by complex story arcs and character development, simple communication among fans via social media networks tends to emphasize only the most exciting aspects of certain characters, and these aspects almost always correspond to hegemonic masculinities. Thus, when celebrating those characters who are seen as having the best chance at surviving, that celebration naturalizes and re-centers those masculinities, allowing for their continued dominance.

This celebration of hegemonic masculinities as the most valuable form of gender in the post-apocalypse finds expression in hundreds of Internet memes. The meme is a visual method of communication that uses a particular format. Most memes consist of one image and some text using the Impact font. Some memes will use several images or will cut and paste pieces of one image onto another. Memes are most often used for humorous purposes or to communicate ideas deemed ironic or ridiculous. However, due to the wide variety of meme types as well as proliferating interpretations, a meme's original purpose may become lost as it enters cyberspace. And because meme creators can rarely if ever be identified, meme interpretations depend entirely upon the context in which they are used.

The difficulties in studying meme culture are multiple. The inherent instability of both the method of communication and the media through which memes are transmitted make tracking patterns a risky business. The memes themselves are almost infinitely varied and can be contradictory; additionally, they are used for contradictory purposes. However, I do not feel that this is a futile exercise. My emic perspective, while it forces me to interrogate my own positionality and ability to critique this work effectively, has also provided me with long-term access to insider spaces and allowed me to observe patterns that have remained remarkably consistent over the years of the show's run.[8]

Among the patterns uncovered in my study of meme use among *Walking Dead* fans is a tendency to use memes nonironically to celebrate masculine-coded behaviors of female characters while also belittling or erasing their feminine-coded aspects. One early example of the tendency to vilify traditional femininities surrounds the character of Lori Grimes. From a fan community perspective, Lori arguably remains the most hated character to have appeared on the show. This has much to do with the way the show makes her a bastion of traditional femininity in that she relies on the men to take on leadership roles and the supposedly more difficult work of procuring food, shelter, and dispatching the undead. Lori, unlike some of her fellow survivors, clings to the traditional gender binary in both her daily decision-making and in considering their long-term situation. In the post-apocalyptic narrative of *The Walking Dead*, such femininity is doomed to suffer, and fans have no problem denigrating Lori on multiple levels.

One recurring theme in Lori memes is her seeming inability to control her son. Lori is blamed repeatedly for losing sight of Carl in tense situations. Captions for these memes include statements such as, "Wants to play housewife during the apocalypse. Doesn't even keep track of her kid," "Don't question my parenting. Shit, where's Carl?" and "I've got 99 problems, but Carl ain't one." Read without irony or context as memes often are, these examples reveal that Lori is expected to maintain pre-apocalyptic standards of motherhood—a task she is stereotypically suited to as a woman. When she is perceived as failing to maintain said standards without redeeming her usefulness in other ways (such as by killing zombies), she is rejected by most fans.

Other major recurring themes in Lori memes are a supposed promiscuity as well as a willful, manipulative quality. Despite the difficult circumstances in which she finds herself in the show's first season, with her husband's almost-certain death and her dependence for survival on his best friend Shane, she still receives the labels of "whore" and "slut," as evidenced by many a meme. Creative examples play upon Lori's involvement with two police officers, such as one using a promotional image and the caption, "I fucked the sheriff and I also fucked the deputy." In the case of Lori, the "joke" that she is a "slut" is based on sexist attitudes about the purity and faithfulness of women—particularly married women—both before and after the apocalypse and despite the (apparent) death of a spouse.

While Lori is vilified for her supposed sexual promiscuity, Shane does not receive this same treatment. Shane memes more often comment on the idea that he has been driven insane (or "inShane") by his love for Lori and his jealousy of Rick. The popular fan joke about "going full Shane" is a direct reference to the former police officer's deranged behavior at being denied a familial relationship with Lori and Carl. But while his behavior is mocked in memes, it is not tied to slut-shaming. In fact, Shane does have a sexual encounter with another character, Andrea, while he is supposed to be pining for Lori, but memes tend to punish *Andrea* for this encounter rather than Shane. One example, created after Andrea begins her relationship with the villainous Governor in the third season, uses an action shot of Shane gesturing to Andrea that is captioned, "Listen up, if I ever die, find the creepiest asshole possible to be slutty with." The meme almost literally points a finger at Andrea both for having multiple relationships—though not at the same time—and for not realizing the Governor's evil nature sooner. At the same time, it ignores Shane's own multiple sexual encounters. Thus the notion of "sleeping around" is protected as a male activity and admonished as a female one.

Rick, for his part, is perceived as the double victim in this love triangle, since he is "betrayed" by both his wife and his best friend. Not only that, he is seen as further victimized when he re-engages in his relationship with Lori, who fans often view not only as "slutty" but also scheming. Fans continue to interpret Lori as "playing" both men, manipulating them in order to get her way. There are several memes that highlight this supposed manipulation, but one expresses it rather plainly with a shot of Lori surrounded by a thick black border, and a caption that reads, "Hey, can you watch Carl for a sec? I need to confuse my two boyfriends." Ultimately, Lori is not only a "slut" for having "two boyfriends" but also overtly calculating via the assumption that she is deliberately sowing confusion. Thus, she embodies the worst of many stereotypically feminine traits.

For female characters who demonstrate masculine-coded traits, fans highlight those traits in order to show their appreciation for the character. From her introduction at the end of the second season, Michonne has had many a meme dedicated to her skill in battle and her general ferocity. Michonne's weapon of choice is the katana, which sets her apart from the group and requires physicality to wield. Overall, Michonne is considered a fan favorite because she is a "badass," which is very much reflected in her memes.

One of the most popular Michonne memes uses an action shot of the first time viewers see her on screen, when she happens upon a panicked Andrea in the forest. Michonne's face is hidden by a hood, but she is immediately recognizable to readers of the comic books by the katana as well as by the two walkers in chains behind her, their arms and lower jaws removed. The caption of this meme reads, "Michonne: what Chuck Norris has nightmares about." The mention of actor Chuck Norris, who is not involved in *The Walking Dead*, refers to the bevy of Chuck Norris jokes that became popular beginning around 2005. These jokes, on the whole, emphasize Norris's toughness and hypermasculine persona. For Michonne to be understood as a figure to be feared by Chuck Norris, the meme implies that she must trump his toughness by a large margin. Her toughness is, by extension, also associated with the masculine.

Another meme in the form of a "demotivational" poster[9] features an action shot of Michonne fighting with the Governor. She is reaching for a piece of glass while he holds her down with his arm around her neck and torso. The caption reads, "Michonne is such a bad-ass that she can carve you up even without her katana." The action sequence in the episode concludes with Michonne taking out one of the Governor's eyes with the piece of glass, so the caption merely anticipates the action rather than making a joke. However, the "badassery" of Michonne is exemplified in her skill with hand-to-hand combat and quick thinking against a male aggressor who is portrayed as a psychopath.

The celebration of Michonne's strength and skill are further compounded by race. While hers is not the first role played by a black woman on the show, it was one of the most anticipated thanks to the popularity of the character in the comic books. Because she was introduced as a fighter (television viewers were not provided background about how she learned to use the katana, for example), her memes rarely portray her as "weak" in the same way they do other women characters. Rather, her strength is as consistently visible as her sword. It becomes difficult not to equate Michonne's meme representation with the stereotype of the "Strong Black Woman" (SBW). As

American Studies scholar Kimberly Springer explains, the discourse surrounding the SBW "assumes that a black woman has *too many obligations* but she is expected to *handle her business*."[10] But as Springer says, while this discourse may seem empowering, it can also have the effect of perpetuating a culture of silence around and erasure of real suffering by African American women in order to maintain that image of "strength." In meme form, the portrayal of Michonne as a Strong Black Woman de-emphasizes her complexity as a character. In one example, Michonne holds the katana while the caption reads, "Strong, independant [sic], black woman who don't need no man." This caption can be interpreted as positive in one sense as it battles more generalized stereotypes of women as weak and dependent on men for their survival.

At the same time, the invoking of the SBW contradicts the actual storyline; in fact, Michonne is traumatized by the zombie apocalypse and seems to be suffering from post-traumatic stress disorder (PTSD), and her involvement with the main group of survivors indicates that she is indeed seeking help. While the meme is generally understood as a playful reference to the SBW, when placed in conjunction with other memes of its type, collectively they serve to characterize Michonne's "strength" as consisting of her prowess as a zombie killer without also recognizing her complexity and strength as a survivor. Despite the attempt to be positive, these memes both reflect and perpetuate normative racist and sexist representations of black women in popular culture.

Michonne's representation in memes, although it clearly has some connection to the Strong Black Woman stereotype, is far more often associated with the masculine or even hypermasculine, and it is in that capacity that she is valued as a member of the group. These two representations are not unrelated; the bodies of black women have long been simultaneously maligned and fetishized for their physical strength and competitive capabilities, which are generally more associated with black masculinities than they are with femininity.[11] Emphasis on her skill in battle, long a masculine-coded trait, combined with a certain portrayal of aggression and competitiveness in her memes, serve to masculinize Michonne and set her apart from white women characters in particular. One meme displays Michonne's famous "side-eye" facial expression in several screen shots with the caption, "Dafuq ... ju lookin' at?!?!" This meme portrays Michonne as overly aggressive and threatening, a method reserved for her alone among other women characters. The use of the informal language in expressing a sentiment that can be read as a threat racializes Michonne's perceived aggressiveness even further. But as with the memes that celebrate Michonne's strength, these representations of her character, racialized as they are, are received in a positive manner because they have been masculinized. Unlike Lori, the Michonne portrayed in these memes does not use underhanded manipulative tactics to "handle her business." She is direct, and her aggression is not complicated by a surplus of stereotypically "feminine" emotionality such as crying or histrionics. While fans may mock her lack of range in facial expressions, they simultaneously recognize how her strength has resulted not only in her own survival but also the survival of the group. The threat that Michonne embodies, since it is not directed at her fellow survivors but rather at the undead menace, is not only acceptable but also appealing.

While the assertion and celebration of Michonne's masculinity may not be seen as objectionable in the context of the post-apocalyptic world in which she lives, the emphasis by fans on her "badassery" makes her contribution to the universe of *The Walking Dead* less complex. In the season four episode "Infected," viewers learn that part of Michonne's trauma stems from the loss of her three-year-old son. Meant to complicate her character by providing her with a connection to motherhood, this revelation is ignored by fans in memes. Instead, one meme chooses to poke fun at Michonne's reaction when she is asked to hold Rick's infant daughter Judith. Michonne picks up the baby by the armpits and holds her there while the child cries in discomfort. Eventually, Michonne relents and puts Judith to her chest, beginning to cry herself. This is the first indication to viewers that there might be more to Michonne's past than was previously known. The meme, however, centers on the image of Michonne holding the baby away from her with an uncomfortable expression on her face. The caption, "Michonne Loves Babies," can be read as sarcasm since the word "Loves" is highlighted with a different color. While the scene in the show makes it plain that Michonne does not hate babies, the meme's creator makes the choice to argue (falsely) that she does in order to convey humor. The effect of this, even if fans understand that Michonne does not really hate babies, is to emphasize once again Michonne's perceived lack of femininity.

One meme makes a direction connection between Michonne and hegemonic masculinities. A simple shot is accompanied by the caption, "I'm starting to see Michonne as the female Daryl in badassery." Rather than accepting Michonne's characterization for its own sake, the meme creator links her to one of the most popular male characters on the show, seemingly unable to resist defining her "badassery" in stereotypically masculine terms. The fan base for Daryl Dixon is arguably the largest of any character past or present, and it is rooted in large part in his exemplary ability to stay alive. He is portrayed as ultra-masculine: eschewing guns most of the time, he wields a crossbow (a close-range weapon that constantly puts him in harm's way as well as creating opportunities for gory zombie kills), and he often rides a loud motorcycle, the act serving as a rude gesture in the face of the undead horde. To see Michonne as "the female Daryl" is indeed to link her to masculinity as it is traditionally associated with "maleness"; as such, she is not even a Strong Black Woman any longer. Again, it is important to point out that Michonne's popularity does not suffer for this comparison or for her perceived lack of femininity. Opposed to Lori's overabundance of traditional (and failed) femininity, Michonne's lack only makes her stronger, more capable, and ultimately more well-liked.

Another character around whom many memes circulate is Carol Peletier. While initially she was cast aside by many fans as zombie fodder or, worse, a loathsome stereotypical representation of the abused housewife, her complex evolution into one of the show's premiere survivors has made her an audience favorite. Fan attitudes toward Carol's "badassery" are evident in now numerous Carol-centric memes. In the majority of these memes, Carol is characterized in ways that demonstrate a sense of power, aggression, and physical strength—traits commonly associated, of course, with hegemonic masculinities.

Several memes attempt to show Carol's progression as a character. One in particular creates a season-by-season presentation of Carol's evolution, though the last shot projects into "Season 20." This last shot is actually from the climax of the film *Aliens* (1986) when Sigourney Weaver's character, Ellen Ripley, battles the alien mother. The meme creator replaces Ripley's face with Carol's. This meme is meant to convey the idea that Carol's ability to be strong and aggressively "take on the bad guy" grows with each season and that, eventually, she will match or perhaps even surpass one of the most iconic female heroes of the action genre. By replacing Ripley's face with Carol's, the meme creator implies that the only way Carol can be more "badass" is by continuing to emphasize those hypermasculine qualities Ripley possesses. It is these hypermasculine traits that make Carol a "badass," and the use of these memes by numerous fans suggests the popularity of this part of her evolution as a character.

Carol memes not only make connections between Carol and Ripley but also between Carol and male action heroes. The most common among these are the Terminator, played by Arnold Schwarzenegger, and John Rambo, played by Sylvester Stallone. One Rambo meme uses two shots—the first of Rambo and the second of Carol's face covered in mud and hiding in foliage—and a caption stating that Rambo has in fact been trained by Carol. A second simply replaces Rambo's head with Carol's. The caption of this meme reads: "Who are you? Your worst nightmare." A third meme has no caption but shows a figure with Rambo's bulging muscles and Carol's intense, open-mouthed expression firing a machine gun. Memes such as these make clear the connection that many fans have made between Carol's actions and hypermasculinity. More than this, however, fans use these memes to demonstrate their approval of her aggression, as they occur consistently in comment sections on Facebook and other social media outlets where *The Walking Dead* is discussed.

More specific Carol memes celebrate the hypermasculine qualities of some of Carol's biggest scenes and story arcs. Two groups of memes in particular stand out: "coughing" and "flowers." The coughing memes refer to the season four episode "Isolation" when audiences learn that Carol has killed and burned two minor characters in order to prevent the spread of a deadly sickness. Memes in this group portray Carol in multiple ways. On one hand, fans seem to acknowledge that her actions may have been excessive, with one meme showing her with a flamethrower and a caption stating, "I heard somebody was coughing." Most consistently, though, Carol has become someone to fear. In one such meme, the caption manipulates a well-known speech from the season four episode, "Isolation," by the character Hershel, who says, "You step outside, you risk your life. You take a drink of water, you risk your life. And nowadays you breathe, and you risk your life. Every moment now, you don't have a choice. The only thing you can choose is what you're risking it for." In the meme version, a picture of Hershel is overlaid with a caption that reads, "Cough around Carol, you risk your life." Yet another coughing meme shows Carol's face next to a bottle of the over-the-counter cold medication Nyquil, and the caption manipulates Nyquil's slogan to read, "The nighttime sniffling, sneezing, coughing, aching, so-Carol-doesn't-kill-you-in-your-sleep medicine." And while it may seem as though being afraid of her or displaying her as "going overboard" in her responses to threats are negative, they are not used in this manner by fans. Instead, being afraid of Carol is overwhelmingly preferable to seeing her as the timid, "weak," and abused housewife. Her strength of will and ferocious practicality are viewed, through these memes, as the inevitable and welcome response to living life in the zombie apocalypse *and* to overcoming her "victim wife" status.

This celebration becomes more complex in analyzing the "flowers" group of memes. The phrase "look at the flowers" refers to a scene in the season four episode, "The Grove," after the group has been attacked at their prison home and forced to split up. Carol and Tyreese find themselves traveling with two young girls, Lizzie and Mika, and the baby Judith. They find an abandoned home and discuss the possibility of living there, but their plans are thwarted by the discovery that Lizzie is mentally unstable and has killed her younger sister. After discussing the incident, Carol and Tyreese come to the conclusion that Lizzie must be killed in order to protect Judith. Since Tyreese has sworn off killing the living, the job falls to Carol. She leads Lizzie to a field and tells her to look at the flowers. While Lizzie is distracted, a weeping Carol takes out a handgun and pulls the trigger.

The details of these actions are important because they reveal the complexity of Carol's character: she loves Lizzie like a daughter and yet is able to kill her for the greater good. The interaction between the two can be read as a substitute for the relationship between Carol and her own daughter, Sophia, which audiences will never witness since Sophia died in the second season. The episode also demonstrates how Carol's practicality comes from a need to protect the group's children both by taking deadly action on her own and by teaching them how to protect themselves. Indeed, Carol's act may well have stemmed in part from guilt, since it was Carol who taught the children how to use knives against walkers (and thus who taught Lizzie how to use a knife on her sister). Above all else, Lizzie's murder is ultimately rooted in Carol's being a mother.

In the "flowers" memes, however, there are no mentions of motherhood, maternity, or any particular understanding of Carol's actions that could be coded as traditionally feminine. In the first panel of one meme, the Governor, Gareth of Terminus, and Rick are each declaring their strongest combat assets: a tank for the Governor, cannibals for Gareth, and Daryl and Michonne for Rick. In the second panel, Carol stands alone, and the caption reads, "That's cute, bitches.... I got flowers!" In the third panel, all three men are shown with their hands raised in surrender. While this meme can be read in isolation as a celebration of the power of the feminine over the masculine, such a reading is out of place with both the meme itself and in the context of the "flower" meme group. These memes typically show Carol with a weapon in hand and with copy that is meant to evoke fear of Carol *through* the symbol of flowers (the irony of which is what makes the memes amusing). None of these "look at the flowers" memes come close to evoking the complexity of Carol's character; rather, they simplistically equate the phrase with a show of aggression that is in keeping with Carol's meme characterization as a terrifying death machine. And again, the memes are used most often to approve of another comment on social media or to demonstrate how much the poster appreciates Carol as a character, particularly her "strength" or "badassery." Thus, the use of these memes celebrates stereotypically masculine traits in a female character while simultaneously erasing her feminine ones. Carol's maternity and protectiveness are not what make her a "badass" for many fans; her fear-inducing practicality and her ability to shoot a child in cold blood do.

Through the third season, there were few memes of Carol. One of the most popular actually mocks her lack of characterization. The meme uses a shot from inside the prison (the group's home throughout the season) and shows Rick and Carol hugging. The caption reads, "Thank God, Someone to take care of the baby." The meme recognizes that, up to that point in the show, Carol was relegated to the background—looking after Judith and otherwise maintaining the group's prison home. In particular, she is seen as a surrogate mother for Judith, a decidedly minor job in the context of a show where killing zombies is the highest priority. Carol's feminine duty of looking after children is not given much airtime, consistent with how the show depicts any activity not involving violence and gore. The only time a female activity is centered in this post-apocalyptic universe is when Lori is giving birth to Judith, but only because that scene does involve action, gore, and ultimately tragedy.

It is not until Carol begins to take on some of the more masculine-coded attributes and behaviors that fans begin to pay attention to her as more than a subject of ridicule or scorn. As the numerous Carol memes demonstrate, what is important to many fans is a show of strength that is connected to masculinity, even hypermasculinity. One simple meme very much demonstrates this connection. The meme consists of an almost complete body shot of Carol from the third season. A white circle has been drawn around her groin region, and the caption simply states, "Lady Balls." The implication here is obvious: in order to do what she does, Carol must have testicles. Like Michonne, she is directly linked to the supposed masculinity that is a "natural" part of maleness. Further, her supposed male parts are something to be celebrated, since her actions tend on the whole to be good for the group. If Carol is equated with hypermasculinity as well as with survival, then, logically, hypermasculinity is seen as necessary for survival. In this sense, the Carol memes serve the project of maintaining the centrality of hegemonic masculinities by celebrating the hypermasculine actions of a woman who has become a hero both within the group and among fans.

Meme culture depends to some extent on repetition. The repeated use of a particular background image provides information as to how we are meant to "read" the image and its accompanying caption/s. Additionally, repeated use of a particular meme serves in some cases to narrow that meme's message as the community comes to understand it in a particular way. The success of memes depends on a consensus regarding how certain characters are evolving on the show. Well-known memes such as those discussed above, while they may seem clichéd to some fans, still communicate widely-held beliefs about characters. In the cases of both unpopular characters such as Lori and popular characters such as Michonne and Carol, those beliefs coincide with larger discourses about what it means (or what some think it *should* mean) to survive in a post-apocalyptic world. Significantly, the survival narratives that create many enthusiastic fans also serve to maintain patriarchal gender hierarchies despite what may well be the progressive aspirations of the show's producers. In fact, the celebration of masculine-coded characteristics in female characters by fans serves to re-articulate, if not always explicitly, that survival in this new "savage wilderness" is as much a masculine endeavor as it ever was.

Notes

1. Nerd HQ, "A Conversation."
2. Cronon, "The Trouble with Wilderness," 78.
3. Katerberg, *Future West*, 20.
4. See Young, "Walking Tall or Walking Dead?" and Graves, "There's a New Sheriff."
5. Garland, Phillips, and Vollum, "Gender Politics," 69–70.
6. Sugg, "*The Walking Dead*," 798–99, 810.
7. Salter and Blodgett, "Hypermasculinity," 402.
8. My impetus for this study comes from a folkloric interest in fan communities as well as my own experience as a fan of the television show. Over the course of my involvement in fan communities on social media, the repeated use of certain memes as a way of communicating widespread fan feeling struck me as noticeably gendered. The choice of which memes to use was made directly from these observations, as I decided to focus on some of the most popular and enduring (to the point of cliché) of these images.
9. Demotivational posters are memes designed to parody the traditional motivational posters that are often used in corporate and school settings. While the original motivational poster features a generic picture of a landscape or familiar object (such as a rose) and a broadly uplifting phrase, the demotivational poster is meant to be ironic at best and demoralizing at worst, usually pairing a sarcastic or cynical comment with a less than flattering picture. The intent is to "discourage one's moral strength and diminish one's self-esteem," according to knowyourmeme.com. As their use has become more widespread, the demotivational poster meme has incorporated an element of crude or crass humor, often straying from the original ironic or sarcastic intent.
10. Springer, "Divas," 252.
11. Sociologist James McKay and cultural anthropologist Helen Johnson have explored the ways in which African American women in sports, such as tennis stars Serena and Venus Williams, are subjected to sexist and racist stereotypes that work to both denigrate and fetishize them. See McKay and Johnson, "Pornographic Eroticism," 491–504.

A Woman's Work Is Never Done

Mothering and Marriage

ELIZABETH ERWIN

Despite the soaring popularity of AMC's *The Walking Dead*, there has been from the beginning a contingent of critics who have argued that the show advocates a patriarchal world order in which women are resigned to sexist gender tropes. In her essay "Women in the Zombie Apocalypse," Ashley Barkman writes, "In *The Walking Dead*'s post-apocalyptic world, the roles of men and women are clearly demarcated by a feminist's nightmare: men 'hunt' while women 'gather'—traditional gender roles are almost organically claimed."[1] Simon Abrams of *The Village Voice* echoes this sentiment when he writes, "Kirkman's ideas of the hunter/gatherer/provider societal norms seem to govern the show's characters and leaves the females to occupy antiquated gender roles."[2] And while Kay Steiger suggests that the much maligned laundry scene from "Tell It to the Frogs" could be read from a feminist perspective because it passes the Bechdel test, she also notes that "stereotypical attitudes about gender roles" are prevalent to the point of being distracting.[3]

While these readings of the text rely heavily upon scene analysis, they fail to take into consideration full character arcs. I posit that the way in which women are portrayed on the show is actually a subversive illumination of the limitations imposed by the two most traditional roles of women: marriage and motherhood. In episode three, there is a critical moment in which the women of the series lament their laundry assignments while the men of the group hunt and chase frogs. This conversation foregrounds for the viewer that women in the apocalypse revert to traditional, domestic roles while men assume the responsibility to protect and to provide. And yet, it is precisely the roles of wife and mother that are ultimately portrayed as *destructive* in the character arcs of the show's three original mother figures: Lori, Andrea, and Carol. In each case, the character goes through a divestment period in which she steps outside her prescribed role in order to achieve independence. Her ability to survive the apocalypse as a contributing member of the community is ultimately dependent upon whether she willingly returns to the role of wife and/or mother. Those who do return to their conventional domesticated roles perish, while those who do not live to fight another day.

In a majority of American cinematic horror films, women who step outside of the confines of normative society, for example by being unapologetically sexually active, become victims of the monster, while those women who exhibit conservative feminine traits, such as chastity, or who exhibit androgynous or masculine traits stand a much better chance of survival.[4] *The Walking Dead* takes this trope and extends it. Women who conform to the patriarchal power structures that render women "the nurturer" are destroyed, while those women who fight against these structures survive. In *The Walking Dead* universe, in other words, women's survival is dependent upon breaking free from the roles of wife and mother. She, and by extension the audience, are fighting the threat of the zombies but, more importantly, she is also fighting the greater monstrosity of a patriarchal world order that renders as non-normative women who are not married or mothers.

The Walking Dead succeeds in tying the classic horror view of the feminine to the normatively sexual and reproductive woman. Women who reflect this femininity face a higher degree of jeopardy than those who occupy a non-traditional sexual/reproductive space. At the heart of the show's radical statement about women is a new contextualizing of how the role of the grotesque functions within horror. Certainly the zombie, with its decaying body and transgression against socially constructed imaginings of life and death, qualifies as the grotesque. Yet, this concept is uniquely applied in *The Walking Dead,* as it is the zombie child body that creates an internal struggle between desire and disgust in biological mother, Carol, and surrogate mother, Andrea. Typically, zombie children on film consume their mothers physically (*Night of the Living Dead* [1968], *Burial Ground: Nights of Terror* [1981], *Wicked Little Things* [2006], and *The Children* [2008]), but in *The Walking Dead* this consumption is figurative—consuming the maternal role not the woman herself. A mother is only a mother in relation to her child, and the show uses the zombified child as a means of freeing the female character from this role. Her identity as a mother dies and is replaced with an identity coded as masculine. The show isn't interested in purification for the zombies but in using the monstrosity of the child zombie as a way to push characters into a state of transgression—specifically, to push the women confronted with the abject child-zombie to shed their conventional roles as mother.

In the case of Carol, the grotesqueness of the zombie child is used as a means of rebirth for the character. Upon seeing that her daughter, Sophia, has become a walker, Carol experiences a guttural agony on par with childbirth. Her reaction is not just emotional, but manifests itself in physical ways such as her inability to remain standing. It is through the death of her child, however, that Carol is able to undergo a rebirth of an identity not tied to motherhood. Similarly, it is the zombie state of her sister, Amy, for whom she has acted as a surrogate mother, that first grants Andrea power. Refusing to allow the men of the group to kill Amy, Andrea takes hold of the gun that will come symbolically to represent her independent identity. A close reading of the character arcs of Lori, Andrea, and Carol, in short, reveals the traditional roles of wife and mother to be ultimately destructive in this new, apocalyptic world.

The wife of Rick and the mother of Carl, Lori begins the series separated from her husband. Mistakenly believing Rick to be dead, Lori becomes involved in a romantic relationship with Shane. There is a domestic quality to the relationship that is evident in Shane's position as substitute father to Carl. The very first time the audience lays eyes on Lori, she is being reprimanded by Shane for wanting to head away from the camp alone in order to put up warning signs along the highway. Her decision is not only obviously irresponsible from a personal safety standpoint but also, as Shane points out, puts Carl in jeopardy of losing his mother. "I'll tell you what, girl.... You cannot walk off like that, all half-cocked," he says. "Look, if you don't wanna do it for my sake or for your sake, that's fine. But just.... You do it for him. That boy has been through too much. And he's not losing his mother too" ("Days Gone Bye"). Not only does Lori accept being spoken to as a child, a fact underscored by both Shane's demeanor and his use of the word "girl," but her easy acquiescence to her partner suggests that she accepts Shane's suggestion that her role as mother trumps any other role she may play within the group.

It should be noted that Lori willingly supports the gendered division of labor that catapults the men of the show into positions of authority over the women. Given Lori's role as the wife to the leader of the group, this willingness to take on a more subservient position to her husband makes sense. Lori derives power over the other women of the group via her relationship with Rick: she is the one who manages the work of the other women and who prioritizes job details. Andrea critiques this power imbalance among the women when she lashes out at Lori for her "Queen Bee" behavior. Lori's response, that she is working to provide stability for the men of the group, is telling for both its shades of delusion and the way it reinforces her own role as someone who is defined solely as wife and mother.

For a character whose identity is grounded in her domestic roles, Lori certainly cannot be considered a model mother. In fact, one of the reasons cited by fans for their dislike of the character is her borderline neglect of

Carl. For example, Lori asked "where's Carl?" before inevitably discovering her son in a dangerous situation to such a degree that fans actually created a drinking game around the frequently-occurring scenario. That the show implied Lori was an irresponsible mother is important when compared to Carol's biological motherhood and Andrea's surrogate motherhood. For Carol and Andrea, motherhood prevents each woman from accessing the skills and gifts that make them capable of survival. Because they are reactive to the world, by virtue of wanting to protect their charge, they don't learn how to proactively take power until that responsibility is eliminated. Lori's version of motherhood, however, isn't just destructive to her but to the group as a whole. Her failure to monitor Carl's activities puts members of the group in repeated danger. And while it may seem unfair to place the burden of child monitoring at Lori's feet, it is important to remember that this is precisely the type of gendered division of labor for which the character advocates throughout the series.

When Lori discovers she is pregnant in season two, her first instinct is to terminate the pregnancy. Yet, she quickly abandons the idea, again putting the group at increased risk, as a baby's cries are certain to gain the attention of walkers. Her pregnancy also impacts the group's mobility as it is noted that the group must move into the prison to accommodate Lori's due date. It is a bit of pointed commentary that Lori's demise comes as a literal result of her unwillingness to divest herself from her role as mother when the character dies after an emergency C-section. In the end, it is left to another man in her life, her son Carl, to shoot her in the head in order to prevent her return as a zombie. This moment not only showcases the destructiveness of motherhood in *The Walking Dead* universe, but also suggests that male children have an implied authority over their mothers.

Although motherhood in horror is often tied to the spectacle of birth, the act of mothering has just as much a complicated cinematic history as does biological motherhood.[5] While it is the mother herself who disrupts the status quo in films centering on biological motherhood, representations of symbolic or adoptive motherhood cast the child as the agent of disruption in cinematic horror. In *The Walking Dead*, symbolic motherhood and domesticity are represented in the narrative journey of Andrea, a civil rights attorney who is forced to adapt to unaccustomed gender roles in the apocalypse. Interestingly, the single Andrea (and later Michonne), unlike the married Lori, is never given a surname, highlighting the way in which the married women on the show are known via their association with their husbands and not as individuals. We learn that Andrea was in the middle of a road trip with her younger sister, Amy, when the zombie epidemic struck. With twelve years between them, Andrea is fiercely protective of Amy and is a decidedly maternal figure to her younger sister. Despite Andrea's feminist leanings and advanced education, she takes her assignment to do the laundry and cooking willingly since it allows her to stay focused on Amy.

And yet, while Andrea begins the series as a mother figure, it is still acknowledged that she is a character whose abilities transcend this role. The same is not true of the character of Lori. Not only is she introduced solely in terms of her relationships to males (Rick, Shane, Carl), but she rigidly advocates an adherence to traditional expectations of gender. For instance, in "Tell It to the Frogs," Lori tells Carl that she can't help teach him to catch frogs because "she's a girl." Her distinction between men and women also extends to how the chores are distributed, as evidenced in "18 Miles Out" when Lori tells Andrea to let the men handle guard duty and suggests Andrea could better serve the group by doing laundry. Certainly, the age of the children being mothered, both figuratively and literally, could explain why Andrea doesn't see her skills marginalized to the degree Lori does. But both Amy, when she decides to go to the RV alone, and Carl, who wanders off at every given opportunity, express a belief in their own invincibility that is representative of childhood naivety. The difference between Andrea and Lori seems to have more to do with how fully they embrace the domesticity of motherhood and the power imbalance of a traditional, heteronormative romantic relationship.

Andrea's willingness to participate in a patriarchal social structure disappears in the wake of Amy's death, however. Instead, Andrea develops an aptitude for sharpshooting and insists she be given a gun and a position guarding the camp from attacks. This move from nurturer to protector is not without its critics. Lori, in particular, makes note of Andrea's supposedly shirking laundry in order to do "men's work." As the series progresses, Andrea has a brief sexual relationship with Shane and forges a deep friendship with Michonne. But these relationships exhibit neither domestic nor maternal traits, and Andrea continues to fulfill the role of able warrior.

Andrea's role changes again, though, when she enters into a relationship in season three with the Governor: their relationship evolves quickly and takes on a decidedly domestic flavor very much akin to marriage. Andrea's status as more than just a lover is emphasized by repeated references to her as "the First Lady of Woodbury" as well as by community members seeking her out to have their messages delivered to the Governor. In this new-found role, Andrea finds her skills as a warrior continually marginalized by the men around her. She is quickly removed from her assignment guarding the wall and, when the town is attacked, is not allowed to defend against the intruders but is asked to go check on the other women and children. It is important to note that Andrea, while initially annoyed by her new subservient position, nevertheless accepts it because of her feelings for the Governor. As her isolation increases and the Governor's perversions become more pronounced,

Andrea does make some half-hearted attempts to break away. For instance, she is told by Carol to give the Governor the best night of his life and then to slit his throat as he sleeps. Andrea follows Carol's advice but finds she is, in the end, unable to kill her lover. Andrea's decision to place her romantic love for the Governor above her own best interests effectively seals her fate and leads to the character's demise. It's worth noting, moreover, that Andrea's death comes as a result of the actions of her romantic partner. Andrea does regain a bit of her power when she decides to end her own life before becoming a walker, after she is bitten. But that decision still comes as a result of a series of events that left her weakened because of her role as de facto wife.

Vastly different to the trajectories of both Lori and Andrea, Carol's character arc is a clear statement of the self-reliant power that occurs once a character is divested of her roles as wife and mother. Aside from Lori and Jessie Anderson (who appears in later seasons), Carol Peletier is the only other character the audience sees engaged in the performance of motherhood for a significant amount of time. This role is explicitly showcased in the first episode in which Carol appears. In each of her scenes, the audience observes her engaged in work stereotypically assigned to stay at home mothers. From caring for her daughter, who never leaves her side, to preparing meals, to ironing clothes, Carol is the very definition of traditional motherhood. That this performance is at least somewhat bound up with her role as an abused wife is something that the series will grapple with in later seasons. But at least initially, Carol represents an American cultural notion of motherhood that is expressly tied to the feminine and is therefore perceived as inherently weaker. Carol's arc remains the most explicit breakdown of the nuclear family depicted on the show. Not only does she lose her spouse, but she also loses her child. Divorced of the roles with which she most identifies, Carol is thrust out of the gender roles that comprise her identity.

A crucial moment for Carol is when Ed is killed and Carol is released from her role as wife. Although she embraces violent brutality when she takes a pickaxe to her late husband's head, a moment that could be read as masculine given the weapon choice and close proximity to the victim, the potentially engendered act is nullified by the audience's awareness of Carol's abuse. This knowledge situates the act away from violence, which traditionally reads as masculine, and into the realm of justice, which has far more androgynous implications. As a result, the act is not enough to move Carol out of the domestic sphere, especially as scenes of Carol cooking and caring for Sophia follow. Ultimately, it is not enough for Carol to be divested of her role as wife in order for her to escape the domestic sphere. She must also disassociate from her role as mother.

Interestingly, Carol's first act of protecting the group comes when she is still actively entrenched in her performance of motherhood. When the group finds themselves trapped in the CDC, it is Carol who provides the means of escape when she pulls a grenade from her "mother's bag." The implications of gender contained in this scene are hard to ignore. Carol's retrieving the item from a large bag she is rarely ever seen without brings to mind the stereotypical assumption that women are nurturers and, whether it is with a diaper bag or a purse, are always prepared. The fact that she pulls a weapon from her bag could have been a radical comment on gender if not for Carol's having given the grenade to Rick. Instead of detonating the grenade herself and saving the group, Carol continues to participate in a patriarchal social structure by depending upon a male to be the one to take action. The real character shift for Carol only occurs after she discovers her missing daughter, Sophia, has died and returned as a zombie and she is forced to watch Rick kill Sophia. Carol's demeanor in the wake of these losses shifts radically. She moves from occupying an exclusively nurturing role to one of fierce indispensability. She becomes a warrior, a hunter, and a healer, growing into a valued and trusted leader of the group.

This autonomy is first tested in the wake of Lori's death. Given Carol's former role as mother, it would make sense that she would step in as the primary, maternal caregiver to Lori's newborn, Judith, when Rick is unable to divorce himself from his own grief to care for the infant. Yet, Carol resists this role. While she changes diapers and participates in the feedings, she doesn't assume primary responsibility for Judith. Rather, she continues to develop as a warrior and provider for the group, leaving the child's daily care to Beth, a child herself. By resisting the role of mother and the engendered performance that it necessitates in Carol's mind, she begins to assimilate into a more androgynous role within the group. While her outward appearance still suggests traditional femininity (she trades the shapeless clothes she wore when with Ed for jewel-tone tank tops that are body conscious), she is now seen as a contributing member of the group with a skill-set beyond the domestic.

The season three episode, "Indifference," is pivotal in the character development of Carol. In the wake of her admission that she killed two group members in a bid to prevent the spread of the flu virus, Rick banishes her from the group, leaving her to face the apocalyptic world alone. Consider their final exchange:

> CAROL: "I could have pretended that everything was going to be fine. But I didn't. I did something. I stepped up. I had to do something."
> RICK: "You're not that woman who was too scared to be alone. Not anymore. You're gonna start over—find others. People who don't know. You're gonna survive out here. You will."

What is particularly fascinating about this scene is Carol's reaction to the banishment. She accepts Rick's decree with little argument. There are no emotional pleas for forgiveness, but she does pointedly state that she stepped up and made the hard decision, suggesting her growing lack of respect for Rick's milquetoast brand of leadership. Her commitment to advocating for her actions in the face of Rick's judgment is a powerful shift from season two when Carol's displeasure over Rick's keeping the fact they are all infected with the virus a secret found voice in her complaints to Daryl but only indirectly to Rick himself. Season two Carol still existed primarily in the domestic sphere, but this Carol has broken free of those confines and is committed to making her voice heard.

Her refusal to once again occupy a "mother" position is again tested in season four when, on his deathbed, a father asks Carol to care for his two young daughters, Lizzie and Mika. She agrees, but it quickly becomes apparent that Carol is not interested in a traditional form of mothering. Not only does she reprimand the new orphans for being reluctant to kill their father before he turns into a zombie, she also explicitly tells Lizzie not to call her "mom." In a sense, she is exhibiting the type of traditional behavior society expects from fathers. She will provide for the children, she will protect the children, but she will not nurture or coddle them. It's a pretty bold character development, especially when juxtaposed against the Rick and Carl storyline in which Rick literally lays down his guns so as to become a more nurturing and positive force within Carl's life. Unlike Andrea's representation of symbolic mothering, which served more as a contrast to Lori's biological mothering, Carol's story is more in keeping with the tropes of horror.

It is no secret that motherhood in American horror is so often maligned that it has become its own sub-genre. Yet, motherhood, specifically the "crazy mother" construct, is often tied to biology. Whether insanity is bred from an unknown source, as with Nola in *The Brood* (1979), or through pronounced trauma, as with Madeline in *Grace* (2009), the connection between mother and child and a madness shared is made overt through the gory specter of childbirth. Even films where the "crazy mother" trope is used in relation to adult offspring, the biological connection between mother and child exists as a definable undercurrent to the relationship. Sometimes this undercurrent is suggested, as in *Carrie* (1979) or *Scream 2* (1997), and other times it is glaringly explicit, such as in *Braindead* (1993) when an adult child literally returns to his psychotic mother's womb. Yet, for the genre's symbolic mothers, the genesis of the horror often resides with the child. Instead of being "crazy mothers," these women who engage in symbolic mothering, whether it be via formalized adoption or being thrust into a mothering situation unexpectedly, are often depicted as being victimized by a mentally unstable child and/or cursed child. Examples of films in which this motif is present include *The Omen* (1976), *The Good Son* (1993), and *Orphan* (2009). *The Walking Dead* reflects this form of symbolic motherhood in its depiction of the relationship between Lizzie and Carol. Lizzie is an orphaned child who continually attempts to force motherhood on Carol, despite Carol's vocal resistance. Lizzie becomes the de facto agent of disruption instantly identifiable to horror film fans, and her escalating efforts to force a familial bond underscores Carol's deep commitment to resisting symbolic motherhood.

Carol's refusal to occupy a caregiving role is somewhat diminished when she encounters Tyreese, Lizzie, Mika, and Judith out on the road. The quartet, having just barely escaped the prison as it is overrun with walkers, joins with Carol, and the group holes up in a seemingly idyllic cabin. At first, Carol adapts to her new role by baking with the children and discussing with Tyreese the possibility of staying in the home and living like a family unit. She never assumes the traditional role of "mother," however. In many respects, the dynamics within the home are a fascinating reversal of conventional gender. While Carol assumes the more masculine activities traditionally associated with fathers, such as digging a hole for burial, lugging water to the house, and cleaning the guns, Tyreese assumes the duties traditionally associated with motherhood. He is almost exclusively shown to be the one caring for Judith and he is the one who marvels at their ability to cook in a kitchen that still has an operating gas stove. More pointedly, Tyreese is the one to comfort Carol when she questions whether she is too hard on the girls. So while motherhood is still tied inextricably to the feminine, it is a role now being performed by a large, African American man.

Carol's performance as the head of the household is visually depicted in a landmark scene in the season four episode, "The Grove," that is as shocking as it is groundbreaking. Upon returning to the cabin, Carol and Tyreese discover that Lizzie has murdered her sister and is about to kill Judith in order to prove to Carol that zombies are people too. Realizing that this new world does not allow for Lizzie's mental illness to be realistically treated, Carol makes the gut-wrenching decision to shoot the girl in the back of the head. Not only does this scene solidify how completely Carol has removed herself from the domestic sphere, it also highlights the show's complicated approach to gender dynamics. It is hard to dismiss the radical visual image imparted of a woman, who also happens to be bereaved mother, assassinating a child at point blank range while a man whose stature is the very definition of physical strength watches on because he is emotionally incapable of pulling the trigger. While the psychological reverberations of this act are still unfolding for Carol, her decision expressly to eschew motherhood and adopt a more masculine presence within a family structure clearly comes at great emotional cost.

Further revelations of Carol's abilities once unshackled from motherhood come when she is able singlehandedly, in the first episode of season five, to save the rest of the group from Terminus, a cannibalistic community that has taken the others hostage. In an echo of when Carol supplied Rick with the grenade that ultimately allowed the group to escape from the CDC, Carol this time saves the group by creating her own grenade and launching it herself ("No Sanctuary"). She acts independently and in a way that conveys she is no longer tied to the feminine, a disassociation made plain by her donning the blood of walkers in order to remain undetected.

Carol's subsequent arrival in Alexandria offers up new insight into how the show portrays and interprets gender within the domestic sphere. Unlike the rest of her family, Carol recognizes immediately the importance of disguising the threat of her true self so as to assimilate within the gated community. She appears purposely klutzy around the weapons and takes up refuge in the kitchen where she makes casseroles for the community, which she then dispenses with a smile. At this point the audience recognizes that Carol's return to the role of happy homemaker is as ridiculous as Daryl declares her new wardrobe of soccer-mom cardigans. By portraying herself as the weak and ineffectual "mother" of the group, however, Carol is able to navigate the Alexandria community covertly. She recognizes that the domestic sphere is seen as non-threatening and sets out to use that assumption to her advantage. It's an overt acknowledgment to the audience that domestic work is inextricably linked to a perception of weakness. In using the kitchen, arguably the room in a home most connected to motherhood, as her war room of sorts, the show suggests that the domestic sphere, at least when used as a guise, can serve strategic purposes.

Yet, while domestic work gets a reframing at this point within the show, motherhood does not. As with Mika and Lizzie, Carol is tempted to "play mother" when a young child, Sam, reveals that he lives in an abusive household. The boy recognizes in Carol an ability to protect, something that Carol feels she was unable to do for Sophia. As with Mika and Lizzie, Carol assumes a position in relation to Sam that is more often associated with fatherhood. She protects and defends him but she never indulges him. In fact, she does the exact opposite when she lays out a gruesome scenario that awaits Sam if he reveals her secrets. Carol, herself, notes the shield her happy homemaker façade provides when she threatens Sam's father with a knife to his throat telling him that no one will ever believe someone who makes casseroles for the community capable of such a threatening act.

Her storyline stands in obvious contrast to that of Jessie Anderson, Sam's mother, an abused wife with whom Carol identifies immediately. Jessie is a direct reflection of the Carol we met back in season one. She is defined wholly in terms of the domestic and she is unable to protect her children. In the show's most overt nod to the destructive force motherhood potentially plays in a woman's life, Jessie is killed in season six when she refuses to relinquish the hand of her young son who is being consumed by zombies ("No Way

Out"). But Carol, who was forced to relinquish Sophia and has since resisted becoming a traditional mother to the children who cross her path, lives to fight another day. Still, Carol's fragmented emotional state and her unwillingness to kill as of season seven indicates that this approach, though a means of self-preservation, has severe emotional and psychological costs.

The subversive, feminist undertones of the show with regard to marriage and motherhood are not limited to just the original, female characters. While Michonne's first appearance is strategically androgynous, and assessing her position on the show is made difficult by her lack of a backstory, in the season four episode, "Claimed," the audience finally learns what it had long suspected: Michonne was a mother before the outbreak. Yet, short of one dream sequence in "After," viewers never see Michonne in the role of mother and so understanding the impact of her son's death upon her character development isn't possible. This dream sequence deserves exploration, however, for its unique commentary on motherhood. The scene functions as both a nightmare and a memory and is a distinct form of storytelling not often utilized in the show's narrative. In horror films, nightmares and memory are inextricably linked and serve to underscore the significance of a particular traumatic event. Moments in which the viewer is unable to distinguish between reality and dream are especially useful in creating a visualized depiction of transformation. By giving the audience enough markers by which to distinguish that this is the character we have come to know and then placing the character in a situation that instantly reads as unusual, we are forced to question why the sequence is so disruptive to how we view Michonne and what it can mean for the character going forward. In the scenes preceding Michonne's nightmare, her trauma becomes more and more pronounced. Not only do we witness her having to destroy Hershel's zombie head, but she soon finds herself traveling alone with two new "pets" (walkers in chains), a clear visual callback to her initial appearance in the series. And yet, while we understand that the character is dealing with emotional upheaval after the fall of the prison, the ultimate source of her trauma remains unclear until her nightmare.

Because we aren't often privy to the depiction of dreams within *The Walking Dead*, Michonne's nightmare stands out primarily because of its uniqueness. In fact, Daryl's hallucination of Merle taunting him while he lay injured in a ravine in the season two episode "Chupacabra" is the show's only true equivalent. Just as the scene in which Daryl hallucinates Merle was meant to convey a particular relationship dynamic, Michonne's experience is used to underscore the character's evolution and to situate her in two distinct realms. There is the pre-apocalypse Michonne whose demeanor is explicitly feminized and maternal and then there is the warrior Michonne of present whose appearance is decidedly ungendered.

Yet, unlike Daryl's hallucination, which is firmly located in reality, the tone of Michonne's nightmare is closer to fantasy. It harkens back to a seemingly idealized time that, as the scene progresses, we realize may not have been so idyllic after all. In the nightmare, Michonne occupies an explicitly domestic space. Not only do we see her preparing food for the men who are sitting at the table and waiting to be served, but she also cradles her son to her bosom. At no point does her partner or his male friend participate in this domestic work. Her appearance is highly feminized and stands in stark opposition to the gender-neutral garb she wears when audiences are first introduced to the character. This softer visual distinction of another time and place indicates that, at least in Michonne's nightmare, her role as a mother is inextricably linked to her passivity. The camera seems to linger on Michonne as she snuggles her child, and the distinctly maternal moment is designed to be recognizable and horrific given that we know the ultimate fate of her son.

To date, Michonne is the only character to be visually situated in a pre-apocalyptic setting in which no other survivors are present. That this foray should be so unequivocally linked to motherhood suggests that the show is making a larger statement about gender roles and survival. The scenes that follow provide additional context for how we should interpret Michonne's nightmare. When we see her awaken screaming, it is clear that the emotion fueling her is the loss of her son. And yet, that loss comes with a difficult acknowledgment of how her passivity as a mother led to Andre's demise, a point underscored in a subsequent conversation with Carl in the episode "A." The show further advances its portrayal of Michonne's motherhood in the season four episode, "After," when Michonne takes refuge among a herd of zombies. In the herd, she sees a zombie with well-maintained braids and feminine clothing and with whom she identifies as her pre-apocalypse self. As she looks at the zombie, a moment of recognition flashes across Michonne's face indicating that Michonne now sees her former self and the role she inhabited as a deadening one. By literally walking alongside her zombie doppelgänger, Michonne's ability to survive and seemingly flourish once she no longer inhabits the role of mother is pointedly conveyed.

Her evolving friendship with Carl places Michonne in the role of emotional caretaker but still the relationship, founded on jokes and a shared love of comics, is more akin to friendship than it is maternal. That bond changes in "No Way Out" when Michonne saves Carl's life by killing another child. Season seven concluded with Rick and Michonne becoming romantically involved and creating a family unit with Carl. It remains to be seen whether Michonne will function explicitly as a mother-figure for Carl, and, if so, what impact that will have on the character's ability to function as a warrior.

If past motherhood, via Michonne, is an opportunity to illustrate implicitly the cultural construct that connects passivity to motherhood in a fundamentally detrimental way, prospective motherhood, depicted in Maggie's character arc, is a much more explicit indictment of the traditional domestic sphere. While both critique the ways motherhood affects the perception of how a woman should function in the public sphere, prospective motherhood in *The Walking Dead* universe challenges the audience in a much more direct way because it confronts our expectations as to how a woman should behave if she is about to become a mother.

A self-described tomboy, Maggie bursts on the scene as a capable woman whose gathering abilities are a valuable asset to her family. In a moment that calls to mind Michonne's rescue of Andrea later in the series, Maggie is first introduced to the group when she rides up and saves Andrea from a walker attack with the aid of a bat. She is the quintessential "white knight," and the group's first awareness of her is as a person with valuable warrior skills. Because Maggie is not introduced in the domestic sphere, she is able to dictate to the group her value. This is made obvious when Lori reprimands Andrea for her lack of domestic work, but doesn't include Maggie's lack of contribution in this area in her diatribe.

Her relationship with Glenn extends Maggie's status as an empowered female. She is the sexual aggressor in the relationship as well as the one who insists upon keeping it casual. It should be noted here that this is another example of the show expressing a white woman's autonomy in relation to a non-white male. As with Carol and Tyreese, the role race plays in Maggie and Glenn's relationship's power dynamics is worthy of further analysis. As television depictions of heterosexual romance often place the male in the position of determining the pace of a relationship with the female trying to convince the man to commit, the inversion of that trope enables the audience to see Maggie in a romantic light while simultaneously maintaining her autonomy. This not only opens up narrative possibilities for the character but ensures that her power as a warrior is not eclipsed. As the relationship deepens and Maggie begins to voice her love for Glenn, her character is still depicted as a warrior. From helping to guard the prison, to supply runs, to dispatching of zombies, Maggie never retreats to the kitchen.

However, there are early indicators that her relationship with Glenn is altering both her perception of self and how the other survivors view her. When Maggie is abducted and sexually assaulted by the Governor, Glenn's reaction casts her in the role of victim. It is a label that the group quickly internalizes, as evident in Hershel's questioning of whether Maggie is "up to" a supply run. In the season three episode "Home," it becomes clear, however, that Maggie is not interested in seeing herself as a victim:

> You want me to say he made me get naked and stand in front of him? He came up behind me. Pushed himself against me. Put his hands all over me.... He slammed my head down and bent me over a table. Either I take off my shirt or he would take off

your hand. I just listened to Merle beating the shit out of you in the other room. What could I do?

This speech reveals that while Maggie does not want to be perceived as a victim, she realizes that her relationship with Glenn makes her vulnerable in a way she wasn't before. It is telling that Maggie's solo runs eventually give way to runs with Glenn. It would be easy to discount this evolution as a necessity. After all, there is strength in numbers when it comes to fighting walkers. Yet, Michonne continues to make solo expeditions long after Maggie ceases to do the same.

Prospective motherhood also plays a part in shifting Maggie away from her warrior roots. In the season three episode "30 Days Without an Accident," Glenn suggests that Maggie not go on a run, and she acquiesces to his request. Given that the run in question is essential, it is a curious decision for a character who never wanted to be coddled. At the end of the episode, it is discovered that Glenn and Maggie both thought that Maggie was pregnant. In this case, even possible motherhood is enough to move the character from the public (warrior) sphere into the traditional domestic sphere. Not only does this imply the limitations of motherhood, it also elevates the threat to Maggie. In this apocalyptic world, it is essential for women and men to maintain their combative abilities through constant vigilance. Maggie's decision to stay home and rest in her love nest with Glenn in order to protect her possible pregnancy increases her vulnerability. Maggie initially contests this increased vulnerability in the season six episode, "Same Boat," when Carol argues that the now pregnant Maggie has no right to be out in the field. Maggie dismisses Carol and the two soon find themselves captured by Negan's group. After a particularly bloody and brutal fight for survival, Maggie acknowledges that her pregnancy has altered the risks she is willing to take when she tells Glenn, "I can't anymore." And yet, Alexandria's walls do not protect Maggie from health complications, which emerge almost immediately after she decides to step away from her warrior persona.

In the wake of Glenn's brutal death at the hands of Negan, however, Maggie ascends to a position of power at the Hilltop community in season seven, despite her pregnancy. From her dress to her demeanor, all markers of femininity have been eliminated as she works to avenge her husband's murder. Her impending motherhood has also undergone a shift. She is no longer shown performing domestic acts but instead is shown being the beneficiary of those acts. For example, she delights in eating an apple pie that was baked in honor of her protecting the community. Thus, while it remains to be seen how caring for a child will affect Maggie's development, her pregnancy at least signals that the show is proposing a radical take on motherhood, suggesting that it isn't motherhood itself that is destructive but the way in which the role is positioned in the domestic sphere.

Television horror offers a new vehicle by which to expand the subversive potential of the horror genre. Unlike in film, where the audience is only able to experience the characters for a short amount of time, the structure of television allows for the presentation of much more complex characterizations. With a show as popular as *The Walking Dead*, criticism is inevitable. But the charges of sexism levied against the show with regard to its female characters are not justifiable. By occupying a space between societal definitions of life and death, zombies by their very nature are uniquely qualified to deconstruct the illusion of our social order. In doing so, they show societal categories such as gender role and social expectation to be permeable and not fixed.

NOTES

1. Barkman, "Women in a Zombie Apocalypse," 99.
2. Abrams, "Think *The Walking Dead*?"
3. Steiger, No Clean Slate," 100–13. Named for cartoonist Alison Bechdel, the Bechdel test looks at conversations between two women that occur in a work of fiction and considers whether those conversations are based on something other than men.
4. Clover, "Her Body, Himself," 82–87; Svehla and Svehla, Introduction, 3–12.
5. For a representative sample of mothering in horror films see the following: Katherine and Damien in *The Omen* (1976), Susan and Mark in *The Good Son* (1993), Anna and Samara in *The Ring* (2002) and Kate and Esther in *Orphan* (2009).

"We ain't ashes"

Daryl, Carol and the Burning Away of Traditional Gender Roles

CATHERINE PUGH

The enduring relationship between Daryl Dixon and Carol Peletier is one of the most compelling of AMC's *The Walking Dead*. Introduced as outsiders to the main group of survivors and with seemingly little in common, they establish an unlikely friendship. Daryl, an unsophisticated "redneck" skilled in hunting and tracking, is initially seen by many in the group as nothing more than a drifter and a liability, although his survival skills soon make him useful in the post-apocalyptic world. Carol is a meek and mild-mannered wife and mother, soft-spoken and easily frightened. At first, they appear to embody horror tropes—the violent, masculine redneck and the scared, incapable feminine victim. As the series continues, however, gender tropes are challenged, inverted or manipulated through Daryl and Carol. They both come from abusive backgrounds that leave them damaged emotionally—Carol at the hands of her husband, Ed, and Daryl by an abusive father and neglectful upbringing. The two recognize the pain that the other carries and are able to empathize and respond to it. Stephen Kuniak and Megan Blink note that, because her "traumatic background relates to Daryl's upbringing and because they share past feelings of powerlessness, worthlessness, and isolation, Carol challenges his negative self-concept.... Despite Daryl's pulling himself away from many personal relationships, Carol continues to see his true nature."[1] The emotional and narrative development of each throughout the series mirrors the other—their relationship catalyzing some of the changes as well as reflecting them.

The post-apocalyptic world forces survivors to re-evaluate their identities, evoking a key theme of the genre: when stripped to a primal level, who are you at your core? Particularly in early seasons, Carol and Daryl's development is rooted in confronting the gender and social conventions that they have been conditioned to follow. They meet the challenges of the post-apocalyptic world through phoenix-like regenerations of identity, a progression underlined on screen by evocative images of fire. As the series continues, they explore the limitations of their social identities—particularly traditional gender roles—ultimately choosing to reject them. Both Daryl and Carol have been conditioned to believe that they are worthless and have adopted gendered behaviors accordingly: Carol is overwhelmed by trauma and becomes passive ("feminine"); Daryl fights to ignore his traumatic past and becomes aggressive ("masculine"). Repeated trauma and suffering in the post-apocalyptic landscape, however, allows them to challenge these core aspects of their identity as the slate is wiped clean, enabling change. How much of a character's old identity is taken forward into the new world is up to them as the old world is burnt away, both literally and metaphorically. Many of the potential havens in *The Walking Dead*, such as the Centers for Disease Control, Hershel's farm and the prison are destroyed by fire, forcing the survivors to move onto the next "home." Daryl and Carol in particular have a notably powerful relationship with fire imagery as it echoes their own journeys of destruction and rebirth, journeys centered on transformed gender roles.

Daryl and Masculinity

Various scholars, including Shelley S. Rees and P. Ivan Young[2] have explored *The Walking Dead* within the framework of the American western genre. In particular, they propound Rick as the ideal of the western sheriff, complemented by various shots throughout the series that are framed to invoke genre tropes, such as Rick riding into Atlanta on horseback or his, "lone, straight-backed walk … whatever Rick is walking toward remains behind the viewer and thus unknown."[3] Daryl represents a different version of masculinity. Rees suggests that his skills as a hunter and tracker place him, "in the role of Indian sidekick to Rick's Lone Ranger persona, an image reinforced by Daryl's crossbow and arrows."[4] Rees further argues that "Daryl's connection to nature and his outsider status in relation to the more middle-class members of Rick's group recall the western genre's fraught portrayals of Native Americans."[5] Daryl's is thus a more marginalized masculinity.

Daryl's connection with nature is supported by his animalistic behavior. He is often seen crouched down with cat-like movements, creeping towards a target or with his hands ready for attack. His woodsmanship, survival skills, and experience at hunting and tracking code him not only as masculine, but as animal. He does not like indoor or enclosed spaces; during season two, he rarely comes into the farmhouse and camps away from the group, sleeps on the porch in Alexandria, and is obviously very uncomfortable in the moonshiner's cabin that is reminiscent of where he grew up. Strangers and new characters tend to note Daryl's animalistic appearance or behavior as an insult or to dehumanize him. Negan and the Saviors treat him like an abused pet, feeding him dog food, attempting to break him in like a horse, denying his name, and (after initially keeping him naked) forcing him to wear a uniform and go barefoot. Negan refers to Daryl as his puppy ("Hostiles and Calamities") and suggests that they train him ("The Day Will Come When You Won't Be").

For the most part, however, Daryl's connection with animals is presented in a positive light, particularly his affinity with the tiger Shiva, who sits with him peacefully before nuzzling his hand ("New Best Friends") and during "Forget," when Daryl joins Aaron in an attempt to capture a black stallion and bring him into the safety of Alexandria. In both cases, animals who are part wild and part domesticated (Shiva is from a zoo and Daryl notes that the stallion used to belong to someone) are used to represent Daryl's emotional state. Parallels can be drawn between Daryl and the horse in particular: both are wild and reluctant to follow Aaron inside the walls despite the offer of sanctuary. Furthermore, tigers and horses—especially black stallions—are mythically aligned with independence, freedom, movement, power, and strength, all attributes associated with Daryl. Aaron tries to tempt both Daryl and the horse without necessarily taming them. The horse rejects Aaron, resulting in its death at the hands of walkers. Meanwhile, Daryl's feelings of being an outsider have been exacerbated by the group's arrival at Alexandria, causing him to revert to being quiet and wary. Just as Aaron tries to bring the horse inside the walls, he attempts to involve Daryl in the community, suggesting that Daryl attend a party at Deanna's house. After they fail to retrieve the horse, Daryl observes the party from a distance before walking away. Aaron notices and invites Daryl to have dinner with himself and his boyfriend, eventually leading Daryl to accept Aaron's offer to work alongside him as a recruiter. Through the incident with the horse, Daryl realizes that Aaron is attempting to help them both find a potential home, inspiring his tentative steps toward becoming part of the community.

Daryl's affinity with nature is typical neither of the western hero nor the redneck antagonist from the city-revenge sub-genre of horror as Carol Clover has defined it in her book *Men, Women, and Chain Saws*.[6] The hero is usually tasked with overcoming nature and conquering the land. The horror redneck, while firmly associated with the wilderness, has little respect for nature. There is no valorization of the natural world to be found in these texts; instead nature appears violent, repulsive and chaotic. Although Daryl is more than aware of this aspect of nature—indeed he has grown up with it—he also has a spiritual connection with the landscape. The season two episodes "Cherokee Rose" and "Chupacabra" underline this relationship. Furthermore, as Rees notes, "both take their titles from supernatural beliefs expressed by Daryl."[7] It is to Carol, significantly, that Daryl brings the Cherokee Rose, to comfort her over Sophia's disappearance. The image of Daryl presenting the delicate, white flower in a beer bottle evokes his struggle with different parts of his identity. Rees argues that "Daryl's commitment to finding Sophia signifies a subconscious desire to align himself with innocence and empathy, to restore the group,"[8] yet he clearly has difficulty letting go of who he believes he is.

The conflict between who Daryl really is (and has the potential to become) and who he believes he is (or has to be) is made more overt in the following episode, "Chupacabra," when Daryl is thrown down a steep ridge into the creek below. Injured and in great pain, he hallucinates Merle berating him for rejecting his "kin," claiming that no one but Merle cares for him and that Rick's group see him only as "redneck trash" and that they will "scrape you off their shoes." Merle encourages Daryl to resort to savagery and "shoot your buddy Rick in the face for me." Kuniak and Blink argue that:

> These statements, coming from Daryl's unconscious mind, reflect his internal dialogue and relate to his self-identity. At this point, Daryl's identity within the group, his *social identity*, is evolving from a liability to an asset. Daryl has difficulty accepting this identity as he has been conditioned to believe he is "nothing." However, he begins to challenge these beliefs with statements to Merle such as "You talk a big game, but you were never there." Though Daryl has begun the transformative process, it is clear that his worst fears still haunt him and his relationships.[9]

It is only by challenging these beliefs that Daryl is finally able to climb out of the ravine, in an echo of the hero's journey/hero's ascent out of the underworld.[10] In "Home," when he is finally confronted with Merle in the flesh, Daryl is able to express his disillusion out loud, asserting that he belongs with the group, not with Merle.

Daryl's past haunts him again in season four, first by the moonshiner's cabin that is so similar to where he grew up and then by the Claimers ("Us"). In "Still," supported by Beth, Daryl realizes how much he has changed and rejects a return to the past by burning down the cabin and giving it the finger as he leaves—a clear moment in which fire represents transformation. When Beth is kidnapped, Daryl is left devastated and vulnerable, temporarily drawn to the Claimers (despite immediately sensing their antagonistic nature) because he can relate to them. Jonathan Hetterly writes, "The Claimers challenge Daryl to face his own identity and answer the questions 'Who am I?' 'Who do I belong with?' and 'Why?'"[11] The Claimers are typical of Clover's urbanoia rednecks, who prey on "soft" city people through rape and destruction. Their overt and savage masculinity is appealing to Daryl because he believes that he understands it, tempting him with regression to the worst stereotypes of the horror redneck. Daryl ultimately rejects the Claimers, however, "recogniz[ing] that any traits and characteristics he and [Claimer] Joe share are superficial, outward, or outdated. The Claimers, unlike Daryl, exhibit behaviors associated with psychopathy, including violence, sexual offenses, and absence of empathy. Joe represents a less mature version of Daryl or a version of what Daryl might have been if he had fallen in with the wrong group."[12] The Saviors, particularly Dwight, are another example of what Daryl could have become. Negan and the Saviors attempt to recruit Daryl by offering him a life of comparative luxury. Despite both temptation and torture, Daryl refuses to utter the words, "I am Negan," and to give up the identity he has fought so hard for. Instead, he reclaims his own name and asserts that he "ain't never gonna kneel," echoing his declaration to Merle in "Chupacabra" that "I ain't nobody's bitch." Significantly, it is confronting his guilt over Glenn's death, breaking down and crying, that helps Daryl to hold on to his identity, underlining the importance of expressing emotion in order to retain identity.

Carol and Femininity

As Carol evolves throughout the series, in parallel with Daryl, she gains independence and agency. This process moves her through several roles within the group, many of which are tied to her gender. Each season assigns her a traditionally female role, which is later utterly destroyed, often by the death of a loved one. In season one, Carol is a wife—but a specific type of wife. She is cowed, passive and highly domestic, seemingly having little life outside of her home and marriage as well as being a victim of domestic violence. She identifies herself in terms of this domestic role, such as mentioning how much she misses her washing machine ("Tell It to the Frogs"). Ed's death removes this default setting, allowing her to start developing independence away from his influence, such as choosing clothes of which Ed would not approve ("What Lies Ahead"). Ed's death moves Carol, in season two, toward the singular role of mother: she is the good mother, the worried mother, the searching mother, the grieving mother, and the nurturing mother figure for the whole group. After the death of Sophia—and after the initial grief over her fate has faded—Carol rarely identifies herself as a mother again and has a troubled relationship with being seen as one. She admonishes her ward Lizzie for accidentally calling her "mom" ("Indifference"), firmly rejects Sam, and reacts badly when Tobin suggests that she retains a maternal outlook ("Not Tomorrow Yet").

At the beginning of season three, Carol is shown to be a competent nurse, efficiently attending to Hershel's amputated leg and caring for the pregnant Lori. Hershel trains her to assist him during Lori's upcoming labor, and she takes full responsibility for this once Hershel's injury puts him out of commission, practicing a caesarean section on a deceased walker. However, when Lori goes into labor, Carol is not there, nor is she present during the infant Judith's first few days to help either as a nurse or in a maternal role. Although she is later seen caring for Judith, she does not take on the primary childcare role, whereas once she would have been seen as the natural choice. Season four sees Carol moving even further away from conventionally feminine roles—indeed, she starts adopting such roles only for disguise. She secretly schools children in survival skills, under the pretense of the more maternal, innocent "storytime." Her authority over her charges is clear; she is referred to as "ma'am" by all children and teenagers except Carl and Beth, distancing Carol from them emotionally. When asked by Lizzie and Mika's dying father to look after them as her own, she agrees, but maintains a teacher/mentor-student relationship rather than a maternal one. Her role as mentor does not end when she is exiled from the prison by Rick; Lizzie and the other children are inspired by Carol's lessons to fight the Governor's attacking forces ("Too Far Gone"). Carol puts additional distance between herself and Mika as the latter reminds Carol of her daughter Sophia, but for that reason, Mika's death at the hands of Lizzie causes her even more pain. Carol is left with no more students to mentor as her entire class is deceased by the end of the season. Yet she remains responsible for them to the end, her shooting of Lizzie protecting not only those around her but the girl herself.

Season five opens with Carol overtly taking on a warrior role, breaking into Terminus in a blaze of glory to rescue the trapped survivors. She is presented not only as a fighter, however, but as the warrior-mother associated with the horror and thriller genres and epitomized by Ellen Ripley in *Aliens* (James Cameron, 1986)—women who become the ultimate bad-ass in order to defend or rescue children (not necessarily their biological children). As Carol attacks Terminus, she demonstrates cunning as well as proficient combat skills, creating a diversion and covering herself in guts to move unnoticed through the walkers. Throughout the series, Carol has gradually developed fighting skills, but her attack on Terminus is her crowning moment. Her time as warrior is cut short, however, first by being hit by a police car in Atlanta, transforming her into a patient and hostage for whom the group must bargain ("Consumed"), and later by the group's arrival at Alexandria ("Remember"). Once inside Alexandria's gates, Carol plays at being passive, domestic and unskilled in order to gain a tactical advantage, but this necessitates her having to hide her abilities by taking on "feminine traits" and behaviors.

Carol becomes one of the leaders of the survivors throughout seasons five and six, standing alongside Rick and Daryl. This progression begins during season four when she and Daryl become members of the council that runs the prison, but it really comes to the fore from the latter half of season five onwards. Carol, Rick, and Daryl are the most suspicious of Alexandria and discuss contingency plans away from the others, including the option of taking over the town if needed ("Remember"). Carol has the confidence of both men over other potential leaders such as Michonne, Glenn, and Maggie. Season six also leads to the emergence of old roles, however, roles that trouble her leadership and that Carol has difficulty in navigating after so many regenerations. In Alexandria, Carol returns to domesticity, baking for the community, including the primarily-suburban custom of delivering food to a grieving family (a gesture that is instantly and brutally rejected). She becomes one of Judith's primary caregivers, listening to a baby monitor while she cooks, and is declared a hero by the Alexandrians for her recipes ("JSS"). Although some of this behavior is part of her cover as the incapable, invisible member of the group, she confides in Sam that, in her pre-apocalypse life, cooking distracted her from feeling sad. After the Wolves attack Alexandria in season six and Carol reveals her warrior-self to the townspeople, she commits to an almost obsessive level of baking, indicating her distress by making cookies for the entire community.

Indeed, the attack forces Carol to confront the consequences of her warrior-self, as she starts to keep a list of all the people she has killed and begins to question whether it was necessary ("Start to Finish"; "No Way Out"; "Not Tomorrow Yet"). She finds a crucifix to turn into a weapon but then keeps it, demonstrating a desire to return to the faith that she had long since rejected ("The Same Boat"; "East"). The mentor and mother roles are revisited through Carol's fraught relationship with Sam and, later, the pregnant Maggie. Carol becomes particularly protective of Maggie, ultimately attempting to detain her during the attack on the Savior Outpost ("Not Tomorrow Yet"). However, it is during the episode "The Same Boat" that Carol is confronted, like Daryl is in the Claimers, with what she could have been in her alter ego, Paula. Not only does Paula have a similar background to Carol (timid, unappreciated by a dominating and needy man, in a traditionally female role/job, and subject to domestic abuse), but she was the mother of four daughters, representing Carol's four lost children (Sophia, Lizzie, Mika, and Sam). Like Carol, post-apocalyptic life has hardened Paula, making her an aggressive, wary, and authoritative leader. Whereas Carol has retained her "feminine" cunning, playing the weak and bewildered victim, Paula revels in her new role. She expresses disgust towards Carol, calling her pathetic and wondering how she has managed to live for so long. Yet it is Carol who ultimately survives, deeply disturbed by the encounter with her alter-ego, and in the next episode, "East," Carol leaves Rick's group, stating that she does not want to kill again, abandoning her roles as leader and warrior as well as her fledgling romance with Tobin.

Despite the tragedy that Carol suffers, each ending allows her to develop and, in some cases, thrive. As old Carols and old roles "burn away," new ones form to take their place, allowing Carol to find her position in the group and the post-apocalypse world. Carol's latest regeneration is more problematic, though. Past roles that reappear during seasons five and six force Carol to re-evaluate who she is, ultimately causing her to reject all the former identities she has established while with the group. The figurative fires that have enabled her rebirths suddenly become too bright and overwhelming. Instead of allowing them to burn her away in order to regenerate into the next stage of her development, she regresses, running away to isolate herself from the group and from herself. She creates an idealistic and safe haven for herself, a pleasant, fire-warmed home with a plentiful supply of food and a mailbox. She cooks and reads and turns away all visitors—except for Daryl of course. She expresses fear at being consumed by violence and guilt at the potential vulnerability she has created in the group by leaving.

Challenging Gendered Narratives

The narrative arcs of both Daryl and Carol resist the highly gendered conventional romance plot, including the trope of the male hero "getting the girl." Alan Kistler and Billy San Juan note that this narrative occurs in the Rick/Shane/Lori/Carl relationship, with Rick, "enduring hardship in order to save a damsel," which "plays into the masculine narrative. The damsel eventually falls in love with the man for his valiant actions and self-sacrifice, which serve as emotional and sexual reinforcement.... The woman becomes a prize to obtain, the man's due, a ball that he must retrieve from an obstacle or opponent who guards it."[13] Daryl, however, receives no such reward for the hardship he endures during, for instance, his search for Sophia in season two. His dedication catalyzes the beginning of his and Carol's friendship, but there is no romantic or sexual motivation in his tireless search. Carol is not a prize or object; Daryl empathizes with her grief and it is his desire to abate that grief that prompts him to bring her the Cherokee Rose, a gesture of comradeship and empathy rather than romance. It is also heavily implied that Daryl empathizes with Sophia herself, despite having never interacted with her on screen, demonstrated through their traumatic backgrounds and Daryl's story of being lost in the woods as a child ("Save the Last One").

The rejection of the masculine romantic hero narrative also occurs in later seasons. For example, in season four Daryl (at first) reluctantly protects Beth with no expectation of romantic reward. Indeed, the trope is subverted somewhat, as it is Daryl that is eventually won over by Beth (whether romantically or platonically). The "reward" of affection and home for fulfilling the guardian role is swiftly rescinded, though. Moments after Daryl suggests that he and Beth could try to live in the funeral home, walkers break in and chase them out, leading to Beth's kidnapping ("Inmates"; "Still"; "Alone"). In season six, Daryl gradually bonds with Denise, becoming protective of her in a sibling-like relationship that involves no sexual desire from either party. He is visibly upset by Denise's death, particularly as she is accidentally shot with Daryl's stolen crossbow in an attack aimed at Daryl himself. After Abraham's death in "The Day Will Come When You Won't Be," Negan taunts Rosita, causing Daryl to attack him despite being heavily injured and warned that resistance would be punished. Here, the motif of the hero defending the lady's honor is swiftly, violently punished with Glenn's death and Daryl's imprisonment. Indeed, in a direct inversion of the hero narrative, instead of being rewarded for his masculinity, it appears that when Daryl becomes particularly close with a female character he is punished for his transgression. Carol is the exception, further underlining the bond between them. Daryl and Carol are a constant to each other, maintaining a balance in their parallel experiences.

Carol also experiences punishment for following conventionally gendered narrative trajectories. In "The Grove," for example, Carol, Tyreese, Lizzie, Mika, and Judith stumble upon a fairytale cottage in a pecan grove. All seems idyllic—and the nascent "family" enjoys cozy fireside scenes. Each quickly settles into their familial role: Carol and the girls prepare food, Mika plays with a doll, Tyreese relaxes in the father's chair. Mika and later Tyreese express a desire to stay, and Carol agrees. However, in the scene immediately following Tyreese and Carol's conversation about staying at the house, they find Lizzie standing over Mika's corpse with a knife. All hope of regaining domestic normality is viciously denied and Carol, Tyreese, and Judith abandon the house at the end of the episode.

Indeed, Carol and Daryl are punished whenever they dare to want a home of some kind, particularly if it conforms to traditional gender expectations. It appears they cannot have partners, children, or a stable home. Admitting their desires leaves them vulnerable, their hoped-for domesticity destroyed. Daryl suggests that he and Beth stay in the funeral home and it is immediately overrun; Carol agrees to stay in the pecan grove and within minutes it is ripped apart by violence. The fact that the episodes in which these events occur focus exclusively on each potential family unit (Daryl and Beth in "Alone"; Carol, Tyreese, Lizzie, Mika, and Judith in "The Grove") and are screened consecutively (with the action possibly occurring concurrently) underlines the idea that Daryl and Carol exist in parallel, mirroring each other through the same themes and desires. Despite trying to shut the door on the horrors of the outside world and settle down, their homes are desecrated and abandoned.

By the middle of season eight, both Daryl and Carol are in the process of another major regeneration that further complicates their relationship to traditional gender roles. It is not insignificant that these regressions take place while they are separated, although they continue to mirror each other even when apart. Both characters are faced with the re-emergence of old roles that they had long-since left behind. Although they may regress to old behavior, the people they were have been burned away; they must find new ways to deal with the return of old wounds. Carol, who tried so hard to isolate herself, has returned to warrior status out of necessity, donning the Kingdom's armor. After Ezekiel's breakdown, she is forced to assume temporary command of the Kingdom, and while she tries to take up her own missions, she is confronted by yet another child looking for guidance ("The King, the Widow, and Rick").

After suffering greatly at the hands of the Saviors, Daryl appears to be regressing to the aggressive and hostile masculinity he exhibited at the beginning of the series. Brutally beating Fat Joey into a bloody pulp ("Hearts Still Beating"), remorselessly killing Morales (despite recognizing him) and a surrendering Savior (despite Rick's promise that they would not harm him) ("Monsters"), Daryl's hatred of the Saviors is causing him to become more violent and less compassionate. It also leads him to question Rick's orders, and he teams up with Tara to attack the Saviors' compound and physically fights with Rick when the latter refuses to use hard-won weapons against them ("The Big Scary U"). The trauma Daryl suffered echoes his childhood abuse, and his former coping mechanisms have re-emerged. Attempting to obliterate the source, as well as emotionally distancing himself from the group (particularly Rick), is typical of early-series Daryl. He is in danger of burning out or burning up all around him.

Daryl is, however, by no means lost. At the season eight mid-season finale, he is reunited with his much-loved wings jacket, which previously had been taken from him by Dwight. The jacket, which first appeared around the beginning of season two, marked the start of Daryl's transformation and has become one of the defining markers of his character, even included in the opening credits along with other significant objects associated with specific characters, such as Rick's gun and Glenn's watch. When Daryl is stripped of his jacket after his capture by the Saviors, he is also stripped of a significant part of his identity, and it is during this period of time that his behavior takes on a much darker streak. Therefore, its return may symbolize another transformation. Certainly, at the end of the episode, Daryl is back in the center of the group, head bowed and cradling Judith ("How It's Gotta Be").

Phoenixes

Carol and Daryl's narrative arcs mirror each other not only as they are denied traditionally gendered narrative arcs but also as they become emotionally stronger, able to claim agency over their abusive pasts and become something new. Throughout the series, they remain allies and friends, helping each other to find their place in the group. At different times, they leave (or discuss leaving) the other survivors because they do not believe that they can fit in, yet they are later accepted back and claimed as family.[14] They both "die" and are resurrected: Carol is thought to be dead in season three after going missing in the prison, and Rees argues that Daryl's visions in "Chupacabra" and subsequent escape from the ravine are framed as a resurrection, down to the Christ-like wound from the arrow.[15] Both are, moreover, thought to be walkers on their initial return to the group. In season six, they both survive gunshots within hours of each other ("East"; "Last Day on Earth").

They are also both initially held back from their new becomings by a controlling, masculine figure, the death (both real and presumed) of whom helps to catalyze their transformation. Merle and Ed represent Daryl and Carol's old lives; their destruction allows a cathartic release that paves the way for future development. In *The Walking Dead*, significance is attached to who "puts down" a loved one or stops them from becoming a walker; it is seen as a duty and an expression of love. Daryl states that Merle was frequently absent from his life when they were growing up, something that is reflected in Daryl's many searches for different characters (Merle, Sophia, the Governor, Beth among others) as well as his role as a recruiter for Alexandria, despite his declaration that he is "done looking for people" ("Nebraska" and echoed again in "The Next World"). Merle disappears from Daryl's life twice on screen, once after his escape from the rooftop in Atlanta and once after his death at the hands of the Governor. By the time Daryl finds Merle the second time, he has been reanimated as a walker ("This Sorrowful Life"). A visibly devastated Daryl pushes Merle away several times before he is able to kill him, just as he has done figuratively throughout the season.

In the same way that Daryl claims responsibility for Merle's second death, Carol is adamant that she needs to do the same for Ed. In the season one episode, "Wildfire," after Ed is killed in a walker ambush, Daryl is seen destroying the brains of the dead before burial. Carol interrupts him, proceeding to violently and repeatedly strike Ed with the pickaxe. Laura Kremmel notes that Carol's actions combine hatred, mourning, and domestic responsibility, writing that she is, "cleaning up after Ed one last time and combining (marital) responsibility with an element of revenge."[16] Kremmel goes on to note that when Ed's corpse is shown from Carol's point of view, it is markedly more human than when shown from Daryl's perspective. Therefore, she suggests that "Carol projects her memories of suffering onto [Ed's corpse], enabling her long-awaited moment of liberation."[17] It is not insignificant that this scene is Carol and Daryl's first interaction on screen, uniting them in trauma and an understanding of the complex nature of abusive relationships. Daryl hands Carol the pickaxe without question, their quiet—if violent—interaction demonstrating a deeper understanding of each other from the beginning.

Fire is a recurring and potent theme in *The Walking Dead* and crystallizes the mirroring, and the parallel regenerations, of Carol and Daryl as images of fire, smoke and ash follow them throughout the series. Daryl's mother was "burnt to nothing" ("Hounded"); he burns down the moonshiner's cabin with Beth ("Still"); he self-harms by burning himself ("Them"); he is betrayed by Dwight in the burnt forest ("Always Accountable"); he blows up a group of Saviors and helps save Alexandria by dramatically setting the lake on fire ("No Way Out"), and he witnesses Negan burning a Savior's face ("Sing Me a Song"). Fire has particular significance for Carol during her most brutal moments: her burning of Karen and David during the prison flu epidemic ("Infected"), her attack on Terminus ("No Sanctuary"), witnessing an Alexandrian being set on fire ("JSS") before she reveals herself as a fighter, and setting the fire trap for the Saviors in "The Same Boat."

Fire often specifically marks Carol's and Daryl's transformations throughout their development, demonstrating not only violence and power, but also the potential for good and bad. It represents death and rebirth during significant changes in Carol's and Daryl's stories as well as highlighting many of the mirroring moments between them. In "New Best Friends," Carol and Daryl are reunited after Carol leaves Alexandria and Daryl is (unbeknownst to her) kidnapped by the Saviors. After an emotional reunion, they talk by the fire before Carol serves a meal in a tableau of the home life they both desire in one way or another. The fire and candlelight suggest a warm and comforting ambiance after the trauma that both characters have experienced. However, the events of the scene, when juxtaposed against the soft, intimate light, create an uneasy and bittersweet undertone. Although the fire itself is not destructive, it provides an evocative setting for a scene filled with lies, guilt, tears, and goodbyes.

Carol's and Daryl's evocative relationship with fire imagery reaches its pinnacle in the season five episode "Consumed." Fire appears throughout the episode, such as Daryl using it to distract walkers, the extreme close-up of him lighting a cigarette as Noah is under attack, and the burning bodies of the mother and daughter found at the shelter. Fire or smoke mark every one of Carol's flashbacks; she sees smoke and flames as the prison burns, she watches the fire as she burns the bodies of Karen and David, and smoke is seen in both the flashback of Lizzie and Mika's burial and Carol's attack on Terminus.

Joined by fire, Carol and Daryl also mirror each other on screen during "Consumed." For example, as Carol leans back on the bed at the shelter, the camera switches to an overhead shot. With Daryl's shadow on the bed next to her, it appears as though Carol and Daryl are lying next to each other even before he lies back. Additionally, Carol is on the left of screen and Daryl on the right for almost the entire episode (certainly during all key moments). Both times that they stand together and look out of the window, moreover, they echo each other's stance. It is during these sequences that they are able to discuss difficult subjects, their mirroring suggesting comradeship and comfort, showing mutual support despite being unable actually to look at each other. During the first window scene, they stand next to each other with their left shoulders angled towards the window/camera. After a few moments, Carol holds onto the strap of her backpack while Daryl holds his crossbow strap in the same way. The gesture is both companionable and defensive, the position of their bodies and fists invoking a fighting stance. The second window sequence puts Carol's right shoulder and Daryl's left shoulder against the glass, forming a triangle against it in another defensive posture.

Throughout "Consumed," Carol and Daryl talk about the pain and possibilities of starting over and of moving on from who they once were. Carol tells Daryl, "It's like you were a kid. Now you're a man." Although Daryl was arguably more "masculine" at the series' start, he has had to accept "feminine" traits such as compassion, empathy and affection in order to become a man. Carol goes on to talk about the burning away of her old identities, noting the continued cycle of burning and regeneration:

> Who I was with [Ed], she got burned away and I was happy about that. I mean, not *happy*, but.... And at the prison I got to be who I always thought I should be. Thought I should've been. And then she got burned away. Everything now just consumes you ("Consumed").

Janina Scarlet writes that, "Ultimately, opening up to painful experiences and being true to our core values and to ourselves seem to be the key ingredients in overcoming trauma."[18] By going through a phoenix-like progression of burning through trauma only to emerge as someone new, Carol and Daryl not only build new identities, but new gendered identities for their post-apocalypse world. Feminine tropes do not make Daryl weak or passive, and it is not masculine tropes that make Carol strong and powerful. It is the rejection and blending of traditional gender expectations that forge Daryl's and Carol's capable and resilient identities. They may get burned away, but Daryl and Carol continue to prove that there is always something more to be brought to life.

Notes

1. Kuniak and Blink, "Hillbilly to Hero," 240.
2. See Rees, "Frontier Values," and Young, "Walking Tall or Walking Dead?"
3. Rees, "Frontier Values," 81.
4. *Ibid.*, 90.
5. *Ibid.*
6. Clover, *Men, Women and Chain Saws*, 124–37.
7. Rees, "Frontier Values," 91.
8. *Ibid.*, 91–92.
9. Kuniak and Blink, "Hillbilly to Hero," 238–39.
10. See Rees, "Frontier Values," 91–92, and Kuniak and Blink, "Hillbilly to Hero," 238.
11. Hetterly, "Case File V," 220.
12. *Ibid.*
13. Kistler and San Juan, "Masculinity Narratives," 48.
14. Carol wants to leave because she believes the others see her as a "Burden" and Daryl as a "Henchman" ("Beside the Dying Fire"); Daryl leaves to be with Merle ("The Suicide King"); Carol is exiled ("Indifference"); Daryl temporarily joins the Claimers ("Us"); Carol prepares a car but is interrupted by Daryl ("Strangers"); Carol leaves so she will not be called on to kill again ("Twice as Far"); Carol isolates herself ("The Well"); Daryl is taken prisoner by the Saviors and forced to act against his family and friends ("The Day Will Come When You Won't Be," "The Cell," "Service").
15. Rees, "Frontier Values," 91.
16. Kremmel, "Rest in Pieces," 88.
17. *Ibid.*
18. Scarlet, "The Walking Traumatized," 190.

The Beauty of Beth Greene

Deborah Kennedy

"Beautiful." This is the word Hershel Greene uses to describe his daughter Beth singing. The song brought solace to the group of weary travelers, who, in the opening episode to season three, "Seed," had finally found a place to stay (at an abandoned prison) and a moment to remember what it was like to hear music. Beth sang a cappella the traditional folk song "Parting Glass," with her sister Maggie joining in midway through, their voices rising against the night sky, a reminder of the beauty of the human spirit and the necessary tenderness that keeps humanity going, even in a dangerous post-apocalyptic world. Beth Greene is not in Robert Kirkman's original graphic novels but was invented for the AMC television series, and her role continued for four seasons. Viewers saw her character develop in a realistic way, as the setting shifted from the idyllic family farm in the country, through the confines of the prison and the backwoods of Georgia, and finally to her last scenes in the dismal hospital in Atlanta. Most important is the coming-of-age story arc involving Beth and Daryl Dixon. The main characters on the show must bring out the best parts of themselves in order to achieve the heroic identities for which they are known, and, in the course of which, questions are constantly raised about moral choices and about gender expectations. Beth's character, I argue, stands as a positive female role model, with unique strengths and abilities, adding to the show's diversity of female characters.

One might describe Beth as more traditionally feminine than some of the other women in the series, and that in itself adds realism and depth: the women are not one-dimensional cardboard clones of each other. *The Walking Dead*, moreover, has its roots in the gothic literary tradition, which has bearing on both characterization and setting. Beth's character is sweet, young, and beautiful, much like the admirable heroines of the eighteenth-century gothic novels of Ann Radcliffe, and these originating gothic texts can provide a valuable framework for viewing the AMC series. Beth's innocence and creativity (the latter demonstrated by her interest in music and writing) are among the details that link her to the enduring role not of gothic victim but of gothic heroine. Radcliffe's heroines are known for their artistic qualities, like the virtuous Emily St. Aubert in *The Mysteries of Udolpho* (1794), who sings, plays the lute, and writes poetry: for her, music has a healing influence, and "it was seldom that her sufferings refused to yield to the magic of sweet sounds."[1] Often in a state of peril in an old castle or a ruined abbey, the traditional gothic heroine must make her way through mysterious passages or shadowy forests.[2] All the while, her heroic status emerges from a combination of femininity, virtue, and a courageous willingness to stand up to evil.

Literary critics distinguish between the female gothic, associated with the happy endings and strong heroines of Radcliffe's novels, and the male gothic of Horace Walpole's *Castle of Otranto* (1764) and Matthew Lewis's *The Monk* (1796). The latter, with their high death counts, bloody violence, and supernatural forces (which Radcliffe eschewed), were the progenitors of works of horror fiction and film that indulge in excess.[3] As an outgrowth of the gothic genre, *The Walking Dead* is powerful because it moves beyond mere gore to address matters of ontological significance. Although known for its display of the gruesome visages and eviscerated bodies of the victims of the zombie virus, the AMC series is character-driven at its core, as well as possessed of a distinctive narrative complexity.[4] The use of color imagery in the television series, for instance, allows for repeated contrasts between stark daylight and darkness, green fields and dirty concrete interiors, and the horrifying and often heart-rending transformation of the human form. Heroism and labyrinthine settings are inherent to the gothic, undergirding the tone, characterizations, and landscapes of *The Walking Dead*. The opening title sequence, in particular, recreates the gothic by using fragmentary images of ruined buildings depicted in the sepia tones that point to a fraught past. David Huckvale has demonstrated how similar filmic imagery owes a debt to Radcliffe's early architectural and landscape descriptions.[5] These visual and tonal elements contribute to the sense of pathos that pervades the series, in keeping with the melancholic key of the gothic as a genre.

The Greene family is introduced in season two of the series, and most of the action takes place at their family farm in rural Georgia. Rick Grimes, his family, and a small band of fellow survivors take refuge there after being forced to leave their camp outside of Atlanta at the end of season one. They join the small multi-generational group of relatives and neighbors who have congregated at the farm where they have been able to live in relative self-sufficiency. Although the comic books include several different family members, the television series focuses on Hershel Greene and his twenty-two-year-old daughter Maggie, adding the new character Beth as a daughter from his second marriage to Annette (who is dead). In both versions of *The Walking*

Dead, they are keeping infected relatives alive in the barn, in the hopes of finding a cure. Beth Greene is a gentle young woman who adheres to the values and Christian beliefs of her father, the heroic Hershel. She is not a stereotypical sulky teen, nor a vain prima donna, and both her delicacy and her strength of character serve as the bedrock for her development through four seasons of the series. In a traditional gendered division of labor, she helps to maintain a sense of normalcy in the home through her domestic duties of cooking and keeping house. She shows an independence of mind when she resists others' assumptions that she is engaged, having only briefly dated her boyfriend Jimmy (who later dies saving Rick).

To some extent she is sheltered from the worst of the apocalypse, but her sensitive nature makes it hard for her to deal with the violent circumstances around her. There is a pivotal moment when, after the walkers being held in the barn have been shot, Beth kneels down to cradle the body of her mother. Like a ghost of her former self, Annette is still wearing earrings and has her hair pinned up, though she is riddled with signs of death in a scene of profound visual juxtapositions ("Nebraska"). She almost attacks Beth, who suffers a breakdown and later tries to kill herself ("18 Miles Out"). Beth's attempted suicide has some parallels with the sicknesses or fainting spells of otherwise resilient gothic heroines. Once Beth recovers, however, she gradually develops some of the new skills needed for survival.

In season three, the character of Beth becomes more defined. Her unique qualities (like her love of music) come to the fore, and she is positioned as a nurturing figure, despite her youth. Having been forced to flee the farm after it was overrun by walkers, the group has been on the road for about eight months. In the first episode ("Seed"), the focus is on the ensemble cast, whose efficient search for food and weapons conveys how practiced they have become at life on the road before they take shelter at the prison. During that period, a mother-daughter bond has developed between Lori and Beth. Lori's soulful self-reckoning has made her a stronger woman: she has had to carry the burden of not knowing whether her baby's father is Rick or Shane, and this has caused a painful rift in her marriage. Yet, in one scene when Lori is helping Hershel outside, the smile exchanged between her and Rick holds the promise of reconciliation. At that exact moment, though, they are under siege by walkers, and events ensue which lead to Lori's tragic death. The timing is something characteristic of *The Walking Dead*, where possibilities of future happiness are often violently disrupted. Lori is separated from Hershel and from her friend Carol Peletier, the only two people who were trained to deliver her baby. Instead, when she goes into labor, she is with her twelve-year-old son Carl and Beth's sister Maggie, who has to perform a crude caesarean section ("Killer Within"). Lori faces her inevitable death with something more than stoicism, with a kind of grace that elevates the discourse of the show and works against the gruesomeness of the subsequent defilement of her remains. Amidst the darkness and the unsanitary conditions of the prison, and with the final words of blessing for Carl, the story offers something else: the luminosity of the maternal.

It should be noted that in the course of the series, Beth is aligned with three maternal figures: her mother Annette; her neighbor Patricia (with whom she shares a physical resemblance); and finally Lori. Thus, Beth inherits and carries forward the traditional feminine role of nurturer. For example, in a deleted scene from the fifth episode of season three, "Say the Word," it is Beth who helps Carl deal with his mother's death.[6] Carl asks her if his mother is in heaven and what happens when someone dies and then turns into a walker. Does their soul go to heaven first, before they turn? It would have been valuable to include this scene in the televised episode because it demonstrates the importance of religious beliefs and the attempt to marshal one's faith as one adjusts to how the world has so horribly changed.[7] The question of religion, along with readings from the Bible, recurs throughout the series, and this scene is one of the most life-affirming examples. Thematically it connects to the previous episode in the near contemporaneous assertion of faith in God made by T-Dog (Theodore Douglas), as he proved himself to be, like the Roman soldier, faithful unto death. Beth explains to Carl that belief in heaven helps, and that she believes her own mother and his mother and others they have loved are in heaven and looking down on them. The scene is filmed in close-ups of Beth and Carl as they share these innermost thoughts and questions. It is a quiet and truthful conversation, like a pool of light, a testament to the depths of both of their characters and to Beth's spiritual strength and her ability, despite her own youth, to offer guidance to someone else. Here she follows in Hershel's footsteps—and likely those of her late mother Annette too—as her Christian upbringing has shaped her outlook on life.[8]

After Lori's death, Beth becomes the primary caregiver for the baby. The significance of taking care of Judith is seen in the way that the responsibility is shared and the way that her very existence is a symbol of hope. Everyone wants to keep that little baby alive, and the episode title "Say the Word" refers to Daryl's immediate response to going to find baby formula. He and Maggie find the supplies at an abandoned day care center. When they get back, Beth prepares the bottle, but it is Daryl who gives it to Judith, cradling her in his arms, a positive example of the gentler side of the man of action. Later, Rick discusses the baby's name with Carl, who suggests the name Judith, after his third grade teacher, Mrs. Mueller ("When the Dead Come Knocking"). Honoring a beloved teacher is also a reminder, in the midst of chaos, of the importance of education and of generational continuity. Life does not go on unless someone is taking care of the children, and the AMC series respects that role, allowing for those quieter domestic scenes that contrast the fast-paced excitement of action sequences.

Beth, who is now seventeen, tells Carol that she always wanted to have a child, implying that maybe she never will in this post-apocalyptic world. Carol reflects on her late daughter Sophia and on her troubled marriage. As a character, Carol maintains her maternal role, but she has added to it a combat role in her refusal to be re-victimized. In another gender reversal, for instance, she will teach the genial Axel how to load a gun. As that relationship just begins to blossom, Axel is shot, and in a posthumous sort of heroism his body saves Carol by shielding her from the flying bullets during the Governor's attack on the prison ("Home"). With violence ever erupting it is hard to feel safe in the prison, but in the midst of it all, the recurring scenes of Beth with the baby establish a sense of home. Often seen carrying Judith, Beth is presented in a posture reminiscent of archetypal portraits of Madonna and child. In a manner suitable to the almost miraculous birth of Judith, such iconographic effect pays tribute to Lori and to all the lost mothers.

The second half of the third season concentrates primarily on the territorial disputes between the Governor at Woodbury and Rick at the prison, yet questions about the role of women are still brought to the fore in important ways. In one scene in the midst of the tense negotiations between Rick and the Governor, Beth begins to sing the soulful "Hold On," transforming the bleak atmosphere in the prison ("I Ain't a Judas"). Her voice is stronger than it has ever been and once again brings comfort in desolate times. The scene concludes by seguing into Tom Waits' original rough-hewn version of the song, shifting from the ethereal quality of Beth's vocalization to a return to the unrelenting business of dealing with trouble.

Indeed, among the women on the first five seasons of the AMC series, Beth is unique in her calm belief in the importance of the arts, and this includes not only music but also writing. To put this in context, one can trace throughout *The Walking Dead* different manifestations of the act of writing. Certain scenes involving the written word are central to the series, beginning with the words scrawled on the locked hospital cafeteria doors when Rick Grimes wakes up out of his coma in the first episode of the series. The words "Don't Open Dead Inside" deliver a simple message that crawls up out of a gothic literary past: a warning about monsters and secrets ("Days Gone Bye"). It is a defining image for the series as a whole. In the landscape of the gothic, there are places one should not go but where the hero or heroine inevitably must go, whether an area of a castle that is off limits or, in this case, a room made dangerous because of the monsters trapped inside. The hurriedly but purposefully scrawled words function as an important message for others. Such forms of textuality are key to the gothic tradition. Letters, wills, and diaries, for instance, play an important role in the gothic, as in the case of the prisoner's fragmentary memoir in Ann Radcliffe's *Romance of the Forest* or the scientist's laboratory journal in Mary Shelley's *Frankenstein*.[9] In *The Walking Dead*, the phrase "Don't Open Dead Inside" haunts every episode. Other short scrawled signs with directions or messages are seen from time to time. Morgan Jones paints cryptic statements like "Away With You" on buildings around his neighborhood, and he keeps a diary of sorts by writing on the walls of his house, a display of both his own mental distress and the drive to record the events of the present ("Clear").

These gothic-style warnings are very different from the type of writing in which Beth engages, which has a creative and constructive basis, most obviously seen by the fact that she keeps a journal. Even in the age of the internet, handwritten journals continue to be highly valued, and with *The Walking Dead's* reversion to a kind of pre-modern society they are even more useful. Writing in a journal helps to bring order to Beth's world, and it is an act of hope implying that there will be a future time in which the journal will be read. One of the few other characters depicted in the act of writing is Milton Mamet, from the town of Woodbury, who is often surrounded by research notes. He told Hershel that he was making a record of events to be kept for posterity, so the people of the future would know what had happened ("Arrow on the Doorpost"). However, Milton, with his experiments on walkers, is akin to the figure of the mad scientist, a type of Victor Frankenstein, though he will end up trying to save Andrea at the cost of his own life. Where Milton's notebooks represent more of a scientific record, Beth's writing, by contrast, is associated with hope for the future and the importance of the imagination. In the prison, Beth is shown in her bedroom (a decorated cell) writing in her journal, like any young woman of her age would be in other circumstances.

From a literary point of view, this expressive mode of writing is often a refuge for a gothic heroine, who, time and again, can be found writing letters or poetry, and it provides a similar refuge here. The opening episode of season four, "30 Days Without an Accident," takes its name from the workplace safety calendar that Beth has kept, which in itself is a kind of diary (and an expression of hope). She marks off the number of days that have passed in a phase of relative peace: thirty days since any crisis. That ends, however, when she learns that her boyfriend Zach was killed on a supply run. Wanting to be the one to break the news to her, Daryl is troubled when she barely reacts. She seems not to care, but this is a temporary coping mechanism, a way to protect herself from the shattering reality of death. Beth is not without a bit of an edge, singing indie songs to Judith rather than lullabies. But she continues to help others, her nurturing presence providing comfort for many, including Michonne. In these episodes, she has less screen-time with Maggie, who is the more action-oriented of the sisters and now in a marriage of equals with her husband Glenn Rhee. For Beth, writing in her journal provides an outlet for her to express her feelings and to manage and escape from the realities around her. Thus, there is great poignancy when the words of Beth's journal are read out (in a voiceover) in the episode "Inmates," as she and Daryl run for safety after her father is killed at the prison. The hopeful words she wrote about making the prison into a real home are juxtaposed with the cruel reality of the violence that broke out there and that ultimately destroyed it. Beth burns those early pages of the journal, but not the whole journal. She eventually starts to write again, having resilience enough to know that from the ashes of the prison there can still emerge a new day: a new chapter is inevitably written.

That new chapter of life occurs in the season four episode "Still," one of the best of the series and one that centers solely on Beth and Daryl. It also highlights Beth's personal journey, thus showing how the world has changed for women. This formative episode finds both characters learning from each other and becoming the better for it. With his physical courage, hunting skills, and keen moral sense, Daryl has proven himself a hero of the series, and Beth brings out even further depth to his character.[10] Beth and Daryl travel through the woods to a golf course and then to a ramshackle cabin, criss-crossing formerly demarcated worlds of privilege and poverty. Their own social class differences rise up in cantankerous moments when Daryl disparagingly compares Beth to a spoiled college girl, and when Beth, for her part, assumes Daryl has been in prison. Both are wrong, and they have misjudged each other based on appearances. But it is their ability to move beyond these preconceived ideas and beyond their distinctive social class backgrounds that enables them to value each other for who they are and to move forward with a mutual respect and an affection that is a kind of love. Perhaps it could turn into something more, but time is not on their side.

By paying attention to Beth's perspective, this episode also tells the story of how the normal day-to-day life of a woman has been drastically altered. For example, clothing and fashion are so much a part of socialization into the female world, and yet they are thoroughly under siege in the new world order of *The Walking Dead*. Since the characters in general are often on the run, their clothing is limited to what they can wear or carry. In many cases they are reduced to having only whatever clothes they are in, usually jeans and the shirt on their backs. As a result, their clothing is dirty, torn, and stained from fights against zombies. Even the clothing of the walkers is a source of pathos, as in the blazer of the solitary walker in the fields in season two, or the once-pretty dresses of any number of female walkers, which point to their earlier lives. For survivors, obtaining new clothing is part of the adjustment to a new way of doing things. Characters must take whatever they can find, whether it be supplies from the trunks of abandoned cars or items left in shops or houses found along the way.

So when Beth and Daryl search the golf club, including its store, in "Still," one feels a moment of relief when Beth is able to "shop." To get there, however, they have to pass through ransacked rooms littered with corpses. Once in the store, Beth chooses a new short-sleeved yellow shirt and a white cardigan for herself, throwing out the stained and tattered top she is wearing. But the pleasure of the moment is swiftly disrupted when they come upon the body of a rich woman propped up in the corner, a shocking instance of sexualized class violence. Beth's reaction is one of compassion, and she and Daryl place a sheet over the woman's body. Then, a minute later, the front of Beth's new white sweater is sprayed with the blood of a walker that Daryl fends off. She is rightfully upset, though Daryl silently dismisses her concern, as if to say this is the way it is now; you can't worry about such things. But for Beth it is something more; as a young woman, a clean and attractive appearance has always been important to her. The sweater is ruined, and the simple pleasure of something so normal is destroyed. The message is clear: nothing can stay pretty; nothing can stay clean. Significantly, this is another way that women in particular have to adjust because it has traditionally been women who carefully select clothes, who sew, and who go shopping, for themselves and for their families. In the quick and violent dirtying of this garment (and of the yellow top she keeps), the feminine world is impinged upon again, and Beth's reaction shows the emotional cost of this kind of loss.

The labyrinthine clubhouse is rife with still more challenges. Beth insists on having her first drink in the bar, expressing her frustration at having had this rite of passage taken away from her too. Daryl objects to her wanting a girlie drink like Peach Schnapps, and, instead, they end up having moonshine found in a cabin in the woods that has a distillery or still, from which the episode takes its name. But hard liquor is traditionally a man's drink, and it seems that yet again in this new, rough world, options for women are limited. One might argue that symbolically the shift from Peach Schnapps to moonshine also demonstrates a loss of civilization, as things are reduced to a basic level, an equality of roughness.

Beth and Daryl's time at the cabin in the woods is revelatory for both characters. Beth is very feminine in her appearance and manners; she is pale and thin, with blonde hair that sometimes takes on an angelic glow. By contrast, Daryl has dark hair, a brooding air, and a strong muscular physique. This visual contrast complements the way that each scene brings them closer together, whether it is arguing about the walker pinned to the tree, or talking in the moonlight on the porch. In the former case, Beth painfully admits what others must think of her, yelling at Daryl in the memorable line: "I know you look at me and you just see another dead girl" ("Still"). She knows she is not a fighter like Michonne, or Carol, or Maggie, and that fact makes her aware of her own impending mortality, even though she still retains, against those odds, a sense of hope for the future. When they burn down the cabin, Beth helps Daryl to exorcise the memories of his own fraught childhood, and it would not be too much to say that they both rise anew, Phoenix-like, from the ashes. They help each other to face their demons, and a beautiful bond emerges between the two characters.

The potentialities of new forms of family life are raised through the chronicle of their travels together, which continue in the next episode, "Alone." In a stroke of irony, their happiest moments occur in a funeral home, of all places. With its gleaming white clapboard siding, the building is reminiscent of the Greene family farmhouse, and Daryl and Beth see a headstone that reads "Devoted father," making them both think of Hershel. The funeral home has been well cared for, with food left in the kitchen cupboards for anyone needing shelter. When they go downstairs to the mortuary and see two deceased walkers laid out in clothes for a proper funeral, Beth says to Daryl, "Don't you think that's beautiful?" ("Alone"). Her remarks exemplify her humane perspective and also show the ongoing importance of sacred rituals of remembrance in a post-apocalyptic world.[11] Later that night in a memorable scene, Beth sits at a piano in the parlor playing a song, while Daryl lies down in a satin-lined coffin. It is a brazen confrontation with death, marking out Daryl's fearlessness and practicality. The companionable manner in which it is filmed takes away the taboo and washes away any allusions to vampires in their coffins, those other monsters who populate horror stories. The glow of tea-lights and a candelabra soften the conventional gothic setting. Instead, in a new version of the Southern Gothic family, Daryl finds the coffin comfortable, and they both relax in each other's company while Beth plays the piano and sings a slow-paced ballad.

The next day there are further echoes of the American dream when a stray dog comes to the door and they want to adopt it and bring it into the house. But the dog is emaciated and skittish and runs off. When Beth starts to write a thank you note to whoever left the food, she reinscribes the value of a traditional genre that is symbolic of orderliness and feminine duty. One can almost imagine life is back to normal, and Daryl contemplates staying there, rather than going on the road again. This feeling of hope is cruelly short-lived, in a reversion to the pressing suspense of gothic horror. A sound at the door is not the happy return of the dog, but an attack by walkers, and as Daryl fights them off, Beth is kidnapped by a group of men driving by in a strange car. Her backpack is left in the middle of the road after she is taken away to the hospital, and its loss is like a premonition of the fate that awaits her there.

In her final episodes, Beth demonstrates both fortitude and vulnerability, as she navigates a new and perilous set of circumstances. When she wakes up in Grady Memorial Hospital in Atlanta in season five, her first instinct is to leave. But her arm is in a cast, she has stitches on her face, and the exits are locked. The hospital is more like a prison or gothic fortress than a place of refuge, and it is ruled with an iron fist by Officer Dawn Lerner ("Slabtown"). For the first time in her life, Beth is truly on her own, having to adjust to a different and menacing environment. Her own values and wholesomeness set her apart from most of the others in Grady Memorial who have been brow-beaten (literally) into following Dawn's regimented way of doing things, which includes making patients work for their keep. Beth's heroism is shown in her manner of standing up to Dawn. The result, though, is that she has made a powerful enemy. Ironically, Beth can out-maneuver a potential rapist (Officer Gorman), but it will be another woman who will take her down. This plot-line is significant because it sheds light on the reality of women's victimization of other women. Like a mean girl envious of Beth's beauty, Dawn on two occasions strikes her in the face so hard that Beth needs more stitches. This creates a type of temporary disfigurement, symbolizing the vulnerability of feminine beauty in the harsh, hard-edged post-apocalyptic world. As a testament of her own modesty and strength of character, Beth does not dwell on this but moves forward. Wearing the dour unisex scrubs, she befriends others in the hospital, enjoying a brief respite of music and conversation with Dr. Edwards, till she is disillusioned by his cowardice.

Throughout her scenes at the hospital, Beth's character functions in a proactive manner, demonstrative of a new level of female agency as she disrupts its hierarchies. She has never been afraid to speak her mind, but this now has the effect of changing the oppressive atmosphere of the closed community at Grady. For example, Beth defends the value of music and art to uplift the human spirit, after Dr. Edwards questions whether his record albums and a purloined Caravaggio painting can bring any transcendence in the world they have now ("Slabtown"). Beth counters his pessimism by describing the Caravaggio (which portrays a scene from the Gospels) as beautiful, and adds that she still sings. Later when she casually hums a song it brings comfort to a suffering Joan, who had been one of the victims of rape in the hospital. Beth also showed the courage of her convictions by confronting Dawn for having allowed some of the officers to take advantage of the women in the hospital. Beth's kindness towards another inmate, Noah, which results in his escape, eventually leads to his informing Daryl and the others of Beth's whereabouts. When Carol is captured, Beth saves her life in a reiteration of her role as an auxiliary nurse, aided by an older ward named Percy.

In the episode "Coda," Rick finally negotiates an exchange of prisoners, and Maggie waits outside for her sister to rejoin the group. When Dawn demands that Noah stay in the hospital, Beth challenges her, risking her own freedom and showing more courage than anyone else in the hospital ever has. The two women have their final showdown, and in a move that seems out of character Beth stabs Dawn, determined to end her tyrannical rule, and feeling this is her battle to fight (not her friends'). But Beth's strengths lie elsewhere, as we have seen, and physical aggression does not come naturally to her, so the stabbing is poorly aimed. She has underestimated Dawn, who automatically shoots Beth in the head and kills her. Daryl retaliates by shooting Dawn, so in the end both women are dead. It would be hard to say that anyone would regret the loss of Dawn, who played the part of the female villain. But the loss of the good-hearted Beth is something else entirely. It is at least some consolation that Grady Hospital is better off than before, with the aptly named Officer Shepherd providing a new form of female leadership. But Maggie is bereft, and returns to the position of her character in the graphic novels, where she is the only surviving member of her family.[12]

In such a world, how does someone like Beth Greene find her place? It is an open-ended question for the AMC series since in some ways her death problematizes the place of the feminine in post-apocalyptic society. Yet, even though Beth dies, she has taught others about the human spirit, about the nature of different kinds of beauty, and about female heroism. Not everyone can be an athletic fighter and leader like Maggie or Michonne, and *The Walking Dead* allows for a wide spectrum of skills and personalities among its female characters.[13] Beth's story is ultimately brought full circle, from life on the Greene family farm to her own Christian burial. In a posthumous pastiche, she is one of several characters who appears in a vision to the noble Tyreese Williams as he is dying ("What Happened"). Images flash and shift from memories to real-time horrors, and amid the sounds floating through the scene, Tyreese hears Beth sing. Later, his sister Sasha forms a deep bond with Maggie as together they mourn their lost siblings. The musical motif continues when, a few weeks after Beth's death, Carl finds a girl's jewelry box, the kind that plays music with a ballerina turning once it is wound ("Them"). It is a rusty old thing, in keeping with their broken and ruinous world, and the tinny sound is nothing like the soaring voice of Beth, but in its femininity it reminds him of her, and it takes on a totemic quality for the mourners. He gives it to Maggie, Daryl repairs it, and in the gift of the music box, something of Beth's sweet spirit is remembered as the group finds their way to their next place of shelter.

NOTES

1. Radcliffe, *The Mysteries of Udolpho*, 5, 9, 14–17, 284.
2. Moers, *Literary Women*, 126.
3. See Botting, *Gothic*, 76–78; and Punter and Byron, *The Gothic*, 278–79.
4. See Bishop, "Pathos," 8–10.
5. Huckvale, *Touchstones*, 47.
6. "Say the Word," Deleted Scene, 3.05, *AMC: The Walking Dead*, DVD, directed by Greg Nicotero (2012; Beverly Hills: Anchor Bay, 2013).

7. Murphy, "Why 'The Walking Dead.'"
8. On Hershel's religious faith, see Cowan, "Maybe Jenner," 24–30.
9. Radcliffe, *The Romance of the Forest*, 116, 127–34, and Shelley, *Frankenstein*, 130.
10. See Kuniak and Blink, "Hillbilly to Hero, 234–45.
11. For a Discussion of Mourning in the AMC Series, See Kremmel, "Rest in Pieces," 80–94.
12. Kirkman, Adlard, and Rathburn, *The Walking Dead*, # 9.
13. See Tothill, "Valkyries Rising," 42–47.

The Sexualized Heroics of Rick and Michonne

Emily Zarka

Readers of Robert Kirkman's *The Walking Dead* might be surprised to know that the backstory of fan-favorite Michonne was first published in the pages of one of America's most famous pornographic magazines. Appearing in the April 2012 edition of *Playboy* magazine, the "Exclusive New Chapter" was advertised on the front cover of the "Sex and Music Issue." Although Michonne had appeared previously in *The Walking Dead #19* (2005), the glimpse of her life at the beginning of the zombie apocalypse did not appear until *Playboy*.[1] No other popular mainstream magazine has carried exclusive *Walking Dead* narrative content, which begs the question, why include one of the most formidable female characters of the entire series in a magazine that features nude women and is targeted at a male demographic?

This essay argues that the choice to publish Michonne's story in such a medium emphasizes the problematic relationship between gender, race, and sexuality throughout *The Walking Dead* series. While other scholars have begun to address the complications of sexuality, gender, and race,[2] the correlations among these elements as exemplified by a comparison of Rick and Michonne has not been the focus of inquiry until now. As both AMC's series and the comics continue to rise in popularity, it becomes even more critical to investigate the broader social and cultural implications of the series in relation to race, gender, and sexuality.

The male and female characters in *The Walking Dead* are subject to different, often opposing, representations in regards to their use of violence and their romantic and sexual relationships. Women in the comic narrative find themselves being demonized and even violently punished for failing to follow heterosexual norms. Despite what may be a female character's superior abilities, the struggle for power and control over post-apocalyptic America finds organization through stereotypically kyriarchal structures, the constructed hierarchies that contribute to systemic oppression. In *The Walking Dead*, race, gender, and age generate the primary power struggles largely occurring between dominant, aggressive, white, heterosexual male characters (Rick/Shane, Rick/the Governor, Rick/Negan). Melissa Lavin and Brian Lowe's work on *The Walking Dead* recognizes the roles of economy, politics, culture, family, and social life to the systems of power the comic "reproduces, resists, and extends," and which, according to Lavin and Lowe, ultimately result in the dismantling of patriarchal-dictated hierarchy as the series progresses.[3] One of the most important relationships of the comic defies this supposed resolution, however. There is no obvious power struggle between Rick and Michonne; indeed, they both play key roles in their group's survival as well as one another's sanity, relying on each other for advice and guidance. Michonne is not only a fan-favorite, but elemental to the progression of *The Walking Dead* narrative, a claim supported by the fact that she is the only other character besides Rick to appear on every compendium cover released so far. An analysis of the physical and visual representation of Michonne and Rick, though, reveals a biased treatment of their characters: their respective physical representations accentuate the dominance of men in the narrative both sexually and authoritatively, which highlights broader suggestions in the text of female sexual repression and punishment, culminating in Michonne's brutal rape. By exploring the differences between Rick and Michonne, it becomes obvious that the fear of a liberated, black woman, even in the apocalypse, is too much of a threat to what remains of patriarchal society.

Current scholarship on Michonne is varied. Katherine Sugg presents Michonne as the "possible exception" to fictionalized women whose identification and agency is entirely contingent on their relationship with male characters, arguing that the TV narrative chooses to emphasize her strength and survival capabilities.[4] Cultural studies scholar Cathy Hannabach believes Michonne is crucial to the television show, claiming that the katana–wielding survivor "remains the most resistant and 'othered' body," in the TV series[5] and, as this essay will argue, in the comic as well—for better or worse. Relying on philosopher James Sterba's theory that neither sexism nor racism can be properly addressed or remedied as separate concepts, but must be addressed in conjunction given their similar theoretical and practical applications,[6] this argument simultaneously discusses race and sex in *The Walking Dead* with Michonne serving to embody these intersections.

Much like the world outside of *The Walking Dead*, the narrative demonizes sexually aggressive women with Michonne suffering most dramatically because of her masculine portrayal of femininity and her status as a black woman, fulfilling the "angry" black woman stereotype. Kevin Thomas Miles asserts, "The ability the body has to 'seep' across boundaries both sexual and racial is not simply scandalous on a social and political level, but more importantly, it is a scandal to reason itself."[7] Hence, such issues can easily be examined in a zombie horror text, where the corrupted and diseased reanimated body shambles among the living as a corporeal incarnation of the body's capacities beyond death, and in which dominance over bodies, both living and dead, contour human relationships and the desperate desire to maintain social order. *The Walking Dead* and Michonne in particular further highlight this theme with their inclusion in *Playboy*, a magazine that at its core is about the exhibition of *female* bodies. Although Michonne is clothed in her origin chapter in the magazine, simply her inclusion among the bare bodies of other women perverts her narrative.

"Okay—so we're both crazy." "Seems like it."[8]

Michonne's portrayal in the series generally receives more positive reactions than Rick's. She proves herself to be a better judge of character, immediately recognizing the Governor's dishonesty and cruelty. She responds to his questions about where they are coming from and who they are with cautiously, lying about their situation, although the Governor dismisses her answers in favor of Rick's. During the interrogation in which the Governor removes Rick's hand, Michonne manages to escape her captor's grasp long enough to rip off the Governor's ear before any of the men in the room can intervene. As Rick lays unconscious, and Glenn cries uselessly in a corner, Michonne strains against the arms of her captor, her face determined even as the Governor promises revenge.[9] Her ability to read the character of others accurately becomes apparent again when the group encounters Aaron, who offers the group shelter at Alexandria. Rick makes the decision for the group to remain on its own, only for Michonne to speak up in favor of joining Alexandria, defying Rick's pronouncement and stating her intent to join the gated community, saying "I remember the Governor, trust me. This man is nothing like him—I can tell." Maggie, Eugene, and Father Gabriel immediately agree to follow her.[10] This interaction underscores Michonne's influence over the group and how the group values her judgment even over Rick's at times. While Rick seems constantly to be making mistakes that put the group at risk, Michonne's actions, even the more extreme and morally questionable ones, do not endanger the group.

Both Rick and Michonne suffer emotionally from the losses of their partners and children. Michonne's boyfriend died in the first days of the zombie outbreak, and her ex-husband and two daughters are presumed to have suffered the same fate. Rick's wife Lori and daughter Judith were killed by the Governor's attack on the prison. These emotional blows manifest as similar psychoses for both characters, with both imagining that they can speak to their dead loved ones. Michonne talks to "herself," saying she knows her boyfriend and his best friend are not really there, but that it makes her feel better:

> I know it seems crazy—and I know I'm probably just imagining it, but ... he speaks to me, my boyfriend ... and I can hear him clear as day. I know it sounds weird, but it helps, y'know? Sometimes I imagine he's in control—like he's helping me ... doing things, almost like I'm not even in control. It makes things easier—easier to deal with.

Responding to this confession with one of his own, Rick confides to Michonne that he has been speaking to Lori: "I know she's only saying what I think she would say—but it seems like I'm really talking to her. I took the phone from the house I found it in—because I couldn't bear the thought of not being able to speak to her again—even though I know it's not really her."[11] It is important to note the differences in these admissions; Rick knows his wife is not present, but Michonne seems unwilling to admit her boyfriend is not "really there." Both relinquish control to the voices they hear, but the difference lies in the gender they assign to those voices. Michonne's reliance on a male figure to provide her with the agency and mental preparedness to survive weakens her character. In contrast, Rick's conversations with Lori are portrayed as a less threatening emotional response, and even their means of communication, via telephone calls rather than conjuring up her presence in front of him, suggests a greater mental stability. Michonne's boyfriend, even as a figment of her imagination, has an active role as he "allows" her to survive in the apocalypse. Rick's hallucinations of Lori display her as passive and supportive rather than aggressive. While both Rick's and Michonne's mental and emotional instabilities must be kept hidden from the others, Michonne's reliance on a non-existent male figure highlights her continued dependence on the patriarchy and weakens her abilities to serve as group leader.

"Oh, what'd you want with that scrawny little white bitch anyway?"[12]

The sexual and romantic relationships of Michonne and Rick are a crucial facet of their visual representation, as their contrasting social demographics and physical attributes merge intimately with their private, sexual personas. Examining the way their sexual relationships are portrayed visually illuminates how the feminine is demonized (Michonne) and the masculine heralded (Rick). Such an exploration offers insight into the classification of

Rick as a main character and Michonne as a merely supporting one, despite their equal importance to the plot and the survival of their allies. Emma Vossen's labeling of the series as "Twilight for Zombie Fans"[13] undermines the complexity of the series, suggesting it is all about sex and romance and completely disregarding the social and cultural implications of the series, especially those of race and gender. Vossen is correct in her statement that Kirkman's apocalypse serves as a catalyst for interpersonal relationships, portraying the drama of humanity more than the horror of reanimated bodies,[14] but this only further supports the argument for reading the series as social commentary. Vossen claims that the social constraints surrounding sexuality are "tossed off" in *The Walking Dead*.[15] The comparison of Michonne and Rick, however, demonstrates that sex within the comic series functions as repressive rather than redemptive, supporting the underlying social hegemony of straight, white men. It is only when characters who defy these cultural codes engage in sexual practices that the discrepancies become obvious, and no one does this more obviously than Michonne.

Pausing to take a brief, macro look at the dynamics of sex and its intersections with identity construction as presented in the comic reveals the wider implications of my analysis of Rick and Michonne's couplings.[16] Within chapters one through twenty-four of the series, looking at major characters, there are twenty men who engage in some form of sexual activity and twelve women. At the end of chapter twenty-four, seven of these sexual active men are alive and only three of the women, resulting in a 10 percent higher mortality rate for sexually active women in the series. Twenty-seven of these sexually active characters are straight. All five homosexual men are still alive, but the one queer woman (Carol) is dead.[17] Six of these sexually active individuals are black, one is Asian, and one Hispanic. The remaining twenty-four are white. Only two non-white characters are alive at the end of chapter twenty-four: Michonne and Heath. Although there is clearly a bias towards heterosexual couples and white sexually active characters in the series, the fact that the only queer characters still alive are men, and only two people of color, suggests that the sexual politics of *The Walking Dead* are influenced by gender and race. To explore all of these couplings and their complexities would require a book of its own, so this argument will analyze only that of Rick and Michonne, while keeping in mind that they represent a narrative-wide theme, rather than existing as individual exceptions.

Michonne serves as the perfect example of queer sexuality in *The Walking Dead*. The term queer is used here as Hannabach employs it in her analysis of *The Walking Dead*, identifying as queer all "practices, embodiments, and desires that resist white, bourgeois heteronormativity and its attendant demands."[18] Not only is Michonne a black, non-traditional woman, but her sexuality can best be described as plastic. Plastic sexuality is detached from romance and performed for pleasure rather than procreation.[19] While Michonne does admit to strong feelings for her sexual partners, particularly Tyreese and Ezekiel, she approaches both for sexual enjoyment rather than in hope of securing a life partner or mate. She is unafraid to approach men already in relationships, and, in some cases, moves immediately to sexual activity with zero provocation. She performs oral sex on Tyreese (who is in a relationship with Carol at the time) despite his initial protests. Unbeknownst to both of them, Carol watches, and the act ultimately results in her attempted suicide.[20] Not only are the other characters in the prison suspicious of Michonne as an outsider, but they now have reason to dislike her because of her disregard of social boundaries—a noted difference from Rick's sexuality as he snuggles in bed with his wife, loyally standing by her despite his knowledge of her affair with Shane and the likelihood that Judith is not his child. The survivors' distrust of Michonne shows that alliances, relationships, and survival within the narrative depend on sex as much as on one's ability to kill zombies.

Even more striking than Michonne's plastic sexuality is her choice in sexual partners. Thus far in the series, the only males she has shown an attraction to or interest in are black. After the death of Tyreese, Michonne engages in a sexual relationship with Morgan, who expresses guilt after their encounters, saying that he still mourns his wife and still feels a loyalty to her.[21] Her next attempted seduction is a failure, approaching Heath (currently in a relationship with a white woman, like Tyreese) with promises of pleasure. In a particularly harsh rejection, Heath says:

> Maggie told me about you and Tyreese. I don't know where I sit with Denise right now, we're figuring things out. And I'm not going to screw that up, okay? I don't know what it is—something where you need to show you're better than other women by getting someone who's unavailable ... it's just not necessary. You're beautiful ... if things go south with Denise, sure. But ... have some self-respect.[22]

Heath's response not only reveals that the other survivors have been gossiping about Michonne's involvement with Tyreese and its effect on Carol; it also makes a dramatic assumption about her personality. By claiming that she needs to have self-respect, Heath tells her that her desires are inherently wrong. Michonne's indifference to existing relationships threatens the social norms of monogamy and therefore the possibility of rebuilding pre-apocalypse patriarchal society. Her status as a black female only exacerbates this "problem," for she is doubly scrutinized as "other." Presented as deviant, the sexuality of the main black female character of the series is immoral, preventing her from having a lasting relationship or gaining the full acceptance and respect of the survivor community.

In contrast, Rick's first lover following the death of Lori is Jessie, whose husband Rick murdered.[23] Jessie should be "off limits" even more so than Morgan and Heath are to Michonne. Her emotional stability seems especially precarious as she engages in a sexual relationship with her husband's killer while their grieving son sleeps in a nearby room, but Rick is never reprimanded or accused of lacking "self-respect" for this relationship. Even after he removes her hand to free his son from the zombies, and leaves her and her son to be eaten alive, his actions seem justified and understandable, while Michonne's do not. This discrepancy is inexplicable unless gender and race enter into the comparison; it becomes clear, then, that in *The Walking Dead* there are different standards for men and women and for different races.

"I'm—I'm not crying for me. I'm crying for you"[24]

Any attempt to discuss Michonne's sexuality in the comic series without addressing the complicated issue of her status as both rape victim and rapist would do a disservice. The official *The Walking Dead Magazine* briefly addressed Michonne's rape by the Governor in their special issue on the women of *The Walking Dead*. Some defend the storyline as realistic, dismissing the claim that including the act is "a disgustingly indulgent display of misogyny and racism"[25] complicated by the historical memory evoked in the power dynamic between a black female and a white male. Lisa Granshaw claims the act is more about power than sex, and that "Michonne's skin color did not matter to the Governor."[26] Michonne's skin color may not matter to the Governor,[27] *but it matters to the reader*. Given the limited depiction of strong women of color in the comic, choosing the most powerful to be a victim of sexual assault hardly seems irrelevant. Moreover, the driving force behind Michonne's punishment is her defiance of gender norms, which are only amplified by her non-whiteness. The patriarchal assertion of power established in the slave system still impacts black women today, driving the stereotype, as bell hooks has argued, that they are sexual, nonhuman savages more easily dehumanized and therefore especially vulnerable to sexual exploitation and rape.[28] Through hooks's argument, no one else but Michonne could be raped because the white, patriarchal society that dominates the apocalyptic world of Kirkman's creation maintains the historical institutionalization of the exploitation of black women. The masculinization of black women also has a long history in America beginning with the early days of slavery. Because black female slaves worked not only inside the home but also in the fields doing physical labor, they became unworthy of the title "woman" having become instead "surrogate" men.[29] When a female character displays aggression, especially if that woman is black, they are labeled as "masculine," making the potential for her portrayal as deviant more acute. This has a policing effect, dissuading other women from engaging in similar forms of opposition.[30] While punishment for attacking the Governor is the explicit cause of Michonne's rape, in the larger context of Michonne's narrative, her assault disciplines her for being black and "deviant."

Michonne refuses to succumb to the Governor's physical and psychological torture. Not only does she not give the Governor the emotional satisfaction of breaking her spirit or getting her to expose the location of the prison, but she decapitates an opponent in the gladiator ring at Woodbury before killing all the walkers that circle the fight, disrupting the Governor's appeasement of his community and forcing the viewers to see the brutality in the practice.[31] Here it seems as if Michonne has resisted her punishment—that she has risen above her circumstances as a heroine, and perhaps even as the hero of the story—but this victory is short lived. She refuses to leave with the rest of the group during their escape, instead returning to the Governor's apartment to lie in wait. What follows is a graphically detailed, *twenty-page* illustration of her assault and torture of the Governor, a dramatic difference from the six-page visual representation of her own rape. Michonne rips out part of the Governor's throat. She strips him, ties his arms to the walls in much the same manner that she was restrained, nails his penis to a wooden board (twice), uses a power drill to wound his shoulder, rips off his finger nails, and cuts off his arm and cauterizes it with a blowtorch. She then sodomizes him with a spoon, using that same spoon to gouge out his eyeball, although at this moment she finally vomits and cries. Before leaving, she cuts off his penis with her katana and leaves him for dead.[32] Regardless of the potentially warranted provocation of these acts, Michonne's use of violence certainly exceeds that of the Governor. Unlike the Governor, who tortured and raped Michonne in part to show his own men his power and retain the illusion of masculinity, Michonne's torment of the Governor serves no one but herself. No other characters are seen being immediately impacted by this event,[33] and the details of the violence seem completely unnecessary.

Kyle Bishop's theory of violence and audience identification in *The Walking Dead* offers an explanation of why Michonne's actions are so vividly depicted. Bishop argues that the depictions of violence are a result of Kirkman's desire that Michonne and Rick be viewed differently. While Rick's acts of barbarism throughout the series are shielded, taking place beyond the bounds of the panels, Michonne's aggression and revenge play out before the readers' eyes, therefore isolating her from feelings of sympathy. Her revenge on the Governor for raping and torturing her, according to Bishop, "has no necessity" and "transcends justifiable retaliation or lawful punishment—she even enjoys herself."[34] Michonne's actions are indeed excessive, but I would argue that the point of the excess is not to condemn "vengeful behavior" generally, as Bishop says, but to punish Michonne specifically for failing to following social norms, thus making the audience question her morality and even her sanity. The intention to distance the audience from Michonne becomes increasingly more difficult to explain without an explanation of underlying misogyny and sexual repression if one examines the other sexual assaults that occur throughout the series. When an all-male gang threatens Rick's son Carl with rape, Rick responds by ripping out the throat of one of them, a brutal act of violence that terrifies the potential rapists. Even after the remaining men run away, Rick prevents Abraham from killing or pursuing them, going after them alone to stab them to death (an act alluded to but not shown in the panels).[35] The hidden violence of the male characters in response to sexual assault emphasizes that men and women are "allowed" to act differently in response to rape, with the male's actions deemed more justifiable. That Rick would retaliate for the attempted rape of his son is a given, making its depiction unnecessary and gratuitous. But Michonne fights back so brutally, her actions must be shown to prove that women are even capable of such violence, with the underlying assumption being that something must be wrong with a woman if she chooses to do so. The violence of men is condoned, or at least understood. Michonne is left an outsider, however, because of the social stigmas that deem women incapable of violence and rape—unless they are severely punished.

"You know this is a fucking disaster already, right?" "I know."[36]

There is some hope that the continuation of *The Walking Dead* comic series will begin to portray men and women more equally, especially in terms of sexual agency. The vestiges of patriarchal hierarchy begin to crumble as the series progresses, with Maggie becoming head of the Hilltop group and with the introduction of two other female survivor group leaders: Magna and Alpha. However, there are hints that women are still incapable of power and control. As Michonne illustrates, women in *The Walking Dead* seem incapable of holding power inside the comic's narrative without being punished for their social transgression as confidant, independent, sexual, and violent women.

Heralding Michonne as a strong, capable warrior only cloaks the institutionalized racism and exploitation of black women inherent in *The Walking Dead* and other media. Michonne represents the threat black women pose to the existing race-sex-gender hierarchy. By emphasizing her "masculinity," aggressive sexuality, and mental instability, *The Walking Dead* succeeds in making her an outsider valuable to the survival of the community but ultimately undeserving of happiness; after all, her success would signify the decline of patriarchal white masculinity.

Notes

1. Michonne's story would be published again in 2013 as the standalone comic "Michonne Special."
2. See Hannabach,"Queering and Crippling," and Vossen, "Laid to Rest."
3. Lavin and Lowe, "Cops and Zombies," 113–14, 119–21.
4. Sugg, "*The Walking Dead*," 803.
5. Hannabach, "Queering and Crippling," 117.
6. Sterba, "Racism and Sexism," 61–71.
7. Miles, "Body Badges," 135.
8. Michonne to Rick. Kirkman, *The Walking Dead*, Compendium Two, Chapter 9.
9. Kirkman, *TWD*, Compendium One, Chapter 5.
10. Kirkman, *TWD*, Compendium Two, Chapter 12.
11. Kirkman, *TWD*, Compendium Two, Chapter 9.
12. Michonne to Tyreese as he expresses guilt in receiving oral sex from her while in a relationship with Carol. Kirkman, *TWD*, Compendium One, Chapter 4.
13. Vossen, "Laid to Rest," 93.
14. *Ibid.*, 88–105.
15. *Ibid.*, 98.
16. Data of sexual relationships in Chapters 1 through 24 was collected using visual analysis, with "Sexual Activity" defined as any sexual or romantic physical interaction between characters implied, referenced in conversation, or visibly shown to the reader in the panels. This included kisses and oral sex as well as vaginal intercourse. Gender determined by labeling of a character's sexual identity as homosexual, heterosexual, bisexual, etc. Determination of a character's race was made by their visual representation (shading of skin, hair texture, etc.) as well as their own self-identification.
17. Carol is labeled as potentially sexually queer for her willingness to engage in a romantic and sexual relationship with both Lori and Rick. By the same logic, she might also be polyamorous or polygamist given that she wants to live as a trio with the two.
18. Hannabach, "Queering and Crippling," 107.
19. Cook, "For a Good Time," 76.
20. Kirkman, *TWD*, Compendium One, Chapter 4.
21. Kirkman, *TWD*, Compendium Two, Chapters 13 and 14.
22. Kirkman, *TWD*, Compendium Three, Chapter 18.
23. Kirkman, *TWD*, Compendium Two, Chapter 11.
24. Michonne to the Governor as he rapes her. Kirkman, *TWD*, Compendium One, Chapter 5.
25. Pokornowski, "Burying the Living," 52.
26. Granshaw, "The Female of the Species," 32.
27. Arguably, larger political and cultural issues regarding race and assault in the United States find footholds here where a white man in a power position rapes a black, female prisoner.
28. hooks, *Ain't I a Woman*, 22–25.
29. *Ibid.*
30. Kramer, "Empowerment as Transgression," 236.
31. Kirkman, *TWD*, Compendium One, Chapters 5 and 6.
32. *Ibid.*, Chapter 6.
33. Assuming that the Governor would have attacked the prison anyway, which is likely.
34. Bishop, "Battling Monsters," 82.
35. Kirkman, *TWD*, Compendium Two, Chapter 10.
36. Michonne to Rick. Kirkman, *TWD*, Compendium Three, Chapter 17.

Rules for Surviving Rape Culture

Natalie Wilson

As a genre, horror often depicts extreme scenes of sexual violence. While various rape-revenge films take male sexual violence to task, scary movies have more generally provided us with sexy damsels in distress, teenagers punished for sexual activity, and a whole host of knives, axes, and chainsaws carving up sexualized bodies in front of willing, eager audiences.[1] Some films meld pornography and horror, such as *Night of the Living Babes* (1987) and *Porn of the Dead* (2006), while, more recently, Eli Roth's *Hostel* films (2005, 2007) brought "torture-porn" to prominence.[2] In contrast to these trends, the zombie genre tends to avoid overt sexualization and has often condemned sexual violence within its narrative arcs. George A. Romero's films, for example, offer a critical take on rape, linking it to the hyper-masculinity called for within patriarchy as a system and the military as an institution.[3] Danny Boyle's 2002 film *28 Days Later* extended the zombie-fueled denunciation of violence against women, framing surviving military leaders as would-be-rapists—and Andrew Currie's satirical film *Fido*, from 2006, alluded to traditional marriage as oppressive at best and as a form of sexual slavery at worst. Of course, some zombie films exude a problematically pro-rape stance, framing the female body as rape-able object, such as the 2008 film *Deadgirl*.[4] Still others present rape as a sort of zombie-ism—as an inexplicable disease which spreads through the culture, rotting the bodies of its victims, as in the 2013 film *Contracted*.[5]

In contradistinction, then, to the long silences and inaction surrounding sexual violence in the real world, especially regarding the legal punishment of rapists, many zombie texts expose and condemn rape culture.[6] While zombie texts have received much scholarly attention in recent years, there has been little sustained examination of the genre's representation of and engagement with sexual violence.[7] AMCs *The Walking Dead*, deemed one of the most successful television series ever made, is particularly ripe for such scrutiny given the series' longstanding engagement with sexual violence—especially as this engagement occurs over a time period in which the concept of "rape culture" established itself on the cultural radar.

Though the phrase "rape culture" arose in the 1970s out of second wave feminism, it did not develop into a widespread concept—so much so as to become part of the mainstream lexicon—until rather recently. Indeed, Kate Harding claims that the phrase is part of "the Zeitgeist of the twenty-first century" in her recent book *Asking for It*.[8] The adoption of the phrase, though, does not indicate there is *more* sexual violence in contemporary society as much as it gives a name to a systematic problem within patriarchy. The longevity of rape as a means of control and as a weapon of war spans recorded history, a fact infamously argued by Susan Brownmiller in her groundbreaking work from 1975, *Against Our Will: Men, Women, and Rape*. The concept encompasses the range of violence that results within contexts that glorify power, aggression, and ownership. Patriarchy is one such context. In such contexts, "a continuum of threatened violence that ranges from sexual remarks to sexual touching to rape itself" is normalized, as argued in *Transforming a Rape Culture*.[9] Rape culture, as such, is an umbrella term referencing the entire spectrum of physical and emotional violence that is carried out between people in intimate relationships (as with domestic violence), between strangers (as with street harassment), as well as acts carried out by an individual (date rape, for instance), or condoned by institutions (rape as a weapon of war). At the heart of such violence is hierarchical power, or what Brownmiller named "the ideology of rape," which makes sexual violence seem a *natural*—or at least to-be-expected—part of culture.[10]

The Walking Dead depicts this type of hierarchy within its fictional landscape, presenting a world plagued by violence as much as by zombies. In addition to having to repeatedly kill the never-ending hordes of walkers that threaten their lives, the characters also must navigate the "mass terrorism" inherent in living in a rape culture.[11] The show features domestic violence, sexual assault, sexual coercion, attempted rape, rape, and sexual enslavement, yet, rather than presenting sexual violence as an aberrant act carried out by individuals, the show sheds light on the contexts within which sexual violence thrives. One such context is post–9/11 America, refracted through the metaphor of a zombified world. Scholars such as Melissa Ames and Kyle William Bishop read the show in this light, though neither focus specifically on rape culture. Bishop sees the "traumatized heroes" of the show "as an indictment of the arguably aggressive stance U.S. politics and foreign policy have taken since 9/11," while Ames emphasizes how the series engages with "anxieties related to shifting gender norms."[12] In what follows, I set out to expand such readings into the arena of rape culture through a consideration of seven episodes in particular, episodes which span seasons one to five: "Tell it to the Frogs," "TS-19," "When the Dead Come Knocking," "Slabtown," "A," "Try," and "Conquer."

Combined, these episodes feature a continuum of violence that presents the terror of living in a zombified world as akin to the terror of surviving within rape culture as a rapeable object. In a sense, the "rape schedule" rules women are trained to follow in the real world are comparable to the survival rules featured in the zombie canon.[13] Rules stipulating how to dress, where to go, how to behave, how much to drink, what to keep in one's bag (a whistle, an alarm, pepper spray) are but some of the "surviving rape culture rules."[14] Such directives are similar to the "survival rules" of zombie texts, which propose that humans can spot or identify zombies, and that following certain protocols will keep one alive.[15] In both types of worlds, fear becomes a companion for those deemed likely to be assaulted, raped, or killed. Rape culture is not like the traditional shuffling zombie, though. It cannot be taken out with a swift swipe of Michonne's katana sword. Yet, *The Walking Dead* offers a list of rape survival rules of sorts, key among them that humans should treat other humans *as humans*, not as property, not as if they were walkers, not as Others to be controlled. In fact, *The Walking Dead* often explicitly condemns treating others as property as well as castigating those who enact unnecessary violence. In so doing, it provides a number of "rules" for eradicating rape culture.

RULE 1: *Silence Is the Enemy*

"Tell it to the Frogs," episode three of the first season, introduces key themes related to interpersonal violence and the power-over mentality that patriarchy calls for. Showcasing violence as a continuum, the episode frames norms of masculinity as leading to escalating cycles of violence. Near the start of the episode, Lori cuts Carl's hair as Shane sits nearby cleaning a gun. Shane tells Carl "get through this with some manly dignity and tomorrow I will teach you something special … to catch frogs." "You and me will be heroes," Shane promises. This exchange sets the "manliness" tone of the episode in which a number of the surviving male characters attempt to secure weapons in zombie-infected Atlanta, while another group stays back at camp.

During the episode, several of the female characters talk and laugh as they do laundry by the river. As they do so, Carol keeps looking back nervously over her shoulder at her husband Ed, who is smoking nearby.[16] Hearing their laughter, Ed stalks up, saying, "you ought to focus on your work, this ain't no comedy club." Andrea, clearly annoyed by his macho attitude, tells him he is welcome to pitch-in. Ed retorts "Ain't my job, missy" and goes on to call her an "uppity smart-mouth bitch." He orders Carol, "Let's go ... come on now, you heard me," but Andrea intervenes, causing him to bark "Don't think I won't knock you on your ass just because you some college educated coos." His behavior appalls the women and visibly frightens Carol. Andrea tries to convince Carol not to go with Ed, but Carol whispers, "It doesn't matter." Ed, frustration rising, snaps at her "You gonna come on now, or you gonna regret it later?" Jacqui interjects pointedly "So she can show up with fresh bruises later?" Ed then warns, "You all don't want to keep riding the bull here." Declaring, "Now I am done talking," he grabs Carol and smacks her across the face. Shane, who had been watching the scene escalate from the sidelines, intervenes. He pulls Ed back, throws him to the ground, and punches him repeatedly in the face, threatening "Put your hands on your wife, your little girl, anyone else in this camp one more time.... I will not stop next time ... you hear me?.... I will beat you to death." Carol, her mouth bloodied, runs to Ed's side, bawling "Oh god, Ed, I'm sorry." This scene, in which Ed takes the women's laughter and camaraderie as a personal affront, highlights his sense of ownership over Carol. When Andrea questions him, he insults her with reference to her gender and class, revealing that she threatens his sense of manliness, framing himself as the bull that is "done talking"—in so doing, he implies his willingness to use force rather than words. This threat, in turn, activates Shane's desire to be top dog. Asserting his higher position on the ladder, Shane mercilessly beats Ed into submission.

Overall, the episode frames men as trying to maintain control via their actions—by catching frogs, procuring weapons, controlling women, and beating other men. Women, meanwhile, are meant to do their chores, mind the children, and keep quiet. Yet, the violence that ensues suggests these gendered expectations are bad for everyone. Recall that near the start of the episode Shane told Carl to "be a man," suggesting that doing so will make him a hero. Yet, within the episode, the violence and cruelty associated with the antagonistic males (Ed, Shane) is condemned. Silencing such issues rather than addressing them is presented as leading to an escalation of violence. Lori's call for silence, for example, in which she instructs Shane to "tell it to the frogs" when he is trying to plead with her not to end their relationship, happens just prior to Shane's violent attack on Ed. Silencing leads to more violence here, as it also does in the next episode under consideration, "TS-19." Before turning to that episode, let's consider the title of the episode in which two intimate relationships take center stage: "Tell it to the Frogs." Frogs have vocal sacs that amplify sound, their croaks sometimes serving as distress signals. On one level, when Lori tells Shane to "tell it to the frogs," she is informing him she does not want to hear what he has to say. On another level though, frogs' ability to amplify sound echoes the anguish Shane is unable to process or voice. As we will soon see, silencing distress only intensifies the sexualized violence around which this early episode circulates.

RULE 2: Keep a Grenade Handy

In the final episode of season one, "TS-19," Shane has spiraled deeper into rage. His descent is mirrored in the group's literal descent into the lower levels of the Centers for Disease Control. Before viewers see what happens at the CDC, however, they are given a flashback to King County Hospital at the onset of the zombie outbreak. In the flashback, Shane is frantically trying to find a way to rescue a comatose Rick. After witnessing combat fighters with machine guns executing everyone in sight, Shane ducks into Rick's room. He listens to Rick's chest but doesn't hear a heartbeat. He then flees, blocking the door to Rick's room with a gurney. Unaware that his actions ultimately save Rick's life, Shane is tormented by this turn of events. Believing Rick dead, though, he pursues a relationship with Lori. After Rick returns alive, Lori is convinced that Shane deceived her and refuses to discuss the matter, as we saw in "Tell it to the Frogs." This silencing causes Shane's frustrations to escalate. During the "TS-19" episode, when a hastily gulped bottle of whiskey is added to his already roiling emotions, Shane sexually assaults Lori in the game room of the CDC. This scene is bookended by the group's arrival and departure from the CDC, a place meant to be safe that turns out to be dangerous– much like the game room itself. This suggestion of entrapment is referenced when the group arrives at the CDC and Dr. Edward Jenner insists everyone submit to a blood test, calling it "the price of admission."

As the episode progresses, we witness Shane drinking heavily. Clearly conflicted about the news that his best friend Rick is alive, Shane struggles to control his emotions. Later, as Lori peruses bookshelves in the game room, Shane leers at her from the doorway, whiskey bottle in hand. Approaching her, he launches into a verbal tirade: "I'm going to tell you a few things, and you're gonna listen." Shane clearly feels wronged by Lori's refusal to continue their relationship. He insists that she loves him, that he truly believed Rick to be dead. Here, though not mentioned explicitly, Shane refers back to the hospital scene that opens the episode, thus structurally allying his attempts to save Rick with his current traumatized state. "You told me my husband was dead," Lori says, but this only heightens Shane's rage. Trapping her against the pinball machine, Shane insists he saved her life, and that she and Carl would be dead if not for him. Shane's traumatic experiences coupled with alcohol and feelings of rejection are ultimately directed at Lori in this violent scene of sexual assault. Lori's eyes are wide with fear as she tries to push Shane away. He puts his hands on her face and throat saying "I love you ... say that you love me too." He then grips her throat and pulls her head back. "Get your hands off me, don't you dare," Lori warns. The camera then cuts to Shane's hand, forcing its way between her legs. At this point, Lori manages to push him away, scratching his face in the process and leaving three clear nail marks that stripe his neck with blood. Shane retreats, violently punching the doorframe on his way out. The camera then cuts back to Lori, who is crying and gripping her head in fear, obviously distressed. This scene, like the one detailing Ed's violence against Carol, echoes how abuse and sexual assault often happens in the real world—by someone the victim knows.[17] Shane insists, moreover, that he loves Lori, a common claim used to justify assault.[18]

The framing of this episode, given the sexual assault at its center, bears closer examination. Opening in a hospital where Shane frantically tries to save his and Rick's life as the outbreak begins, then moving to another place of disease/cure, the CDC, the episode focuses on the breakdown of safe, protective institutions. When Jenner shows them his wife's brain (the titular Test Subject 19), the group stands mesmerized, eager to know what the zombie virus does to the human brain. Explaining, "it invades the brain," Dr. Jenner paints an alarming scenario: "Everything you ever were or ever will be, gone." As Lori watches, the brain shows signs of life. "It restarts the brain?" she asks hopefully. "No," Jenner replies, "just the brain stem," explaining the human part, the "you part," will not come back. Akin to the experience of abuse and assault, the zombie virus changes one forever, invading one's brain/thoughts and destroying the "you" you once were. In a sense, this happens to Lori—she never fully recovers from Shane's attack, showing signs of PTSD up until her death.[19] However, on a more hopeful note, the series will go on to champion the once compliant Carol as forming a new, warrior version of herself. Indeed, Carol's burgeoning heroism comes to life in this episode when the group discovers the CDC is due to explode in less than thirty minutes. They convince Jenner to release them into the entry area, but enforced glass bars their escape. Carol rummages through her bag, telling Rick she thinks she has something that will help. Shane jeers "I don't think a nail file is gonna do it." Here, Carol, the victim of a domestically abusive marriage, trumps the self-appointed hero, Shane. Thanks to her foresight, Carol held onto one of Rick's grenades, an act which makes the group's escape from the CDC possible. The episode closes with the survivors driving away from the burning building ensconced in rubble and ash. However, as with the lingering smoke, the trauma wrought by sexual violence will spread.

RULE 3: Rape Culture Needs to Be Aired

The season three episode, "When the Dead Come Knocking," depicts sexual violence as a torture tactic via a narrative arc focusing on Maggie and Glenn. Working on the Governor's behalf, Merle has captured the couple in hopes of extracting information regarding the whereabouts of Rick's group. Glenn is interrogated and physically beaten by Merle, who calls Maggie derogatory names as he does so, while the Governor threatens to sexually assault Maggie if she does not divulge information. In both cases, sexual coercion and threats are used as torture: in the first, Glenn is accosted by Merle, who, by calling Maggie names ("farmer's daughter," "little bo-peep") emasculates Glenn, insinuating Maggie will suffer if Glenn does not comply; in the second, the Governor threatens to rape/sodomize Maggie if she does not divulge information.

Indeed, the Governor does more than threaten Maggie: he orders her to strip. She reluctantly takes off her shirt and bra, then stands defenseless, trying to cover her breasts with her hands. While verbal threats are made about the removal of Glenn's hand, threats of rape are lobbied at Maggie, indicated by the Governor's removing his belt and positioning himself behind Maggie. He caresses her hair before shoving her head down on to the table, leading her to assume rape is imminent. She, however, refuses to be compliant. "Do whatever you're going to do, then go to hell," she interjects. Ultimately he walks away, but Maggie is still prone and locked in the room with him, leaving viewers to wonder if Maggie is indeed raped. Later in the episode, the Governor brings Maggie, still topless and clearly traumatized, before Glenn. Witnessing the gun at Glenn's head, Maggie promptly reveals the whereabouts of Rick and company. Before letting her go, the Governor hugs her in a sadistic embrace, emphasizing the power he holds over her.

Significantly, the narrative does not simply move on from the assault Maggie endures. Rather, subsequent episodes frame the incident as a form of torture equal to or even worse than other types of physical violence. For example, in "The Suicide King," we see Maggie avoiding Glenn and being comforted by Hershel, her father. Later, in "Home," when Glenn and Maggie finally discuss what happened, she tells him she wasn't raped, presuming it will comfort him, and then asks bitterly if knowing this makes him feel better. Here, the dialogue emphasizes that Maggie continues to suffer from her sexual assault. Departing from real world insinuations that rape must be violent and traumatic to "count," the series suggests that the threat of rape is itself incredibly traumatic.

Various online critics took issue with this episode, however. For example, Doug Barry, in his 2012 *Jezebel* piece, felt the narrative "veered a little too close to the exploitation-territory of *I Spit on Your Grave* or *The Last House* on the Left," suggesting such a move "can (and should) make viewers uncomfortable." Here, Barry dismisses two rape-revenge classics without arguing *why* such content is problematic.[20] The films mentioned, directed by Meir Zarchi and Wes Craven respectively, examine brutal realities of rape and violence within narratives that explore the violent tendencies at the heart of American culture.[21] In claiming that "artistic integrity, plot progression, or whatever other grandiose sentiment we can summon" does not justify airing a rape scene, Barry suggests that rape should not be "aired" at all. Yet, rape narratives are a staple in popular culture. Why then is this particular narrative so problematic? And if media texts don't address such brutal realities, who will? Barry does not address such questions.

In a *Fem2.O* post from 2012, Tizzy Giordano similarly condemns the representation of the near-rape of Maggie, calling the episode a "rape-fest for ratings" that features a "fucked-up striptease."[22] Maggie's terrified face as she removes her shirt is far from strip-tease material, however. The scene is gritty, dark, and cold, much like the sadistic scenes in issues 28 and 29 of the comic, where the Governor repeatedly rapes Michonne. The soul-crushing details of such scenes illuminate the collective trauma of rape culture. For example, in the television series, Glenn is traumatized along with Maggie. His hand is used as a bargaining chip to force Maggie to comply, while her brutalized appearance is used to lead him to believe she has been raped. Significantly, moreover, such scenes are framed so as to denounce the perpetrators. Though Giordano rightly points out "Fake killing fake zombies in a fake post-apocalyptic U.S., that is fantasy. Rape is a reality. It is a dehumanizing, soul-killing reality," her contention that television series should not air rape is not supported.[23] How does not showing this "soul-killing reality" make it any less of a reality? In fact, doesn't *not* showing it make it more able to hide in the shadows and the silences—more able to continue spreading, unabated and under-examined, in the real world?

RULE 4: *Go for the Jugular*

The series' depiction of rape culture within this zombie-plagued world continues in seasons four and five, especially in "A" and "Slabtown." In "A," Joe, the leader of the Claimers, directs threats of rape at Carl and Michonne. Seeking revenge against Rick for killing one of his men in a previous episode, Joe holds Rick and Michonne at gunpoint. Daryl intervenes, saying, "You want blood, I get it. Take it from me, man." On Joe's command, the Claimers start to beat Daryl while another Claimer grabs Carl. Joe says to Rick, "First we're gonna beat Daryl to death. Then we'll have the girl. Then the boy. Then I'm gonna shoot you and we'll be square." The camera cuts to two men holding

Carl to the ground. One forces Carl facedown as he loosens his belt and pants, clearly intending to rape him. As this is happening, Joe says to Rick, "What the hell you gonna do now?" In response, Rick lunges towards him, ripping out his jugular vein with his teeth. Rick proceeds to cut open the man attempting to rape Carl, spilling his intestines to the ground. These are arguably the most gruesome acts we have seen from Rick's character.

Later, Daryl is apologetic, explaining to Rick, "I didn't know what they could do." Rick responds, "It's not on you." Here, though not made explicit, Daryl is presumably talking about the threats of rape—and especially about the attempted rape of Carl—as other types of violence are so common in the narrative that it would be odd to describe them in this way. Daryl insists that Rick's violent response is understandable, though, saying, "What you did last night. Anybody would a done that." Rick replies, "No, not that." This frames the violence as exceptional, as something beyond what is necessary for survival. Rick and Daryl both seem to recognize this shift. Daryl says, "Something happened. That ain't you." However, Rick will soon enact extreme violence against another human—not a rapist, but the abusive husband/father, Pete Anderson. Before that point, however, viewers will watch more evidence that this zombified world is pervaded by rape culture in "Slabtown."

The apt title of this episode links the slab, a common structural element of modern buildings, to rape, a common element in patriarchal societies. The title also denotes a morgue full of dead bodies. The episode bearing this title is set at Grady Memorial Hospital, a place purporting to save people, much as "TS-19" was set at the Centers for Disease Control. As with the CDC, the relative safety of the hospital and its sterile, upstanding appearance will prove deceiving. Indeed, the hospital has a rotten core—a decaying pile of corpses littering its elevator shaft. Symbolic of the rot that undergirds rape culture, this hospital is made up of rotten people—the violent, exploitive leader Officer Dawn Lerner, the predatory Officer Gorman, and the self-serving Dr. Edwards.

In "Slabtown," Beth wakes up in a hospital bed after being kidnapped in season three. She stares at a clock on the wall, watching the seconds slowly tick by. Reminiscent of how time is often counted in seconds during traumatic experiences, this opening foreshadows the tragic events to come. Soon after, Beth encounters Dawn Lerner, decked out in full uniform, who ominously tells her, "You owe us." Here, the dialogue is reminiscent of the notion that women "owe" something to their so-called saviors. As the episode unfolds, Beth witnesses a woman with a bitten arm being commandeered by officers down a hall and forced into a surgical room. Officer Gorman looks on, calling the woman a "smart ass whore." Once in the operating room, the woman resists having her arm amputated. "I am not going back to them!" she shouts. Everyone present, including Beth, holds her down as Edwards cuts off her arm. The scene is redolent of a gang rape, the woman held down against her will by multiple people, her body violated.

The episode ultimately contrasts Beth and others like her in similar positions of powerlessness with those who have authority and privilege (Lerner, Gorman, Edwards). This unequal distribution of power, it is suggested, undergirds and perpetuates the sexual violence that pervades the hospital—and the series. Meanwhile, those in power present themselves as saviors while committing violence, as does Shane, for example. In this episode, Gorman frames himself as Beth's savior, telling her he rescued her from a "rotter." He then says, "one was eyeing your thighs when we showed up. But I got there first," suggesting that her thigh, her body, belongs to him. This feeling of ownership is further emphasized later in the episode when Edwards walks in on Gorman forcing a lollipop into Beth's mouth, an act evoking oral rape, the lollipop suggesting Beth is the innocent child Gorman is forcing himself on. He exclaims, "yeah, that's right," as he shoves the lollipop in Beth's mouth. When Gorman's actions are interrupted by Edwards, he then angrily huffs, "Girl should've been mine."

As the episode further unfolds, it becomes clear that Gorman sexually assaulted the woman who was bitten—a fact corroborated by Lerner when she sinisterly reveals to Beth "The wards keep my officers happy. The happier my officers are, the harder they work." The clear indication is that these "wards" are used as sex slaves for the officers. Lerner's earlier statement to Beth that "It's easier to make a deal with the devil when you're not the one paying the price" reveals she herself does not have to "pay" as she is providing the officers under her command with female wards. In order to escape this fate, Beth plans to break out of the hospital. When she sneaks into Gorman's office to search for the spare elevator key needed to escape, she finds the woman with the amputated arm dead on the floor, presumably having killed herself to avoid further abuse by Gorman. As Beth locates the key, Gorman walks in. He says he won't report her if she agrees to be "friendly." He pushes her against the desk (similar to the way Shane pushed Lori against the pinball machine in season one) and starts to put his arm up her shirt, adding that it will be a "win win situation." Noticing that the woman is about to reanimate, Beth smashes the lollipop jar from the desk over his head, knocking him to the ground. The woman, now a walker, pounces on him, ripping out his jugular (much like Rick ripped out Joe's jugular in "A.") The female ward who chose death over sexual assault thus ensures that Gorman's actions come back to bite him (quite literally) when she reanimates. The episode closes with Beth, still imprisoned in the hospital, watching Carol brought in on stretcher. This structurally allies the two survivors of sexual violence, indicating that rape culture, like the walkers, is everywhere.

RULE 5: Cookies Coupled with Careful Observation Make for a Better Community

With its houses, food supplies, appointed leaders, doctors, and medical supplies, Alexandria promises a normal existence for Rick and company. Its suburban atmosphere allows the group to rest in one place and finally have a bit of relief from their long apocalyptic-induced wandering. Yet, behind its *Leave it to Beaver* exterior, Alexandria hides various unsavory things, much as supposedly normal, nuclear families often shield explosive secrets. Several seasons on, Carol has undergone many transformations: submissive wife, grieving mother, renegade adoptive mother, badass warrior-woman, and now, den-mother.[24] At Alexandria, she bakes cookies, wears comfy cardigans, and offers an ever-smiling face. Underneath her happy-housewife facade, though, she continues her vigilant, always-on-watch persona, one that is quite common for survivors of abuse/sexual violence. In fact, she is the first to recognize, with her knowledgeable survivor-gaze, one of Alexandria's hidden horrors: Pete Anderson.

The neighborhood surgeon, Pete is married to Jessie, a soft-spoken hairdresser. They have two sons: Ron and Sam. Pete is habitually violent and abusive to Jessie, something that leads Jessie to put a bolt inside Sam's closet door so that he can safely lock himself inside his closet when necessary. Carol is quick to spot Pete as an abuser. In "Conquer," convinced of the danger Pete poses to his family, Carol tells Rick "If walkers hadn't killed Ed, I wouldn't be alive right now." Here, the threat Ed posed to her life aligns her with other women of the series that don't survive this traumatic rape culture world such as Lori, Andrea, Joan, and Beth. Once aware of the threat Pete poses, Rick approaches Deanna, Alexandria's leader, telling her, "He's beating his wife, we have to stop him." Yet Deanna evades the allegations, countering, "Pete's a surgeon. He has saved lives." Rick then tries to convince Jessie to take the danger posed by Pete seriously, but, as he is doing so, Pete returns home and orders him to leave. A violent brawl ensues, resulting in Rick and Pete's smashing through a window. As they continue to fight, moving towards the town square as they do so, a crowd gathers to watch. When Jessie tries to break them up, Rick puts Pete in a chokehold. Deanna orders him to stop, but Rick pulls out a gun, arguing that the residents of Alexandria don't understand what it takes to survive. Coming one season after "A," when Rick ripped out another man's jugular to prevent Carl's rape, Rick's claim about survival connects the more general goal of surviving walkers to surviving sexualized violence. Further, suggesting Pete needs to be eradicated, much like the walkers, constructs the perpetrators of sexual violence as posing as much of a threat as zombies do. The sheltered Alexandria community, however, does not see it this way. In the next episode, "Conquer," Rick is put on trial for his actions, a narrative arc which echoes real-life scenarios in which those confronting abusers are punished.[25] Carol, seemingly wise to people's incredulity surrounding matters of interpersonal violence, advises Rick to tell a story that will absolve him of malicious intent. When she indicates she has been telling the townspeople stories since coming to Alexandria, Michonne asks her why. "Because they are children and children like stories," Carol replies. Here, it is implied the townspeople cannot face the truth about the dangers in their midst, whether those dangers be walkers or abusive husbands.

Later, Carol confronts Pete directly under the guise of delivering a casserole to his house. When he asks her to leave, she pulls a knife on him, stating that she could kill him and claim self-defense. She then encourages him to attack her, but he refuses. Calling him weak, she hands him the casserole and departs. Later that evening, Pete steals Michonne's katana sword and goes to the meeting where the participants have been discussing Rick's fate. Screaming "You're not one of us" at Rick, Pete's rampage is interrupted when Reg, Deanna's husband, steps in, an act that results in his throat being slit by the katana sword. After Reg dies in Deanna's arms, she orders Rick to kill Pete, which he swiftly does. Deanna's failure to heed Rick's warning leads to her own husband's death, a twist suggesting that if those who abuse and/or sexually assault others are tolerated, their harmful actions will spread, much like the zombie virus.

Whether the rotting, mindless walkers pose more of a threat than sexually violent predators such as Ed, Shane, Gorman, and Pete is up for debate. If the first few episodes of season seven are any indication, the series' focus on sexual violence will continue. As hinted at in the season seven episode, "Cell," Negan forces Sherry, whom he refers to as Dwight's "super-hot wife," to become his sex slave. As we see her taking a pregnancy test and hear Dwight offer condolences when the test is negative, the insinuation is that Negan is raping Sherry and, further, that she is meant to become pregnant. Though some read Negan as "anti-rape," as he imposes a no-rape policy at Sanctuary, he is indeed raping "his harem of wives."[26] At another point in the episode, Negan tries to reward Dwight by offering him the chance to commit acts of sexual assault. When Dwight declines, Negan mocks him, saying, "I just said it was happy hour at the pussy bar, and Dwight said no." As Negan is arguably the most threatening villain on the show thus far, associating him with raping Sherry (who is portrayed sympathetically) stands as another incidence of the series' condemnation of sexual violence.

Through a progression of narrative arcs, *The Walking Dead* focuses on the cyclical, interconnected nature of domestic abuse, sexual assault, rape, and sexual slavery, suggesting the dominator-model of patriarchy is the "patient zero" of rape culture. As Melissa Leon puts it, "the real source of terror within the world of *The Walking Dead* is not walkers, it's rape."[27] This claim aligns the series with several other zombie narratives that imply patriarchal male violence poses more of a threat than zombies. Though feminist critic Jessica Valenti argues that the lack of on-screen rape and sexual violence makes the show more feminist-friendly than other current fair, I would contend that it's not off-screen violence that gives the series feminist appeal—rather, it's the way show *actually deals with the topic of rape culture*.[28] Instead of sensationalizing violence, eroticizing it, or showing it as an individual tragedy, the series presents violence itself as an infection, generating a list of survival rules along the way. Chillingly, the show suggests that while you might be able to out-live the walking dead, you are less likely to survive rape culture unscathed.

NOTES

1. For analysis of gender within horror films, see, for example, Clover, *Men, Women, and Chain Saws*, and the essays in Grant, *The Dread of Difference*.
2. For a discussion of zombie porn, see Jones, "Porn of the Dead."
3. Wilson, "Re-Composing Zombie Politics."
4. For an excellent analysis of *Deadgirl*, see Jones, "Gender Monstrosity."
5. Wilson, "Re-Composing Zombie Politics."
6. For a discussion of the low prosecution rates of rape and sexual violence, see Harding, *Asking for It*.
7. For an overview of recent zombie scholarship, see Bishop, *How Zombies Conquered*.
8. Harding, *Asking for It*, 7.
9. Buchwald, Fletcher, and Roth, *Transforming a Rape Culture*, xi.
10. Brownmiller, *Against Our Will*, 2.
11. Griffin, *Rape*, 1.
12. See Bishop, *How Zombies Conquered*, and Ames, "The Trauma of (Post-Apocalyptic) Motherhood."
13. Valenti, *Full Frontal Feminism*.
14. See, for example, McEwan, "Rape Culture 101."
15. As in, for example, *Zombieland* (2009) and *Shaun of the Dead* (2004).
16. Ames, "The Trauma of (Post-Apocalyptic) Motherhood."
17. According to RAINN (Rape, Abuse & Incest National Network), 43 percent of rapes are committed by someone the victim knows. https://www.rainn.org/statistics/perpetrators-sexual-violence.
18. See, for example, Katz, *The Macho Paradox*.
19. For an examination of PTSD resulting from sexual assault, see, for example, Kimerling, Ouimette, and Wolfe, *Gender and PTSD*.
20. Barry, "Where's the Line?"
21. Clover, *Men, Women, and Chain Saws*. See especially Chapter 3, "Getting Even," for a discussion of the rape revenge genre.
22. Giordano, "Surprise!"
23. *Ibid*.
24. Ames, "The Trauma of (Post-Apocalyptic) Motherhood."
25. For a discussion of women imprisoned for confronting their abusers, see McCray, "When Battered Women."
26. See, for example, Davis, "The Walking Dead."
27. Leon, "The Walking Dead's 'Slabtown.'"
28. Valenti, "Why Do Women?"

"We can't just ignore the rules"
Queer Heterosexualities

John R. Ziegler

In the world of creators Robert Kirkman and Tony Moore's *The Walking Dead* comics, the structures and strictures of human society have broken down to the extent that protagonist Rick Grimes and his band of zombie-apocalypse survivors butcher and burn a group of cannibals who had eaten their own children before moving on to devouring strangers.[1] In the sixth season of the television adaptation, members of Rick's group preemptively murder members of rival group the Saviors in their sleep ("Not Tomorrow Yet").[2] While moments such as these are intended to raise questions about the ethical assumptions underlying their actions, the characters' behavior is always partly excused by their circumstances. The rules are different now, we are meant to think. However, such radical transfiguration appears not to extend to the conceptualization of the family. The apocalyptic refashioning of social practices makes it all the more striking how tightly the protagonists in both manifestations of *The Walking Dead* cling to the traditional bourgeois nuclear family as an organizing social unit, reflecting both its hegemonic position in contemporary American society and the conceptual and linguistic apparatus by which that position is maintained. Ultimately, the insistent conservativism underpinning familial dynamics in these texts overwhelmingly forecloses possibilities for alternative family arrangements.

The potential for radical alternatives to the traditional heteronormative family unit—a foundational grouping with wide-ranging implications—can best be engaged through the framework of queerness. In *No Future*, Lee Edelman opposes queerness to the social obsession with what he terms reproductive futurism. For Edelman, the figure of the "Child" drives the mechanism by which society thinks itself and functions as an assurance of both individual and collective futures. As a result of this figure's centrality, "the fantasy subtending the image of the Child invariably shapes the logic within which the political can be thought."[3] Political possibilities are thus constrained by reproductive futurism, which preserves "the absolute privilege of heteronormativity by rendering unthinkable, by casting outside the political domain, the possibility of a queer resistance to this organizing principle of communal relations."[4] The consequence of such constraint as it plays out in *The Walking Dead* is the continued dominance of the reproductive, "heteronuclear family … even in a post-apocalyptic world that in many ways might seem to require a more expansive and heterogeneous network of kinship and community."[5] Queerness, in Edelman's view, represents the social order's death drive, and stands outside of the assumption that "the body politic must survive."[6] Reproductive futurism denies and represses that death drive.

The Walking Dead does present the (admittedly incomplete) death of the social order, which Emma Vossen argues allows sexual encounters "almost entirely without any hesitation or heed to heteronormative socio-sexual customs," representing "their liberation in all facets of life."[7] One might expect such liberation to open new spaces for alternative structures. However, neither version of *The Walking Dead* meets the expectation of such spaces, specifically for new kinds of families. Queer family arrangements do not merely fail to materialize; they are often, in fact, actively rejected. The most arresting example of this rejection occurs when Carol proposes a polyamorous relationship to Lori in the comics.[8] Carol tells the pregnant Lori, "I kinda want to *marry* you." "Not just *you*," she explains, "you *and* Rick. Just hear me out—it's not as crazy as it sounds. I mean, I've been thinking about what Rick said, y'know—about how things are *never* going to go back to the way they used to be and how we need to just make a new life for ourselves."[9] Close attention to the specific language used in this and other exchanges regarding sociosexual organization allows us to trace its operations as one mechanism that both reflects and propagates heteropatriarchal ideology, establishing and maintaining the distinctions between the normative and "unthinkable" to which Edelman refers.[10] Carol's phrasing acknowledges that even in the face of sweeping, irreversible social change, her tripartite model of marriage will register as "crazy." Her use of "new life" proposes a new *way* of life, even if she still envisions this new mode through the conceptual framework of marriage. Carol does, however, recognize the potential to create new politico-familial spaces: "This just *makes sense* to me. I love you *both* and we could *all* raise Carl and Sophia and the new baby together. I know it seems weird now but we don't have to follow the *old* rules, we can make *new* ones."[11] She raises the possibility, if not of entirely abandoning existing structuring principles for the family, at least of reimagining them.

Resistance to such reimagining as Carol's arises not only from others but also from the deep-rooted internalization of heteronorms. Carol attempts to reassure Lori that "it'd be *like* we were married, but there wouldn't be a ceremony or anything. That'd be too *weird*." Her care not to appear as if she were undermining traditional marriage demonstrates the ideological dominance of the institution and the difficulty of overcoming its naturalization even for those who are actively challenging it. That she feels discomfort in stepping outside the boundaries of the nuclear heterosexual family testifies to the policing of queer possibility. Indeed, Lori proves effective at such policing by continuous appeals to the very same "old rules" that Carol wishes to reconfigure. She objects that they don't know one another well enough, invokes her small-town Kentucky upbringing, and, finally, again categorizes Carol's proposition as unthinkable, labeling it "insane." Lori equates polyamory with insanity because only by denying its status as rational discourse can she account for its challenge to the heteronormative family.[12]

Ironically, much earlier, Lori herself had defended, in similar terms, what another character thought to be an alternative family arrangement. Erroneously thinking that Dale is participating in a polyamorous relationship with Andrea and her sister, Amy, Donna says, "Look at the three of them ... carrying on in front of *God* and everyone. It's unchristian," to which Lori replies, "So's being judgmental if I remember correctly."[13] Although there is no sexual component to Dale's living with Amy and Andrea, as he later clarifies to Rick, Carol's affirmative response to Lori's defense of the trio suggests that their relationship may represent an influence in her considering different, more collective relational models. Dale's model of collectivity, however, involves no children, those anchors of reproductive futurism to which Lori turns in her final objection to Carol's request for a polyamorous family. Heteronormativity has long weaponized the imagined innocence of children, and Lori employs that exact tactic, crying, "What would our *children* think? Can you imagine how a living arrangement like this would scar them for *life*?!"[14] Her invocation of "our *children*" has less to do with protecting any actual child and more to do with deploying the discursive, regulatory concept of the Child. As Edelman explains, "the image of the Child, not to be confused with the lived experiences of any historical children, serves to regulate political discourse—to prescribe what will count as political discourse—by compelling such discourse to accede in advance to the reality of a collective future whose figurative status we are never permitted to acknowledge."[15] The figurative status of the social (and individual) future should be especially clear in this apocalyptic setting, but reproductive futurism nonetheless tenaciously persists. If Carol is not thinking of the children, then she cannot be said to be thinking at all.

Having had her proposal insistently rejected, Carol chooses a radical queer negation instead. Edelman uses a neologism, *sinthomo*sexuality, to describe a queerness that asserts itself against futurity, "reducing the assurance of meaning in fantasy's promise of continuity to the meaningless circulation and repetitions of the drive."[16] Adopting this position, and in an act that negates the social subject and its future, Carol allows a zombie to tear out her throat, first confessing that "Everyone thinks I'm *crazy*." She compliments her undead executioner, moreover, on how much less judgmental it seems than the survivors, a linguistic choice that echoes Lori's defense of Dale's living with Andrea and Amy.[17]

Carol's scorned proposition and subsequent suicide provide the most straightforward clash between reproductive futurism and queer resistance, but it is far from the only instance. Conflicts such as those surrounding the parentage of Lori's unborn child further demonstrate the tenacity of the reproductive futurist paradigm. In the comic series, after Rick and Lori are first reunited, Lori gives him his wedding ring back, symbol of his comforting position within the family and its promise of a future. Shane and Lori's violation of the boundaries of the nuclear family in his absence, even though done unknowingly, immediately creates tension, however. (One might go so far as to interpret Lori's pregnancy as punishment for her accidental infidelity.[18]) In spite of the fact that Rick admonishes Shane, who worries about stealing guns from the police station, that he shouldn't be "so worried about the *rules*" since they will likely never be the same again, the "*rules*" governing the constitution of the reproductive family unit remain unchanged.[19] Shane and Rick are positioned in competition rather than cooperation with each other because of the unthinkability of alternatives to the two-parent household. This is a competition not just for Lori but also for ownership of the Child, embodied both in Rick's son, Carl, and in Lori's unborn baby. The competition turns violent when Shane threatens Rick with a gun because Rick's return has reduced him to "*nothing*."[20] Because there can only be one head of a nuclear family, Shane believes that killing Rick is "the *only* way" to return to when "Everything was *so* perfect."[21] Instead, Carl, as a representative of futurity, preserves the proper family unit by shooting and killing Shane.

The television version of *The Walking Dead* emphasizes the rivalry engendered between Shane and Rick by heteropatriarchy even more than do the comics. The second scene in the entire series is a flashback in which they discuss the state of Rick's marriage, establishing the potential for conflict through Shane's interest ("Days Gone Bye"). The first episode also establishes Shane's assumption of the missing Rick's place in the family: Shane, unsurprisingly, tells Lori to survive for Carl, the guarantor of the future. In a later episode, Shane orchestrates some fatherly bonding time ("You and me," he says, "Shane and Carl") catching frogs ("Tell It to the Frogs").

As in the comics, Lori returns Rick's wedding band to mark his reinstatement as patriarch and invokes the restrictions of the dominant, monogamous familial structure against Shane, marginalizing and isolating him.[22] When Rick comments during a debate, "If it was your family, you'd feel differently," Shane is incredulous: "What did you say to me? I kept 'em safe, man. I looked after them like they were my own" ("Wildfire"). However, under the rules of the normative heterosexual family, they cannot *be* his own at the same time that they belong to someone else. Shane's final confrontations with Rick center on who can best ensure the future of and through Lori and Carl. Rick employs the language both of ownership ("That is *my* wife. This is *my* son. That is *my* unborn child") and, relatedly, of futurism: "I will stay alive to keep them alive" ("18 Miles Out"). Such statements draw force from the idea that Shane's professed love for Lori, in the monogamous heterosexual ideology that underlies the family unit, is an impossibility. As Rick explains: "I love her. You don't love her. You think you do, but you don't" ("18 Miles Out"). Later, Lori echoes this while referring to how "things got ... confused" and "Whatever the hell happened between us, whatever we *thought* it was" ("Better Angels"; emphasis mine). Again, anything that deviates from the dictate that romantic love can only exist within a single monogamous pair must be categorized and expressed as indescribable (because unthinkable) and thereby rendered nonthreatening.

This unnecessary struggle for ownership carries over into the final, deadly encounter between the two men. Rick frames Shane as a pretender to a title that cannot be shared: "Screw my wife? Have my children—*my* children—call you daddy? Is that what you want?" ("Better Angels"). Shane questions Rick's right to hold this exclusive position, taunting, "I'm a better father than you, Rick. I'm better for Lori" ("Better Angels"). Ultimately, Rick fatally stabs Shane. Carl kills Shane in the comics, and the show's substitution of Rick for Carl puts greater focus on the competition over child and family, but Carl does arrive afterwards and shoots zombie-Shane. His killing of Shane here, framed as it is by Rick's initial belief that Carl is aiming at him, becomes a declaration of choice between filial allegiances. In making this declaration, as in the comic, the Child preserves the integrity of the two-parent nuclear family.

However, Shane's death does not resolve the questionable parentage of Lori's unborn child, later named Judith (who, like Carl, is also a Child).[23] In the comics, Rick insists, in the face of a hesitant response, that Lori's pregnancy "is *good* news."[24] Even during a zombie apocalypse, futurism dictates that reproduction must always be cause for "'Congratulations.'"[25] This maxim, however, conflicts disruptively with the rules governing the monogamous heterosexual reproductive unit. That the child may not be Rick's, like Carol's proposal of polyamory, is quickly labeled unthinkable. Rick acknowledges the possibility to instantly dismiss it: "It's all I'm thinking about. ... I'm trying not to *think* about it. If I dwell on this I'll lose my *mind*."[26] Rick casts a family unit in which he and Lori raise Shane's child as counter to rationality (it makes him lose his mind), unnameable, and even dangerous: "This [birth] could *kill* Lori.... And I—the other thing could kill *me*."[27]

In the television version, Lori considers terminating the pregnancy. This consideration is framed, of course, as the wrong choice. In order to accomplish the termination, Lori has Glenn bring her boxes of morning after pills from a supply run that puts Glenn and Maggie in danger. Maggie's snide comment, "And here's your abortion pills," condemns Lori for putting group members in danger for an anti-reproductive act ("Secrets"). However, viewers are soon rescued from judging Lori because she makes herself throw up the pills she takes. That her decision is meant to be a relief to the audience (in the same way as the suicidal Beth choosing life) is reinforced by the fact that her planned termination would never have succeeded anyway, since the morning after pill cannot induce a miscarriage, even in extreme doses.[28] Whether or not Lori is aware of the futility of her plan, any viewers familiar with the mechanics of such contraceptives would never have had to worry that reproductive futurism was being seriously challenged.

When Rick confronts his wife over the empty pill boxes, he rhetorically locates, as we have seen in previous examples, the non-reproductive outside the realm of coherent thought. He responds to Lori's concern that a baby would live only a "short, cruel life" with a disbelieving "How can you *think* like this?" ("Cherokee Rose"). She admits that she "screwed up," and, although he claims that he wouldn't force her to have a baby, he also equates the non-reproductive with immorality, asserting that "Not even giving it a chance isn't right, either" ("Cherokee Rose"). During this conversation, Lori, for the first time, openly addresses her violation of monogamy with the half-sentence "Shane and I...," and despite Rick's response that he knows, perhaps one reason that Lori dies in childbirth is as symbolic punishment for violating the hetero-norm.

The Child, embodied in actual children or not, is, as we have seen, central to the normative regime of reproductive futurism. We might add to our examples of this centrality by pointing out that in both comic and television versions, Rick does everything for Carl, "the one thing I don't wanna fail," as he puts it ("Cherokee Rose"). In the TV series, Hershel calls children "now, more than ever, our most precious asset" ("Cherokee Rose"). Daryl Dixon became a viewer favorite partly because he would not give up the search for the missing child, Sophia. Tight-lipped warrior Michonne turns out in season four to have been mother to an infant before the apocalypse. As Anna Mae Duane observes, "The victimized child has long functioned as the litmus test for American virtue. We just *know* we're on the right side of [the] battle of good and evil when we are avenging lost little angels."[29] Duane continues, "American adults—even post-apocalypse—are desperately worried about losing the innocent child we rely on to confirm our roles as protectors and heroes."[30] In the same season, even the villainous Governor temporarily becomes just such a child savior, redeemed by the love of a little girl and the chance to reconstruct a nuclear family. The traditional nuclear family itself operates as the socially approved locus for producing and protecting the child/Child. Queer family arrangements must be, as we have seen, repudiated and regarded as irrational. However, the families that I have discussed in detail to this point are composed of the living, and *The Walking Dead* also presents the policing of a second type of (even more radically) queer family: families that incorporate the undead.

Interestingly, and disruptively, in *The Walking Dead*, the centrality of the child/Child can extend beyond death. According to Cory James Rushton and Christopher M. Moreman, "Zombies, as an abject reflection of our individual mortality, and harbingers of societal decay, force the viewer to consider the dark possibilities of a meaningless existence."[31] We can thus think of zombies, which "can be a dominating culture's figures for groups against whom violence and exclusion are systematically performed," through the paradigm of the queer, specifically, of the *sinthomo*sexual.[32] Edelman describes the *sinthomo*sexual as "the shadow of death that would put out the light of heterosexual reproduction," and within *The Walking Dead* universe, zombies take on this role of queer antagonist to reproductive futurism.[33] As such, they represent a threatening, unrestricted expression of drives. If the *sinthomo*sexual represents "the continuous satisfaction that the drive attains by its pulsions and not by its end," then the undead, endlessly consuming, occupy a similar role.[34] Their endless drive to consume simultaneously constitutes, if only as an effect, a drive to reproduce, both of which drives undermine reproductive futurism. As Steve Jones argues, zombies show "the violent potential of the Other that overpowers the accepted system, inevitably dominating via an unstoppable reproductive regime."[35]

It is especially significant that zombies reproduce, through infection or death, outside of the framework of heterosexual sex. Within the dominant paradigm, "the specifically heterosexual alibi of reproductive necessity obscures the drive beyond meaning driving the machinery of sexual meaningfulness."[36] Thus, the asexual method of zombie reproduction is doubly threatening. On the one hand, it provides a future that will bring about its own end: the zombies will either kill themselves off *through* reproducing when they run out of living flesh to consume, or, if they do not *need* to eat, they will be unable even momentarily to fulfill the desire that drives them. On the other hand, zombie reproduction removes the Child and its attendant fantasies from a place of primacy.[37] Zombies' conflation of ingestion and reproduction repositions the latter as mere drive rather than unifying force for the social and individual self and future.

As a result of such potential disruption, zombie-queer families must be purged. In the comics, Hershel creates a sort of extended family by keeping zombified relatives and neighbors in his barn until he figures out how to help them. He argues, "We don't know what they're *thinking*—what they're *feeling*."[38] Television Hershel makes much the same argument. His daughter Maggie reprimands Glenn for using the term "walkers," insisting that they are "Mom, Shawn, Mr. and Mrs. Fischer, Lacey, Duncan" ("Secrets"). However, she quickly comes around, following a close call while procuring Lori's "abortion pills." In the comics, a deadly mishap forces Hershel to help kill all of his undead, demonstrating that his position is untenable. In the television series, a similar massacre ends with Rick shooting Carol's daughter Sophia, who had become a zombie. Sophia's death as a child zombie is the ultimate symbol of the impossibility of the queer inclusion that Hershel attempts. Even a Child, the search for whom propelled the entire season, must be eliminated once she becomes a threat to the futurist family.

Undead children such as Sophia provide a particularly destabilizing example of the way in which the "zombie menaces the integrity of our systems of belonging."[39] As Trevor Grizzell notes, whenever "the social order's Child is deployed to cover up realities of society or individual behaviors, the zombie child shows its instabilities."[40] The zombie child represents a sort of queer negation of the Child. Embracing rather than destroying a zombie child, therefore, undermines the conceptual foundations of the traditional reproductive family. While Hershel attempts to undo or outwait this negation, in the comics, the Governor attempts to preserve his own family by adapting to and partially embracing it. He keeps his zombie niece, Penny, in his dwelling, feeding her human flesh. He also assumes some subjective continuity between her living and dead forms, scolding her, "I raised you better than this."[41] He later saves Penny from being shot, and later still removes her teeth with pliers "for the good of our relationship."[42] By this point, he refers to himself as her "Daddy" and tells her that he will get used to the taste of kissing her.[43] Before he leaves for what will be the last time, the Governor makes sure that she will be well taken care of. In the television version, in which she is the Governor's daughter rather than his niece, he sings to her and is upset that she is more interested in nearby meat than in making eye contact with him. He begs Michonne not to hurt his little girl, and he weeps as he cradles Penny's body after Michonne stabs her ("Made to Suffer"). Other considerations aside, it is the Governor who, in some ways, most radically reconfigures the family and resists futurity. "Because of its ontological liminality, the monster notoriously appears at times of crisis as a kind of third term that problematizes the clash of extremes," as well as the tendency towards binary thought.[44] Through her relationship to the Governor, the monstrous Penny disrupts the boundaries regarding family, subjectivity, and even life, boundaries that someone like Rick would regard as perfectly clear.

In the television series, the threats that Penny presents die with her. In the comics, what finally causes the Governor's death, after all of his horrific deeds, is that Lilly blames him for the fact that she shoots and kills Lori and Judith during the prison assault. She calls the Governor a "monster" and screams, "*A baby!* You made me kill a fucking baby!"[45] In other words, she holds him responsible for the ultimate crime of murdering a child, the most potent symbol of reproductive futurity. The Governor has violated a basic social tenet by choosing a dead child over a living one, a zombie child who subverts the illusions of subjective wholeness, who can reproduce outside heterosexuality, and who signifies no social futurity. This choice cannot be made without social retribution, which Lilly provides by killing the Governor.

When Rick, in the comics, faces a similar choice between a living and a dead child, between futurism and negation, he, as the hero, sides with the former. He has begun forming a new nuclear family with a woman named Jessie and her son. He tells her, however, "if I have to choose between my child or someone else's child.... I'm going to choose mine *every* single time."[46] As the town is overrun by zombies, Jessie's son is bitten, but she refuses to let go of either his hand or Carl's, leading Rick to sever her hand at the wrist. Jessie dies because she clings to a dead child, while Rick literally cuts off that connection and chooses futurity over oblivion, even at the cost of his new family unit.

As Jeffrey Jerome Cohen defines it, "the monster is ... a code or pattern or a presence or an absence that unsettles what has been constructed to be received as natural, as human."[47] The zombies in *The Walking Dead* universe, both in themselves and in the social shifts that they bring about, denaturalize the hegemony of reproductive futurism based in the traditional monogamous nuclear family unit. Whether it is Carol's proposed polyamory or the Governor's refusing to remove his zombie daughter from his family, the value of "queer negativity" "resides in its challenge to value as defined by the social, and thus in its radical challenge to the very value of the social itself."[48] Reading such queer resistance into *The Walking Dead* can at the very least call into question the social as currently ordered. It might also allow us to better attend to Margrit Shildrick's call to embrace the potentialities opened up by the monstrous: "Rather than attempting to recuperate the monstrous, might we not refigure it as an alternative, but equally valuable, mode of being, an alterity that ... signals other less restrictive possibilities?"[49] *The Walking Dead's* depictions of threats to futurity and the normative family and of the containment of those threats can help us to think through the problems surrounding queer heterosexualities, particularly how they continue to be policed even in a world where the rules we "invented to make us feel like we *weren't* animals" can be safely ignored.[50] Rick's assertion that *"Nothing will ever be the way it used to be,"* is not, it turns out, entirely true.[51]

Notes

1. Kirkman, *TWD*, Compendium Two, chapter 11 (unpaginated). The quotation in my title comes from Kirkman, *TWD*, Compendium One, chapter 4, and is spoken by Tyreese during Rick's "We *Are* the Walking Dead" speech.
2. Because they share the same fictional universe (including characters and portions of storylines), along with the involvement of Robert Kirkman, I treat the comics and television series here as related texts. While both versions have featured (mostly underdeveloped) same-sex relationships, none have yet involved a "Family," and so these relationships fall outside of my focus.
3. Edelman, *No Future*, loc. 64. All citations of *No Future* are to Kindle edition location markers, as are all citations of other Kindle files.
4. *Ibid.*, loc. 64.
5. Hannabach, "Queering and Crippling," loc. 1951.
6. Edelman, *No Future*, loc. 73.
7. Vossen, "Laid to Rest," loc. 1734, 1766.
8. Kirkman, *TWD*, Compendium One, Chapter 5.
9. Text in the comics occurs entirely in capital letters. In quoting, I alter this but preserve original emphases.
10. Edelman, *No Future*, loc. 64.
11. Prior to this, Carol has kissed both members of her proposed triad individually. When Rick reacts with disbelief, she promises not to tell Lori, to which Rick responds that he will, adding, "She's my *wife* and I *love* her." Kirkman, *TWD*, Compendium One, Chapter 4. Their exchange reinforces normative boundaries, confining sexual behavior to the nuclear family and its version of romantic love. Andrea answers Dale similarly when he mentions a less radical version of Carol's queer heterosexuality. Citing his own age and disability, he suggests that Andrea can have sex with Tyreese if she wishes, without repercussions. Her answer, "Oh, stop it.... *I love you*," like Rick's, collapses love and monogamy in the service of the status quo. Kirkman, *TWD*, Compendium One, Chapter 7.
12. After Lori's baby is born, Rick suggests that it is "best to forget the weirdness with" Carol. He invokes the supposed lack of socially-enforced boundaries while continuing to locate alternate behavioral models outside of those boundaries. "We gotta keep reminding ourselves there's no rules out here," he says. "the way people react to things—their behavior. It's going to be damn erratic ... [H]er advances on us, as uncomfortable as it makes us—maybe we should just forget it." Kirkman, *TWD*, Compendium One, Chapter 7.
13. Kirkman, *TWD*, Compendium One, Chapter 1.
14. Lori later uses devotion to children to justify, albeit apologetically, her distance from Carol subsequent to the proposal: "I'm sorry if we've drifted apart. We were so close until recently. I've just, with the baby and the latter months of pregnancy..." Kirkman, *TWD*, Compendium One, Chapter 7.
15. Edelman, *No Future*, loc. 200.
16. *Ibid.*, loc. 537, 637.
17. Kirkman, *TWD*, Compendium One, Chapter 7.
18. In the comics, Carol's comment to Lori that her pregnancy may be further along than she thought suggests that the child is in fact Shane's. Kirkman, *TWD*, Compendium One, Chapter 3.
19. Kirkman, *TWD*, Compendium One, Chapter 3.
20. Kirkman, *TWD*, Compendium One, Chapter 1.
21. *Ibid*. In the television series, Shane echoes this statement in his final argument with Rick: "You come back here and *destroy* everything" ("Better Angels").
22. In the television version, Lori does ask if Rick *wants* the wedding band back, but

this seems as much a reference to the marital problems hinted at in the series premiere as to a new world order. Rick, of course, replies, "Of course."

23. I should perhaps more properly call this Shane's first death, since he is killed again in both the comic and television series after he becomes a zombie. If we can align the walking dead with the queer, as I will argue later in this essay, then Shane's first death can be read as his social death. In fact, we can compare Shane's accusation immediately prior to his death in the comics that Rick has reduced him to "Nothing" to Edelman's assertion that "*Sinthomo*sexuals ... represent loss itself: represent, more precisely, loss of self, of coherence, of life, and of heirs." Edelman, *No Future*, loc. 1432.

24. Kirkman, *TWD*, Compendium One, Chapter 2.

25. *Ibid*. Edelman's statement while discussing Alfred Hitchcock's 1963 film *The Birds* that "the child means 'meaning' for adults, who can only attain it by virtue of participating in the labor of giving (it) birth" applies equally well here. Edelman, *No Future*, loc. 1904. It also illuminates the fact that Glenn and Maggie, in both comic and television versions, conceive a child of their own.

26. Kirkman, *TWD*, Compendium One, Chapter 2.

27. *Ibid*. This statement takes on additional dimensions if, again, we read death as associated with queerness. Dale reiterates this when he tells Lori that she should never tell Rick if the baby isn't his because "It'll *kill him*. It'll be the one last thing it takes to make him crack." Kirkman, *TWD*, Compendium One, Chapter 2.

28. See Ryan, "*The Walking Dead*." Beth, when suicidal, can be aligned with the *Sinthomo*sexual, criticizing both Lori's reproduction ("You're pregnant. how could you do that?") and the illusion of meaning that it helps to maintain ("It [life']s just so pointless.") ("18 Miles Out").

29. Duane, "'The Walking Dead's' Scary, Necessary Lesson."

30. *Ibid*.

31. Rushton and Moreman, "Introduction," loc. 148.

32. Cohen, "Undead," 405.

33. Edelman, *No Future*, loc. 1745.

34. *Ibid*., loc. 1354.

35. Jones, "Porn of the Dead," loc. 738.

36. Edelman, *No Future*, loc. 244.

37. The fact that everyone who dies becomes undead only intensifies the threat, since everyone will at least briefly experience this queered subjectivity. Zombies are "a danger from without that is already within." Cohen, "Undead," 403. Carol's death in the comics can be seen this way, since it is caused both by a zombie allowed *within* the protective boundaries of the prison and by her own choice of self-negation. As Cohen describes it, "The Monster prevents mobility (intellectual, geographic, or sexual), delimiting the social spaces through which private bodies may move. To step outside this official geography is to risk attack by some monstrous border patrol or (worse) to become monstrous oneself." Cohen, "Monster Culture," loc. 341. Both happen to Carol, who wanders off the map of heteronormativity.

38. Kirkman, *TWD*, Compendium One, Chapter 2. He also says that they may "Wake up *tomorrow*, heal up, and be completely *normal* again." *Ibid*. His desired outcome is always a full return to the normative.

39. Cohen, "Undead," 401.

40. Grizzell, "Re-Animating," loc. 2326.

41. Kirkman, *TWD*, Compendium One, Chapter 5. This type of treatment is limited To his own family, as he keeps other zombies for public fights and a number of zombie heads in aquariums for his own entertainment.

42. Kirkman, *TWD*, Compendium One, Chapter 8.

43. *Ibid*. This scene and these statements also carry incestuous implications, an extreme violation of typical familial boundaries and practices.

44. Cohen, "Monster Culture," loc. 226.

45. Kirkman, *TWD*, Compendium One, Chapter 8.

46. Kirkman, *TWD*, Compendium Two, Chapter 14.

47. Cohen, "Preface," loc. 67.

48. Edelman, *No Future*, loc. 121.
49. Shildrick, *Embodying the Monster,* 67.
50. Kirkman, *TWD*, Compendium One, Chapter 4.
51. *Ibid.*

Afterword
From Identity Politics to Tribalism

Dawn Keetley

While the essays in this collection have illuminated the complexities of identity formation, specifically the imbrications of race, gender, class, and sexuality in *The Walking Dead*, I want to end by offering a different paradigm for understanding AMC's TV series, one that has emerged particularly in its later seasons (four through eight) and that I believe articulates a genuine movement beyond identity politics—and that is, tribalism.[1] *The Walking Dead* has for the length of its run tapped into twinned and contradictory impulses in the twenty-first century: post-racialism (along with post-feminism and post-heterosexism) and a resurgent (post–9/11) tribalism. Political scientist Michael Tesler articulates versions of these impulses in the title of his book on the presidency of Barack Obama: *Post-Racial or Most-Racial?: Race and Politics in the Obama Era* (2016), a title that identifies both the hope that America had moved beyond divisions of race with the election of the first African American president (post-racial) and also the countering (most-racial) reality that Americans became *more* polarized around race—more "tribal"—during President Obama's two terms in office.

Beginning not long after President Barack Obama took office, AMC's *The Walking Dead* contains evidence of both of the competing impulses of Tesler's title: the narrative itself clearly strives for post-racialism, since race is rarely invoked after season three, and was only infrequently invoked before that. In this way, the series tracks the post-racial hope that many scholars identified at the time of Obama's election. As Catherine Squires writes, "post-racial rhetoric surged during the historic 2008 election," as claims about the "declining significance of race" became pervasive. The "post-racial vision of an already-achieved multicultural nation," she concludes, seemed finally fully realized.² Such claims were premature, however. Tesler argues in his 2016 book that the racial divide in fact widened dramatically during the Obama years (2009–2017). As he puts it, "Mass politics was indeed more polarized by and over race during Barack Obama's presidency than it was before his 2008 presidential campaign"—indeed there was a "spillover of racialization," in that a "wide array of Americans' opinions" became "more polarized by racial attitudes and race during the Obama presidency."³ Despite its own hopes to create a "post-racial" post-apocalyptic world, *The Walking Dead* has certainly not been immune to the increasingly polarized discourses around race (along with gender and sexuality), but they have swirled for the most part *outside* the diegetic frame, raising issues that do not seem to matter very much within the narrative itself.⁴

The growing racial divide of the Obama era has been an integral part of what many deem a reinvigorated "tribalism" that intensified especially around the 2015–2016 presidential campaign and the election of Donald Trump in November 2016. Andrew O'Hehir, writing for *Salon*, diagnoses the newly resurgent tribalism under Donald Trump. Trump, O'Hehir writes, "channels primitive and incoherent tribal emotions that stretch way back into our species' history, before America, before modern conceptions of race and nationality, before any of that stuff." Trump's campaign is not about issues, O'Hehir (hyperbolically) claims, but about "the call of the wild, the allure of that long era of cruelty and brutality that preceded recorded history and human civilization, when the weak were ruled by the strong and little or no justification was required to inflict terror and violence on our perceived enemies."⁵ Trump's election, many believe, signaled the triumph of tribalistic tendencies, the resurgence of what we thought was a collective atavism *of the past* incarnate (again) in the contemporary political sphere.

Needless to say, O'Hehir's description of tribalism (while it may or may not describe Trump's America) describes perfectly the world of *The Walking Dead*. It is most likely impossible to map causality here—to assert either that the success of *The Walking Dead* contributed to Trump's success or vice versa—but it is undeniable that *The Walking Dead* has mapped onto the ways in which many political commentators characterize the typical Trump supporter and the particular worldview Trump promotes.⁶ Not surprisingly, perhaps, in an interview in *Forbes*, Trump's son-in-law and campaign advisor Jared Kushner disclosed a strategy to advertise during *The Walking Dead* in order to reach "people worried about immigration," people worried, in other words, about the integrity and safety of their tribe.⁷

Some may argue that *The Walking Dead* taps into a tribalism that is structured around those familiar lines of identity politics (race, class, gender, sexuality, and nation) that structure the contemporary American landscape and that have been so visible in the 2016 presidential election and its aftermath. I want to argue, though, that to the extent that people read *The Walking Dead* this way, they are reading *against* what the series has evolved to become in seasons four through eight. The dominant reading, in my view, tracks away from identity politics and toward a tribal formation that is blind to race, gender, class, and sex. *The Walking Dead* thus offers a utopian alternative to a United States that, in the late 2010s, is increasingly fractured along the lines of identity politics.[8]

AMC's series undoubtedly begins mired in rather conventional identity politics. Merle's racist rant on the rooftop in Atlanta in the second episode of the series is only the most obvious example of how characters, at first, wield racist and sexist stereotypes. The series moves rather quickly, however, to cast these assumptions as fevered delusions, suggesting their obsolescence in the post-apocalyptic world. In the season two episode, "Bloodletting," T-Dog is suffering from an infection from a deep cut on his arm when he says to Dale that since he (Dale) is old and T-Dog himself is "the one black guy," everyone else thinks "we're the weakest." He adds that he'll undoubtedly "be the first to get lynched." Dale is astonished and, indeed, two episodes later (after some salutary antibiotics), T-Dog says to Dale that he didn't mean what he said: "It wasn't me." T-Dog had to be out of his head, in short, to contemplate the possibility that race mattered to his group. In a later episode in season two, "Chupacabra," Daryl falls down a ravine and is stuck by one of his own arrows. In a hallucinatory state similar to T-Dog's, Daryl conjures up his lost brother Merle, who reiterates his view of the world in terms of stark race, class, and political difference. In Daryl's vision, Merle mocks his brother for his allegiance to Rick and the others, telling him that he's aligning with "pansy asses, niggers, and Democrats." The Merle whom Daryl conjures up in his fevered state has a deep sense of identity rooted in white, working-class heteronormativity that is most likely supposed to code as Republican and that is expressly *not* Democrat.

After these hallucinatory moments, however, race, gender, class, and sexuality for the most part disappear from the series as a matter for overt comment, as anything that actually matters. As I mentioned before, though, the identity politics of the series has consumed commentators and fans long after it stopped being an explicit issue in the show itself—not least in the pointed (and, for a while, legitimate) critique of *The Walking Dead*'s "One Black Man at a Time" problem.[9] For the most part, though, and especially after season three, *The Walking Dead* has been orienting us to a new world that aspires to be not only post-apocalyptic and post-nation state but also post-identity politics, encompassing most notably post-racial, post-class, and post-gender politics.

The Walking Dead does not abandon us in a void, however, in an empty space characterized only by the loss of the ways in which people habitually affiliate; it also does not pretend that we have arrived in a place where everyone is equal, where all matter equally to all, where inclusivity reigns and humans embrace, in Peter Singer's words, an "expanding circle."[10] Instead, the show reconstructs social relations through *a post-identity-politics tribalism*. The series represents its characters organizing into tribal formations, in other words, but they are emphatically *not* articulated along the lines of race, ethnicity, gender, class, or sexual orientation. Indeed, *The Walking Dead*'s tribal alliances markedly cross these lines, thus providing a hopeful alternative to that parallel resurgence of "tribal" politics in the 2010s that is very much structured around traditional identity formations of race, ethnicity, nation, class, religion, and gender. *The Walking Dead*, in short, offers a more utopian vision of tribalism than that which is fracturing the U.S. (and much of Europe) in the second decade of the twenty-first century. The series insists that "tribalism" is indeed something that humans cannot get past but also that it is a mutable social formation, one that can be created, broken down, and re-created.

In an influential definition, political theorist Paul James defines tribes as "real, self-reproducing and changing communities framed by the social dominance of face-to-face integration and living in the world today." Crucial to James's definition is face-to-face interaction and what he calls "structures of embodied interrelation," as opposed to the prevailing "modern abstracted communities." He notes that while such "embodied interrelations" are often formed around bonds of blood kinship, tribes are also formed by "fictive blood ties."[11] Thus, it is a crucially important moment, for instance, when Rick says to Daryl in season four, "You're my brother" ("A"). Rick's group has become a "tribe"—significantly a multi-racial tribe—based on embodied kinship relations that are not the less powerful for being "fictive blood ties" rather than biological.[12] Their tribe operates like an extended family, and they implicitly vow (and demonstrate) unswerving loyalty to each other.

Place is also crucially important to the tribal formations of *The Walking Dead*, second only to the bonds of "family"—and thus *The Walking Dead* offers an alternative to the triumph of globalization, of unencumbered, networked space over the enmeshments of local place.[13] As Timothy Morton has pointed out, cultural critics have been pronouncing the death of "localized, particular 'place'" and the preeminence of "homogeneous empty 'space'" since the 1970s. "Our habitual talk," he writes, pits "presence, villages, the organic, slow time, traditions" against "dissolution, speed, modern, and postmodern technocultures." Yet even in our (real) world, place has by no means died, despite reiterated accounts of its death. Instead, as Morton asserts, it is "(the fantasy of empty smooth) space" that has collapsed.[14] In fact, though, neither space nor place has vanished in the early twenty-first century: each remains in a perpetual tension that can be mapped onto the tension between globalism and tribalism. As James points out, despite claims of the historical progression from tribalism to globalism, there is in fact no such progression. James describes the relation between the two formations as a perennial conflict: "Systemic processes of rationalizing homogenization integrate the globe at one level, while ideologies and practices of difference and radical autonomy frame the popular imaginary at another. These are material and lived contradictions."[15] And they are contradictions that have been writ large in the political cataclysms of the 2010s such as Brexit (the 2016 majority vote of UK citizens to leave the European Union) and Donald Trump's victorious U.S. presidential campaign. Both instances represent a citizenry's ongoing struggle over whether to define themselves locally or globally.

In the world of *The Walking Dead*, place, with its political implications of what James calls "difference and radical autonomy," is insistently resurgent. The survivors, who are at first forced by the apocalypse to be nomadic, forced to be dangerously "on the road," have had to fight to carve out and defend habitable places—as humans have throughout our species history. As they find such places, the bonds of tribalism become stronger, and the survivors are willing to go to greater lengths to defend a tribe now rooted in *place* as well as in the "fictive blood ties" of family. The season six episode "Not Tomorrow Yet" represents a monumental turning point for Rick's group, now settled in Alexandria and ready to defend it at all costs. In need of food and refusing to return to a nomadic and scavenging existence, Rick and his group decide to launch a preemptive attack on the Saviors after Maggie works out a deal with the leader of Hilltop: Gregory has agreed to give them food if they can kill the group that is extorting food from them.[16]

In the next episode, "The Same Boat," Rick and his group attack the Saviors' outpost, engaging for the first time in unprovoked brutality, killing the Saviors in cold blood in their sleep. Maggie and Carol even burn a group of them alive. Before that, however, and even more demonstrable of tribal loyalties, Maggie and Carol kill two women who are depicted as *just like them*. Maggie kills a woman, Michelle, who looks strikingly like her and who was recently pregnant, like Maggie. And Carol kills a woman who, as she has, lost daughters in the apocalypse and who was (it is suggested) in an abusive relationship with a man. The episode brilliantly shows how Maggie and Carol are strongly drawn to these women by shared *gendered* life experiences. But in the end, Maggie and Carol refuse the bonds of gender for the *bonds of their tribe*.

Tribalism as an increasingly dominant social formation in *The Walking Dead* is highlighted by other groups that may appear tribal but are not. In season four, for example, Daryl briefly joins up with a group called the "Claimers," a nomadic group held together by a set of "rules" that are, as their leader Joe explains, designed to prevent them "going all Darwin." The

Claimers come to own items and food by being the first to declare "claimed," and theft and lying are violently punished. Even though this group may appear to be a "tribe" in that Joe insists on the importance of a "group" for survival (and the episode is titled "Us"), the notion of tribe is explicitly disavowed both in the group's rootlessness and in their lack of any allegiance to each other. As Joe says, they don't have to be "friendly" or "brothers-in-arms," they just need to follow the rules—and they turn on each other violently when the rules are broken. Daryl rejects this group, saying to Joe, "There ain't no us," and joining forces (again) with Rick, Michonne, and Carl the minute the Claimers run across them. Indeed, Daryl immediately and without any reservations offers his life for Rick, Michonne, and Carl—and it is at the end of this episode that Rick says to him, "You're my brother" ("A").

Negan's Saviors, too, illustrate tribalism by depicting what it is not. Although Negan's group is rooted in a place (the ironically named Sanctuary), it has nothing resembling kinship ties, no face-to-face, embodied interrelations. Negan rules by overpowering and terrorizing those in his group, a strategy glaringly evidenced by the fact that every member of his group must relinquish their autonomous identity and declare "I am Negan." As Negan himself says in the season seven episode, "Cell," "I am everywhere." There is nothing that is not Negan. The Saviors—subsumed by Negan's overpowering will—are fascism writ large. In his essay on fascist masculinities in *The Walking Dead*, Stephen Olbrys Gencarella defines fascism as "staunchly anti-individualist in promoting the state, defined as a people who observe governmental authority,"[17] a description that perfectly encapsulates Negan's rule over the Sanctuary. Gencarella, however, argues that *The Walking Dead* promotes fascism uncritically. In an interview, Sean Collins quotes Gencarella as saying that, while other violent television shows "demonstrate the consequences for violence or debate the ethical complexities of living with others who are different, or show the moral turmoil of people who enact or suffer violence," *The Walking Dead* is "the only show that actively courts, rather than critiques, fascist ethics, and suggest[s] that it's the only viable solution to perceived threat."[18] I would argue, however, that *tribalism* is a more accurate description of the social formation that *The Walking Dead* promotes, and that fascism, as epitomized by Negan, is indeed thoroughly critiqued by the series. *The Walking Dead* offers multiple ways of being a community, a tribe—all of which diverge dramatically from Negan's terrorized and fascistic "community."

Despite the positive characteristics of tribalism—its rootedness in place, its affective and familial bonds—*The Walking Dead* does make the negative consequences of tribalism quite clear. The need to protect the tribe can (and does) lead to brutal violence, as the slaughtering of the Saviors in cold blood in the season six episodes "Not Tomorrow Yet" and "The Same Boat" graphically illustrate. These episodes epitomize what one commentator has pithily described as the tendency of tribalism to encourage "Tribe first. Morals second."[19] Far from blindly promoting this intrinsic quality of tribalism, however, the series puts it in question: one of the series' principal characters, Carol Peletier, leaves her "tribe" because of the violence it demands of her. As Carol says to Morgan, about her decision to leave the people she loves, "If you care about anyone, Morgan, there's a price to pay and you're going to pay it." She adds that she has paid this price and she can't do so anymore ("Last Day on Earth"). Carol goes off to live on her own, temporarily believing that the benefits of her "tribe" are not worth the price.

For all the damage tribalism can do, it is nonetheless inevitably a part of human nature and thus to confront it, as in everything, is much preferable to ignoring it. AMC's *The Walking Dead* functions as one way in which we can bring to consciousness our profoundly human tribal nature. Moreover, and most importantly, *The Walking Dead* makes it clear that however innate the tribal impulse may be, it is not inherently racist (or sexist). Our tribes—our real and embodied communities—are more powerful than what most scientists agree are the finally arbitrary lines of race. Psychologist Joshua Greene describes numerous experiments that unfailingly show that group membership trumps race. Race, he writes, "far from being an innate trigger, is just something that we happen to use today as a marker of group memberships." Humans tend, he continues, to sort people "based on culturally acquired characteristics, such as language and clothing, rather than genetically inherited physical features."[20] *The Walking Dead* demonstrates that what constitutes a "group" can be radically made and re-made. It is a critically important fact about the "tribes" of the series—Alexandria, Hilltop, the Kingdom, the Scavengers—that they are all composed of *men and women of diverse races* (and even, though this is not as well developed, of diverse sexualities). The Kingdom, moreover, is led by an African American man (Ezekiel); the Scavengers by a white woman (Jadis); and at the end of the season seven episode "Say Yes," Rick pointedly refuses to lead his "tribe" alone, insisting that he will only lead if Michonne (an African American woman) leads with him. By season eight, a white woman (Maggie) has ousted Gregory as the leader of Hilltop.

There is a telling moment in the season four episode "Claimed" in which Rick falls asleep while reading the *Selected Short Stories of Jack London*. London was himself notoriously a proponent of a virulent tribalism predicated on what he believed was immutable racial difference. As he wrote in a letter, if a white man should "meet another white hemmed in by danger from the other colors—these whites will not need to know each other—but they will hear the call of blood and stand back to back."[21] After falling asleep to Jack London, Rick wakes up to the presence of (other) white men in the house—the Claimers. Rick does not know them but he does not "stand back to back" with them, does not hear the call of race. Not only do the Claimers fight with each other, but Rick fights with them, not only for his own life but for that of his son and Michonne, an African American woman. In the end, the three of them, a racially-mixed family, walk off together. It is they who stand back to back, bound by the ties of a tribalism that is not a racial tribalism. The irrelevance of Jack London's ideas about racial tribalism in *The Walking Dead*'s world are summed up in that Rick is not shown *reading* the book, only *sleeping with it* as it lies on his chest. So while political commentary of the early twenty-first century has relentlessly bound the current upsurge of tribalism in our real world to xenophobia and entrenched racism, *The Walking Dead* insists, in its more utopian tribal formations, that such does not have to be the case.

Notes

1. For an important discussion of tribalism in *The Walking Dead*, which he calls sectarianism, see Simpson, "Sects and Violence," 165–88. As I do, Simpson sees the sectarianism of the series "as a reactionary backlash to the complexities of living within the postmodern world-without-borders" (169), although Simpson views the sectarianism represented in the show much more negatively than I do. See also Tenga and Bassett, "'You Kill or You Die,'" 1280–1300.
2. Squires, *The Post-Racial*, 4, 6.
3. Tesler, *Post-Racial*, 5–6.
4. See especially Lorraine Berry's articles on *The Walking Dead* as a white patriarchy: "'The Walking Dead'" and "'Walking Dead': Still a White Patriarchy." For my countering view, see Keetley, "Has the *Walking Dead*?" While Berry is addressing only seasons one through three, which do fit her argument more than later seasons, the criticism of *The Walking Dead*'s deficient representation of people of color and women continues. See Zevallos, "The Walking Dead."
5. O'Hehir, "Trump, Sanders and Tribalism."
6. For my description of the shared "structure of feeling" between *The Walking Dead* and the stereotypical Trump supporter see Keetley, "'The Walking Dead.'"
7. Bertoni, "Exclusive Interview."
8. In making my argument about the utopian tribal politics of *The Walking Dead*, I disagree with a countervailing (although thoroughly intriguing) argument, offered by Katherine Sugg, that the series represents a stark neoliberal ideology—a translation into the post-apocalyptic world of enforced "market-based individualism" and relentless self-interest. See Sugg, "*The Walking Dead*," 796, 797, 800. Sugg does argue, though, that the series also critiques the model it represents, mostly through Rick Grimes. As she writes, "the role of white male hero is shown to be a trap within a logic that the protagonist cannot escape." Sugg, "*The Walking Dead*," 810.
9. This problem is well laid out (through season four) in a post on the *Nerds of Color* website. See Jenn, "The Walking Dead's Ongoing."
10. Singer, *The Expanding Circle*.
11. James, *Globalism*, 29, 32, 28.
12. With the impending death of Carl Grimes, expected when season eight returns, there would be no biologically-related characters in the main group of survivors (assuming that Judith is Shane's child, not Rick's).
13. For a very useful definition of globalization, see Schweitzer, *Going Viral*, 71–74. Schweitzer concludes her discussion of *The Walking Dead* by suggesting that the series is a "retaliation against a world where networks have overshadowed individuals, where borders have become ephemeral and irrelevant." Schweitzer, *Going Viral*, 190.

14. Morton, *Dark Ecology*, 9–10.
15. James, *Globalism*, 13.
16. Sugg argues that the constant warring among groups is an illustration of the neoliberal logic of the show, a logic in which one is perpetually "defending oneself against aggressors," but Sugg herself defines neoliberalism as an ideology that relentlessly promotes individualism, and the principal groups of *The Walking Dead* fight *as groups*, not as individuals. Sugg, "*The Walking Dead*," 800, 796–97.
17. Gencarella, "Thunder Without Rain," 128.
18. Collins, "Fascism."
19. Ropeik, "How Tribalism."
20. Greene, *Moral Tribes*, 52.
21. Mexal, "Darwin's Anachronisms," 263.

Episode List

Episodes are listed first by the overall episode number, followed by the episode number for the particular season.

Season 1

1. 1: "Days Gone Bye"—*Directed by:* Frank Darabont; *Written by:* Frank Darabont; Oct. 31, 2010
2. 2: "Guts"—*Directed by:* Michelle MacLaren; *Written by:* Frank Darabont; Nov. 7, 2010
3. 3: "Tell It to the Frogs"—*Directed by:* Gwyneth Horder-Payton; *Story by:* Charles H. Eglee & Jack LoGiudice; *Teleplay by:* Charles H. Eglee & Jack LoGiudice and Frank Darabont; Nov. 14, 2010
4. 4: "Vatos"—*Directed by:* Johan Renck; *Written by:* Robert Kirkman; Nov. 21, 2010
5. 5: "Wildfire"—*Directed by:* Ernest Dickerson; *Written by:* Glen Mazzara; Nov. 28, 2010
6. 6: "TS-19"—*Directed by:* Guy Ferland; *Written by:* Adam Fierro and Frank Darabont; Dec. 5, 2010

Season 2

7. 1: "What Lies Ahead"—*Directed by:* Ernest Dickerson & Gwyneth Horder-Payton; *Written by:* Ardeth Bey and Robert Kirkman; Oct. 16, 2011
8. 2: "Bloodletting"—*Directed by:* Ernest Dickerson; *Written by:* Glen Mazzara; Oct. 23, 2011
9. 3: "Save the Last One"—*Directed by:* Phil Abraham; *Written by:* Scott M. Gimple; Oct. 30, 2011
10. 4: "Cherokee Rose"—*Directed by:* Billy Gierhart; *Written by:* Evan Reilly; Nov. 6, 2011
11. 5: "Chupacabra"—*Directed by:* Guy Ferland; *Written by:* David Leslie Johnson; Nov. 13, 2011

12. 6: "Secrets"—*Directed by:* David Boyd; *Written by:* Angela Kang; Nov. 20, 2011
13. 7: "Pretty Much Dead Already"—*Directed by:* Michelle MacLaren; *Written by:* Scott M. Gimple; Nov. 27, 2011
14. 8: "Nebraska"—*Directed by:* Clark Johnson; *Written by:* Evan Reilly; Feb. 12, 2012
15. 9: "Triggerfinger"—*Directed by:* Billy Gierhart; *Written by:* David Leslie Johnson; Feb. 19, 2012
16. 10: "18 Miles Out"—*Directed by:* Ernest Dickerson; *Written by:* Scott M. Gimple & Glen Mazzara; Feb. 26, 2012
17. 11: "Judge, Jury, Executioner"—*Directed by:* Greg Nicotero; *Written by:* Angela Kang; Mar. 4, 2012
18. 12: "Better Angels"—*Directed by:* Guy Ferland; *Written by:* Evan Reilly & Glen Mazzara; Mar. 11, 2012
19. 13: "Beside the Dying Fire"—*Directed by:* Ernest Dickerson; *Written by:* Robert Kirkman & Glen Mazzara; Mar. 18, 2012

Season 3

20. 1: "Seed"—*Directed by:* Ernest Dickerson; *Written by:* Glen Mazzara; Oct. 14, 2012
21. 2: "Sick"—*Directed by:* Billy Gierhart; *Written by:* Nichole Beattie; Oct. 21, 2012
22. 3: "Walk with Me"—*Directed by:* Guy Ferland; *Written by:* Evan Reilly; Oct. 28, 2012
23. 4: "Killer Within"—*Directed by:* Guy Ferland; *Written by:* Sang Kyu Kim; Nov. 4, 2012
24. 5: "Say the Word"—*Directed by:* Greg Nicotero; *Written by:* Angela Kang; Nov. 11, 2012
25. 6: "Hounded"—*Directed by:* Dan Attias; *Written by:* Scott M. Gimple; Nov. 18, 2012
26. 7: "When the Dead Come Knocking"—*Directed by:* Dan Sackheim; *Written by:* Frank Renzulli; Nov. 25, 2012
27. 8: "Made to Suffer"—*Directed by:* Billy Gierhart; *Written by:* Robert Kirkman; Dec. 2, 2012
28. 9: "The Suicide King"—*Directed by:* Lesli Linka Glatter; *Written by:* Evan Reilly; Feb. 10, 2013
29. 10: "Home"—*Directed by:* Seith Mann; *Written by:* Nichole Beattie; Feb. 17, 2013
30. 11: "I Ain't a Judas"—*Directed by:* Greg Nicotero; *Written by:* Angela Kang; Feb. 24, 2013
31. 12: "Clear"—*Directed by:* Tricia Brock; *Written by:* Scott M. Gimple; Mar. 3, 2013

32. 13: "Arrow on the Doorpost"—*Directed by:* David Boyd; *Written by:* Ryan C. Coleman; Mar. 10, 2013
33. 14: "Prey"—*Directed by:* Stefan Schwartz; *Written by:* Glen Mazzara & Evan Reilly; Mar. 17, 2013
34. 15: "This Sorrowful Life"—*Directed by:* Greg Nicotero; *Written by:* Scott M. Gimple; Mar. 24, 2013
35. 16: "Welcome to the Tombs"—*Directed by:* Ernest Dickerson; *Written by:* Glen Mazzara; Mar. 31, 2013

Season 4

36. 1: "30 Days Without an Accident"—*Directed by:* Greg Nicotero; *Written by:* Scott M. Gimple; Oct. 13, 2013
37. 2: "Infected"—*Directed by:* Guy Ferland; *Written by:* Angela Kang; Oct. 20, 2013
38. 3: "Isolation"—*Directed by:* Dan Sackheim; *Written by:* Robert Kirkman; Oct. 27, 2013
39. 4: "Indifference"—*Directed by:* Tricia Brock; *Written by:* Matthew Negrete; Nov. 3, 2013
40. 5: "Internment"—*Directed by:* David Boyd; *Written by:* Channing Powell; Nov. 10, 2013
41. 6: "Live Bait"—*Directed by:* Michael Uppendahl; *Written by:* Nichole Beattie; Nov. 17, 2013
42. 7: "Dead Weight"—*Directed by:* Jeremy Podeswa; *Written by:* Curtis Gwinn; Nov. 24, 2013
43. 8: "Too Far Gone"—*Directed by:* Ernest Dickerson; *Written by:* Seth Hoffman; Dec. 1, 2013
44. 9: "After"—*Directed by:* Greg Nicotero; *Written by:* Robert Kirkman; Feb. 9, 2014
45. 10: "Inmates"—*Directed by:* Tricia Brock; *Written by:* Matthew Negrete & Channing Powell; Feb. 16, 2014
46. 11: "Claimed"—*Directed by:* Seith Mann; *Written by:* Nichole Beattie & Seth Hoffman; Feb. 23, 2014
47. 12: "Still"—*Directed by:* Julius Ramsay; *Written by:* Angela Kang; Mar. 2, 2014
48. 13: "Alone"—*Directed by:* Ernest Dickerson; *Written by:* Curtis Gwinn; Mar. 9, 2014
49. 14: "The Grove"—*Directed by:* Michael E. Satrazemis; *Written by:* Scott M. Gimple; Mar. 16, 2014
50. 15: "Us"—*Directed by:* Greg Nicotero; *Written by:* Nichole Beattie & Seth Hoffman; Mar. 23, 2014
51. 16: "A"—*Directed by:* Michelle MacLaren; *Written by:* Scott M. Gimple & Angela Kang; Mar. 30, 2014

Season 5

52. 1: "No Sanctuary"—*Directed by:* Greg Nicotero; *Written by:* Scott M. Gimple; Oct. 12, 2014
53. 2: "Strangers"—*Directed by:* David Boyd; *Written by:* Robert Kirkman; Oct. 19, 2014
54. 3: "Four Walls and a Roof"—*Directed by:* Jeffrey F. January; *Written by:* Angela Kang & Corey Reed; Oct. 26, 2014
55. 4: "Slabtown"—*Directed by:* Michael E. Satrazemis; *Written by:* Matthew Negrete & Channing Powell; Nov. 2, 2014
56. 5: "Self Help"—*Directed by:* Ernest Dickerson; *Written by:* Heather Bellson & Seth Hoffman; Nov. 9, 2014
57. 6: "Consumed"—*Directed by:* Seith Mann; *Written by:* Matthew Negrete & Corey Reed; Nov. 16, 2014
58. 7: "Crossed"—*Directed by:* Billy Gierhart; *Written by:* Seth Hoffman; Nov. 23, 2014
59. 8: "Coda"—*Directed by:* Ernest Dickerson; *Written by:* Angela Kang; Nov. 30, 2014
60. 9: "What Happened and What's Going On"—*Directed by:* Greg Nicotero; *Written by:* Scott M. Gimple; Feb. 8, 2015
61. 10: "Them"—*Directed by:* Julius Ramsay; *Written by:* Heather Bellson; Feb. 15, 2015
62. 11: "The Distance"—*Directed by:* Larysa Kondracki; *Written by:* Seth Hoffman; Feb. 22, 2015
63. 12: "Remember"—*Directed by:* Greg Nicotero; *Written by:* Channing Powell; Mar. 1, 2015
64. 13: "Forget"—*Directed by:* David Boyd; *Written by:* Corey Reed; Mar. 8, 2015
65. 14: "Spend"—*Directed by:* Jennifer Lynch; *Written by:* Matthew Negrete; Mar. 15, 2015
66. 15: "Try"—*Directed by:* Michael E. Satrazemis; *Written by:* Angela Kang; Mar. 22, 2015
67. 16: "Conquer"—*Directed by:* Greg Nicotero; *Written by:* Scott M. Gimple & Seth Hoffman; Mar. 29, 2015

Season 6

68. 1: "First Time Again"—*Directed by:* Greg Nicotero; *Written by:* Scott M. Gimple & Matthew Negrete; Oct. 11, 2015
69. 2: "JSS"—*Directed by:* Jennifer Lynch; *Written by:* Seth Hoffman; Oct. 18, 2015
70. 3: "Thank You"—*Directed by:* Michael Slovis; *Written by:* Angela Kang; Oct. 25, 2015

71. 4: "Here's Not Here"—*Directed by:* Stephen Williams; *Written by:* Scott M. Gimple; Nov. 1, 2015
72. 5: "Now"—*Directed by:* Avi Youabian; *Written by:* Corey Reed; Nov. 8, 2015
73. 6: "Always Accountable"—*Directed by:* Jeffrey F. January; *Written by:* Heather Bellson; Nov. 15, 2015
74. 7: "Heads Up"—*Directed by:* David Boyd; *Written by:* Channing Powell; Nov. 22, 2015
75. 8: "Start to Finish"—*Directed by:* Michael E. Satrazemis; *Written by:* Matthew Negrete; Nov. 29, 2015
76. 9: "No Way Out"—*Directed by:* Greg Nicotero; *Written by:* Seth Hoffman; Feb. 14, 2016
77. 10: "The Next World"—*Directed by:* Kari Skogland; *Written by:* Angela Kang & Corey Reed; Feb. 21, 2016
78. 11: "Knots Untie"—*Directed by:* Michael E. Satrazemis; *Written by:* Matthew Negrete & Channing Powell; Feb. 28, 2016
79. 12: "Not Tomorrow Yet"—*Directed by:* Greg Nicotero; *Written by:* Seth Hoffman; Mar. 6, 2016
80. 13: "The Same Boat"—*Directed by:* Billy Gierhart; *Written by:* Angela Kang; Mar. 13, 2016
81. 14: "Twice as Far"—*Directed by:* Alrick Riley; *Written by:* Matthew Negrete; Mar. 20, 2016
82. 15: "East"—*Directed by:* Michael E. Satrazemis; *Story by:* Scott M. Gimple & Channing Powell; *Teleplay by:* Channing Powell; Mar. 27, 2016
83. 16: "Last Day on Earth"—*Directed by:* Greg Nicotero; *Written by:* Scott M. Gimple & Matthew Negrete; Apr. 3, 2016

Season 7

84. 1: "The Day Will Come When You Won't Be"—*Directed by:* Greg Nicotero; *Written by:* Scott M. Gimple; Oct. 23, 2016
85. 2: "The Well"—*Directed by:* Greg Nicotero; *Written by:* Matthew Negrete; Oct. 30, 2016
86. 3: "The Cell"—*Directed by:* Alrick Riley; *Written by:* Angela Kang; Nov. 6, 2016
87. 4: "Service"—*Directed by:* David Boyd; *Written by:* Corey Reed; Nov. 13, 2016
88. 5: "Go Getters"—*Directed by:* Darnell Martin; *Written by:* Channing Powell; Nov. 20, 2016
89. 6: "Swear"—*Directed by:* Michael E. Satrazemis; *Written by:* David Leslie Johnson; Nov. 27, 2016
90. 7: "Sing Me a Song"—*Directed by:* Rosemary Rodriguez; *Written by:* Angela Kang & Corey Reed; Dec. 4, 2016

91. 8: "Hearts Still Beating"—*Directed by:* Michael E. Satrazemis; *Written by:* Matthew Negrete & Channing Powell; Dec. 11, 2016
92. 9: "Rock in the Road"—*Directed by:* Greg Nicotero; *Written by:* Angela Kang; Feb. 12, 2017
93. 10: "New Best Friends"—*Directed by:* Jeffrey F. January; *Written by:* Channing Powell; Feb. 19, 2017
94. 11: "Hostiles and Calamities"—*Directed by:* Kari Skogland; *Written by:* David Leslie Johnson; Feb. 26, 2017
95. 12: "Say Yes"—*Directed by:* Greg Nicotero; *Written by:* Matthew Negrete; Mar. 5, 2017
96. 13: "Bury Me Here"—*Directed by:* Alrick Riley; *Written by:* Scott M. Gimple; Mar. 12, 2017
97. 14: "The Other Side"—*Directed by:* Michael E. Satrazemis; *Written by:* Angela Kang; Mar. 19, 2017
98. 15: "Something They Need"—*Directed by:* Michael Slovis; *Written by:* Corey Reed; Mar. 26, 2017
99. 16: "The First Day of the Rest of Your Life"—*Directed by:* Greg Nicotero; *Written by:* Scott M. Gimple, Angela Kang & Matthew Negrete; Apr. 2, 2017

Season 8

100. 1: "Mercy"—*Directed by:* Greg Nicotero; *Written by:* Scott M. Gimple; Oct. 22, 2017
101. 2: "The Damned"—*Directed by:* Rosemary Rodriguez; *Written by:* Matthew Negrete & Channing Powell; Oct. 29, 2017
102. 3: "Monsters"—*Directed by:* Greg Nicotero; *Written by:* Matthew Negrete & Channing Powell; Nov. 5, 2017
103. 4: "Some Guy"—*Directed by:* Dan Liu; *Written by:* David Leslie Johnson; Nov. 12, 2017
104. 5: "The Big Scary U"—*Directed by:* Michael E. Satrazemis; *Story by:* Scott M. Gimple, David Leslie Johnson & Angela Kang; *Teleplay by:* David Leslie Johnson & Angela Kang; Nov. 19, 2017
105. 6: "The King, the Widow, and Rick"—*Directed by:* John Polson; *Written by:* Angela Kang & Corey Reed; Nov. 26, 2017
106. 7: "Time for After"—*Directed by:* Larry Teng; *Written by:* Matthew Negrete & Corey Reed; Dec. 3, 2017
107. 8: "How It's Gotta Be"—*Directed by:* Michael E. Satrazemis; *Written by:* David Leslie Johnson & Angela Kang; Dec. 10, 2017
108. 9: "Honor"—*Directed by:* Greg Nicotero; *Written by:* Matthew Negrete & Channing Powell; Feb. 25, 2018
109. 10: "The Lost and the Plunderers"—*Directed by:* David Boyd; *Written by:* Angela Kang & Channing Powell & Corey Reed; Mar. 4, 2018

110. 11: "Dead or Alive Or"—*Directed by:* Michael E. Satrazemis; *Written by:* Eddie Guzelian; Mar. 11, 2018
111. 12: "The Key"—*Directed by:* Greg Nicotero; *Written by:* Corey Reed & Channing Powell; Mar. 18, 2018
112. 13: "Do Not Send Us Astray"—*Directed by:* Jeffrey F. January; *Written by:* Angela Kang & Matthew Negrete; Mar. 25, 2018
113. 14: "Still Gotta Mean Something"—*Directed by:* Michael E. Satrazemis; *Written by:* Eddie Guzelian; Apr. 1, 2018
114. 15: "Worth"—*Directed by:* Michael Slovis; *Written by:* David Leslie Johnson-McGoldrick & Corey Reed; Apr. 8, 2018
115. 16: "Wrath"—*Directed by:* Greg Nicotero; *Written by:* Scott M. Gimple & Angela Kang & Matthew Negrete; Apr. 15, 2018

Bibliography

Abrams, Simon. "Think *The Walking Dead* Has a Woman Problem?" *The Village Voice*, April 3, 2013. http://www.villagevoice.com/film/think-the-walking-dead-has-a-woman-problem-heres-the-source-6437961.

Ames, Melissa. "The Trauma of (Post-Apocalyptic) Motherhood: *The Walking Dead's* Social Commentary on Contemporary Gender Roles." Paper presented at the National Women's Studies Association Conference, Milwaukee, WI, November 12–15, 2015.

Bajac-Carter, Maja, Norma Jones, and Bob Batchelor, eds. *Heroines of Comic Books and Literature: Portrayals in Popular Culture*. Lanham, MD: Rowman and Littlefield, 2014.

Balaji, Murali. "Thinking Dead: Our Obsession with the Undead and Its Implications." In Balaji, *Thinking Dead*, ix–xviii. Lanham, MD: Lexington Books.

Balaji, Murali, ed. *Thinking Dead: What the Zombie Apocalypse Means*. Lanham, MD: Lexington Books, 2010.

Baldwin, Martina, and Mark McCarthy. "Same as It Ever Was: Savior Narratives and the Logics of Survival in *The Walking Dead*." In Balaji, *Thinking Dead*, 75–87. Lanham, MD: Lexington Books.

Barkman, Ashley. "Women in a Zombie Apocalypse." In Yeun, The Walking Dead *and Philosophy*, 97–106. Chicago: Open Court.

Barry, Doug. "Where's the Line When We're Talking About Rape on a Basic Cable Series?" *Jezebel*, December 2, 2012. https://jezebel.com/5965006/wheres-the-line-when-were-talking-about-rape-on-a-basic-cable-series.

Baudrillard, Jean. *Simulacra and Simulation*. Translated by Sheila Faria Glaser. Ann Arbor: University of Michigan Press, 1994.

Baxter, Joseph. "The Walking Dead: Norman Reedus Hints a Dark Future for Daryl." *Den of Geek*, October 24, 2016. http://www.denofgeek.com/us/tv/the-walking-dead/259495/the-walking-dead-norman-reedus-hints-a-dark-future-for-daryl.

Beech, Jennifer A., and Matthew Guy. "Rick Grimes, Eastman, and White Power: Resisting the Suture from a Critical Fan Perspective." In Simpson and Mallard, The Walking Dead Live!, 155–64. Lanham, MD: Rowman & Littlefield.

Ben-Zeev, Avi, Liz Scharnetzki, Lann K. Chan, and Tara C. Dennehy. "Hypermasculinity in the Media: When Men 'Walk into the Fog' to Avoid Affective Communication." *Psychology of Popular Media Culture* 1, no. 1 (January 2012): 53–61.

Berger, James. "Propagation and Procreation: The Zombie and the Child." In Gurr, *Race, Gender, and Sexuality in Post-Apocalyptic TV and Film*, 149–163. London: Palgrave Macmillan.

Berry, Lorraine. "'The Walking Dead' Has Become a White Patriarchy." *Salon*, November 11, 2012. https://www.salon.com/2012/11/11/the_walking_dead_has_become_a_white_patriarchy/.

———. "'Walking Dead': Still a White Patriarchy." *Salon*, April 1, 2013. https://www.salon.com/2013/04/01/walking_dead_still_a_white_patriarchy/.

Bertoni, Steven. "Exclusive Interview: How Jared Kushner Won Trump the White House."

Forbes, November 22, 2016. https://www.forbes.com/sites/stevenbertoni/2016/11/22/exclusive-interview-how-jared-.

Bishop, Kyle William. "Battling Monsters and Becoming Monstrous: Human Devolution in The Walking Dead." In *Monster Culture in the 21st Century: A Reader*, edited by Marina Levina and Diem-My T. Bui, 73–85. New York: Bloomsbury Academic, 2013.

_____. *How Zombies Conquered Popular Culture: The Multifarious* Walking Dead *in the 21st Century*. Jefferson, NC: McFarland, 2015.

_____. "The Pathos of *The Walking Dead*: Bringing Terror Back to Zombie Cinema." In Lowder, *Triumph of* The Walking Dead*: Robert Kirkman's Zombie Epic on Page and Screen*, 1–14.

Boluk, Stephanie, and Wylie Lenz, eds. *Generation Zombie: Essays on the Living Dead in Modern Culture*. Jefferson, NC: McFarland, 2011.

Botting, Fred. *Gothic: The New Critical Idiom*. Abingdon-on-Thames: Routledge, 2001.

Brayton, Sean. "The Racial Politics of Disaster and Dystopia in *I Am Legend*." *The Velvet Light Trap* 67 (2011): 66–76.

Brownmiller, Susan. *Against Our Will: Men, Women, and Rape*. New York: Ballantine Books, 1975.

Buchbinder, David. *Studying Men and Masculinity*. Abingdon-on-Thames: Routledge, 2013.

Buchwald, Emilie, Pamela R. Fletcher and Martha Roth, eds. *Transforming a Rape Culture*. Minneapolis, MN: Milkweed, 2005.

Butler, Judith. "Performative Acts and Gender Constitution: An Essay in Phenomenology and Feminist Theory." *Theatre Journal* 40, no. 4 (December 1988): 519–31.

Canavan, Gerry. "'We *Are* the Walking Dead': Race, Time, and Survival in the Zombie Narrative." *Extrapolation* 51, no. 3 (2010): 431–453.

Cardona, Josué, and Lara Taylor. "Diversity and Strength in Zombie Apocalypse Atlanta." In Langley, The Walking Dead *Psychology: Psych of the Living Dead*, 82–92. New York: Sterling, 2015.

Chaney, Jen. "'Walking Dead': In 'Pretty Much Dead Already' They Shoot Zombies, Don't They?" *Washington Post*, November 28, 2011. https://www.washingtonpost.com/blogs/celebritology/post/walking-dead-in-pretty-much-dead-already-they-shoot-zombies-dont-they/2011/11/27/gIQA5Lai3N_blog.html.

Clover, Carol J. "Her Body, Himself: Gender in the Slasher Film." In Grant, *The Dread of Difference: Gender and the Horror Film*, 66–113. Austin: University of Texas Press.

_____. *Men, Women, and Chain Saws: Gender in the Modern Horror Film*. Princeton, NJ: Princeton University Press, 1993.

Cohen, Jeffrey Jerome. "Monster Culture (Seven Theses)." In Cohen, *Monster Theory: Reading Culture*. Minneapolis: University of Minnesota Press.

_____. "Preface: In a Time of Monsters." In Cohen, *Monster Theory: Reading Culture*. Minneapolis: University of Minnesota Press.

_____. "Undead (A Zombie Oriented Ontology)." *Journal of the Fantastic in the Arts* 23, no. 3 (2012): 397–412.

Cohen, Jeffrey Jerome, ed. *Monster Theory: Reading Culture*. Minneapolis: University of Minnesota Press, 1996. Kindle File.

Collins, Sean T. "The Fascism of *The Walking Dead*." *Vulture*, December 13, 2016. http://www.vulture.com/2016/12/the-walking-deads-fascism.html.

Colombe, Audrey. "White Hollywood's New Black Boogeyman." *Jump Cut*, no. 45 (2002). http://www.ejumpcut.org/archive/jc45.2002/colombe/.

Connell, R.W. *Masculinities*. Cambridge: Polity Press, 1995.

_____. *Masculinities*. 2d ed. Berkeley: University of California Press, 2005.

Connell, R.W., and James W. Messerschmidt. "Hegemonic Masculinity: Rethinking the Concept." *Gender and Society* 19, no. 6 (2005): 829–59.

Cook, Denise N. "For a Good Time Just Scream: Sex Work and Plastic Sexuality in 'Dystopicmodern Literature.'" In McGlotten and Jones, *Zombies and Sexuality: Essays on Desire and the Living Dead*, 73–87.

Cook, Karen S., and Eric Rice. *Handbook of Social Psychology*. New York: Kluwer Academic/Plenum Publishers, 2003.

Corasaniti, Nick, and Maggie Habermanaug. "Donald Trump Suggests 'Second Amendment People' Could Act Against Hillary Clinton." *New York Times*, August 9, 2016. http://www.nytimes.com/2016/08/10/us/politics/donald-trump-hillary-clinton.html.

Cortiel, Jeanne. "Travels with Carl: Apocalyptic Zombiescape, Masculinity and Seriality in Robert Kirkman's *The Walking Dead*." In *The Journey of Life in American Life and Literature*, edited by Peter Freese, 187–204. Heidelberg: Universitätsverlag Winter, 2015.

Cowan, Steven B. "Maybe Jenner Was Right." In Yuen, *The Ultimate* Walking Dead *and Philosophy: Hungry for More*, 19–30. Chicago: Open Court.

Cronon, William. "The Trouble with Wilderness; Or, Getting Back to the Wrong Nature." In *Uncommon Ground: Toward Reinventing Nature*, edited by William Cronon, 69–90. New York: Norton, 1995.

Davis, Brandon. "*The Walking Dead*: Where Did Negan Take Daryl?" *Comicbook*, October 23, 2016. http://comicbook.com/thewalkingdead/2016/10/24/the-walking-dead-where-did-negan-take-daryl-/.

Dillard, R.H.W. "*Night of the Living Dead*: It's Not Like Just a Wind That's Passing Through." In *American Horrors: Essays on the Modern American Horror Film*, edited by Gregory A. Waller, 14–29. Urbana: University of Illinois Press, 1988.

Doane, Ashley ("Woody"). "Shades of Colorblindness: Rethinking Racial Ideology in the United States." In *The Colorblind Screen: Television in Post-Racial America*, edited by Sarah Nilsen and Sarah E. Turner, 15–38. New York: New York University Press, 2014.

Dovidio, John F., and Samuel L. Gaertner. "Aversive Racism." *Advances in Experimental Social Psychology* 36 (2004): 1–52.

Dow, Bonnie J. "The Traffic in Men and the Fatal Attraction of Postfeminist Masculinity." *Women's Studies in Communication* 29, no. 1 (2006): 113–131.

Duane, Anna Mae. "'The Walking Dead's' Scary, Necessary Lesson about American Childhood." *Salon*, November 3, 2013. http://www.salon.com/2013/11/03/the_walking_deads_scary_necessary_lesson_about_american_childhood/.

Dulanto, Andrea. "Stranger Than Zombies: Power, Privilege and Lesbian Subtext in *The Walking Dead*." *PopMatters*, February 17, 2013. http://www.popmatters.com/feature/168276-stranger-than-zombies/P1/.

Edelman, Lee. *No Future: Queer Theory and the Death Drive*. Durham, NC: Duke University Press, 2004. Kindle File.

Eldredge, Richard L. "Oh, HELL No! Merle Crashes T-Dog's Walking Dead Viewing Party." *Atlanta Magazine*, October 15, 2012. http://www.atlantamagazine.com/news-culture-articles/oh-hell-no-merle-crashes-t-dogs-walking-dead/.

Emerson, Richard M. "Social Exchange Theory." *Annual Review of Sociology*, 2 (1976): 335–62.

Erwin, Elizabeth. "The Function of Queerness on *The Walking Dead*." *HorrorHomeroom*, March 24, 2016. http://www.horrorhomeroom.com/queerness-and-the-walking-dead/.

Esposito, Jennifer. "What Does Race Have to Do with *Ugly Betty*?: An Analysis of Privilege and Postracial(?) Representations on a Television Sitcoms." *Television and New Media* 10, no. 6 (2009): 521–35.

Fear, David. "Robert Kirkman: Inside 'Walking Dead' Creator's Twisted Mind." *Rolling Stone*, May 31, 2016. http://www.rollingstone.com/tv/features/robert-kirkman-inside-walking-dead-creators-twisted-mind-new-show-20160531.

Fienberg, Daniel. "On 'The Walking Dead' Season 7 Premiere, Sadism and the 2016 Election." *The Hollywood Reporter*, October 24, 2016. http://www.hollywoodreporter.com/fien-print/critics-notebook-walking-dead-season-7-premiere-sadism-2016-election-940835.

Fong, Ken. "Is Glenn Rhee the Most Beloved Asian American Male in the U.S.?" *Angry Asian Man*, November 11, 2015. http://blog.angryasianman.com/2015/11/is-glenn-rhee-most-beloved-asian.html.

Garland, Tammy S., Nickie Phillips, and Scott Vollum. "Gender Politics and *The Walking Dead*: Gendered Violence and the Reestablishment of Patriarchy." *Feminist Criminology* 13, no. 1 (2018): 59–86.

Gavaler, Chris. "Zombies vs. Superheroes: Resurrecting Gender Formulas in *The Walking Dead* and *The Fantastic Four*." *ImageTexT: Interdisciplinary Comics Studies* 7, no. 4 (2014). http://www.english.ufl.edu/imagetext/archives/v7_4/gavaler/.

Gencarella, Stephen Olbrys. "Thunder Without Rain: Fascist Masculinity in AMC's *The Walking Dead*," *Horror Studies* 7, no. 1 (2016): 125–46.
Giordano, Tizzy. "Surprise! Attempted Rape Scene in Episode of 'The Walking Dead.'" *Fem2.0*, November 28, 2012. http://www.fem2pt0.com/?p=17086.
Glenn, Cerise L., and Landra J. Cunningham. "The Power of Black Magic: The Magical Negro and White Salvation in Film." *Journal of Black Studies* 40, no. 2 (2009): 135–52.
Godfrey, Sarah, and Hannah Hamad. "Save the Cheerleader, Save the Males: Resurgent Protective Paternalism in Popular Film and Television After 9/11." In *The Handbook of Gender, Sex, and Media*, edited by Karen Ross, 157–73. Oxford, UK: Wiley-Blackwell, 2011.
Goldman, Eric. "The Walking Dead: What's T-Dog Been Doing All Season?" *IGN*, March 16, 2012. http://www.ign.com/articles/2012/03/17/the-walking-dead-whats-t-dog-been-doing-all-season.
Granshaw, Lisa. "The Female of the Species: The Portrayal of Women in *The Walking Dead* Comic." *The Walking Dead Magazine*, no. 12 (Spring 2015): 28–35.
Grant, Barry Keith, ed. *The Dread of Difference: Gender and the Horror Film*. Austin: University of Texas Press, 1996.
Graves, Abby. "There's a New Sheriff in Town: Hegemonic Masculinity in the Zombie Apocalypse." In Simpson and Mallard, *The Walking Dead Live!: Essays on the Television Show*, 131–53. Lanham, MD: Rowman & Littlefield.
Greene, John, and Michaela D.E. Meyer. "The Walking (Gendered) Dead: A Feminist Rhetorical Critique of Zombie Apocalypse Television Narrative." *Ohio Communication Journal* 52 (2014): 64–74.
Greene, Joshua. *Moral Tribes: Emotion, Reason, and the Gap Between Us and Them*. New York: Penguin, 2013.
Griffin, Susan. *Rape: The Politics of Consciousness*. New York: Harper & Row, 1979.
Grizzell, Trevor. "Re-Animating the Social Order: Zombies and Queer Failure." In McGlotten and Jones, *Zombies and Sexuality: Essays on Desire and the Living Dead*, Kindle File. Jefferson, NC: McFarland.
Gurr, Barbara, ed. *Race, Gender, and Sexuality in Post-Apocalyptic TV and Film*. New York: Palgrave Macmillan, 2015.
Hamad, Hannah. *Postfeminism and Paternity in Contemporary U.S. Film: Framing Fatherhood*. Abingdon-on-Thames: Routledge, 2014.
Handlen, Zack. "The Walking Dead: 'Pretty Much Dead Already.'" *A.V. Club*, November 27, 2011. https://tv.avclub.com/the-walking-dead-pretty-much-dead-already-1798170626.
———. "The Walking Dead: 'Sick.'" *A.V. Club*, October 21, 2012. https://tv.avclub.com/the-walking-dead-sick-1798174687.
Hannabach, Cathy. "Queering and Crippling the End of the World: Disability, Sexuality and Race in *The Walking Dead*." In McGlotten and Jones, *Zombies and Sexuality : Essays on Desire and the Living Dead*, 106–122. Jefferson, NC: McFarland.
Harding, Kate. *Asking for It: The Alarming Rise of Rape Culture—And What We Can Do About It*. Boston: Da Capo, 2015.
Harkins, Anthony. *Hillbilly: A Cultural History of an American Icon*. Oxford: Oxford University Press, 2004.
Harris, Geraldine. "A Return to Form? Postmasculinist Television Drama and Tragic Heroes in the Wake of *The Sopranos*." *New Review of Film and Television Studies* 10, no. 4 (2012): 443–63.
Heldman, Caroline. "The Hunger Games, Hollywood and Fighting Fuck Toys." *Ms. Magazine*, April 6, 2012. http://msmagazine.com/blog/2012/04/06/the-hunger-games-hollywood-and-fighting-fuck-toys/.
Hetterly, Jonathan. "Case File V: The Claimers." In Langley, *The Walking Dead Psychology: Psych of the Living Dead*, 218–21. New York: Sterling, 2015.
Ho, Helen K. "The Model Minority in the Zombie Apocalypse: Asian-American Manhood on AMC's *The Walking Dead*." *The Journal of Popular Culture* 49, no. 1 (2016): 57–76.
hooks, bell. *Ain't I a Woman: Black Women and Feminism*. Boston: South End, 1981.
Horbury, Alison. "Post-Feminist Impasses in Popular Heroine Television." *Continuum: Journal of Media and Cultural Studies* 28, no. 2 (2014): 213–25.

Huckvale, David. *Touchstones of Gothic Horror: A Film Genealogy of Eleven Motifs and Images.* Jefferson, NC: McFarland, 2010.
Hughey, Matthew W. "Cinethetic Racism: White Redemption and Black Stereotypes in 'Magical Negro' Films." *Social Problems* 56, no. 3 (2009): 543–77.
Huntington, Brian. "Robert [Kirkman] on CNBC'S *Closing Bell*." March 22, 2013. http://www.thewalkingdead.com/robert-on-cnbcs-closing-bell/.
Ingraham, Christopher. "Three Quarters of Whites Don't Have Any Non-White Friends." *Washington Post*, August 25, 2014.
James, Paul. *Globalism, Nationalism, Tribalism: Bringing Theory Back In.* London: Sage, 2006.
Jeffords, Susan. "The Big Switch: Hollywood Masculinity in the Nineties." In *Film Theory Goes to the Movies: Cultural Analysis of Contemporary Film*, edited by Jim Collins, Ava Preacher Collins, and Hilary Radner, 196–208. Abingdon-on-Thames: Routledge, 2012.
Jenn. "The Walking Dead's Ongoing Black Man Problem." *Nerds of Color*, October 29, 2013, https://thenerdsofcolor.org/2013/10/29/the-walking-deads-ongoing-black-man-problem/.
Jones, Steve. "Gender Monstrosity: *Deadgirl* and the Sexual Politics of Zombie-Rape." *Feminist Media Studies* 13, no. 4 (2012): 525–39.
_____. "Porn of the Dead: Necrophilia, Feminism, and Gendering the Undead." In Moreman and Rushton, *Zombies Are Us: Essays on the Humanity of the Walking Dead*, 40–61. Jefferson, NC: McFarland.
Joseph, Ralina L. "'Tyra Banks Is Fat': Reading (*Post-*)Racism and (*Post-*)Feminism in the New Millennium." *Critical Studies in Media Communication* 26, no. 3 (2009): 237–54.
Katerberg, William H. *Future West: Utopia and Apocalypse in Frontier Science Fiction.* Lawrence: University Press of Kansas, 2008.
Katz, Jackson. *The Macho Paradox: Why Some Men Hurt Women and How All Men Can Help.* Naperville, IL: Sourcebooks, 2006.
Kearns, Megan. "Nothing Can Save *The Walking Dead's* Sexist Woman Problem." *Bitch Flicks*, May 1, 2013. http://www.btchflcks.com/2013/05/nothing-can-save-the-walking-deads-sexist-woman-problem.html#.V6qVLZMrLuM.
Keetley, Dawn. "Has *The Walking Dead* Killed the White Patriarchy?" *Flow*, December 16, 2013. https://www.flowjournal.org/2013/12/has-the-walking-dead-killed-the-white-patriarchy/.
_____. "Introduction: 'We're All Infected.'" In Keetley, *"We're All Infected": Essays on AMC's* The Walking Dead *and the Fate of the Human*, 3–25. Jefferson, NC: McFarland, 2014.
_____. "'The Walking Dead' and the Rise of Donald Trump." *PopMatters*, March 17, 2016. http://www.popmatters.com/feature/the-walking-dead-and-the-rise-of-donald-trump/.
Keetley, Dawn, ed. *"We're All Infected": Essays on AMC's* The Walking Dead *and the Fate of the Human.* Jefferson, NC: McFarland, 2014.
Kim, Daniel Y. *Writing Manhood in Black and Yellow: Ralph Ellison, Frank Chin, and the Literary Politics of Identity.* Stanford, CA: Stanford University Press, 2005.
Kimerling, Rachel, Paige Ouimette, and Jessica Wolfe, eds. *Gender and PTSD.* New York: Guilford Press, 2002.
King, Stephen. *Danse Macabre.* New York: Berkeley Books, 1983.
Kirkman, Robert, Charlie Adlard, Tony Moore, and Cliff Rathburn. *The Walking Dead: Compendium One.* Berkeley, CA: Image Comics, 2009.
Kirkman, Robert, Charlie Adlard, and Cliff Rathburn. *The Walking Dead: Compendium Two.* Berkeley, CA: Image Comics, 2012.
Kirkman, Robert, Charlie Adlard, Stefano Gaudiano, and Cliff Rathburn. *The Walking Dead Compendium Three.* Berkeley, CA: Image Comics, 2015.
Kirkman, Robert, Charlie Adlard, and Cliff Rathburn. *The Walking Dead*, #9, *Here We Remain.* Berkeley, CA: Image Comics, 2012.
Kissell, Rick. "'The Walking Dead' Ratings Rise with Controversial Episode." *Variety*, October 27, 2015. http://variety.com/2015/tv/news/the-walking-dead-ratings-rise-1201627223/.
Kistler, Alan, and Billy San Juan. "Masculinity Narratives in the Post-Apocalypse." In Langley,

The Walking Dead *Psychology: Psych of the Living Dead*, 42–50. New York: Sterling, 2015.
Kramer, Michael R. "Empowerment as Transgression: The Rise and Fall of the Black Cat in Kevin Smith's *The Evil That Men Do*." *Heroines of Comic Books and Literature: Portrayals in Popular Culture*, edited by Maja Bajac-Carter, Norma Jones, and Bob Batchelor, 233–43. Lanham, MD: Rowman and Littlefield, 2014.
Krans, Brian. "Hypermasculinity in Advertising." *Healthline*, March 3, 2013. http://www.healthline.com/health-news/mental-masculine-ads-distort-mens-perceptions-030313.
Kremmel, Laura. "Rest in Pieces: Violence in Mourning the (Un)dead." In Keetley, *"We're All Infected": Essays on AMC's* The Walking Dead *and the Fate of the Human*, 80–94. Jefferson, NC: McFarland, 2014.
Kuniak, Stephen, and Megan Blink. "Hillbilly to Hero: The Transformation of Daryl Dixon." In Langley, The Walking Dead *Psychology: Psych of the Living Dead*, 234–45. New York: Sterling, 2015.
Kunyosying, Kom, and Carter Soles. "Postmodern Geekdom as Simulated Ethnicity." *Jump Cut*, no. 54 (2012). http://www.ejumpcut.org/archive/jc54.2012/SolesKunyoGeedom/.
Langley, Travis, ed. The Walking Dead *Psychology: Psych of the Living Dead*. New York: Sterling, 2015.
Lavin, Melissa F., and Brian M. Lowe. "Cops and Zombies: Hierarchy and Social Location in *The Walking Dead*." In Gurr, *Race, Gender, and Sexuality in Post-Apocalyptic TV and Film*, 113–24. London: Palgrave Macmillan.
Leon, Melissa. "The Walking Dead's 'Slabtown': The Real Source of Terror Isn't Walkers, It's Rape." *The Daily Beast*, November 2, 2014. https://www.thedailybeast.com/the-walking-deads-slabtown-the-real-source-of-terror-isnt-walkers-its-rape.
Lotz, Amanda D. *Cable Guys: Television and Masculinities in the 21st Century*. New York: New York University Press, 2014.
Lowder, James, ed. *Triumph of* The Walking Dead: *Robert Kirkman's Zombie Epic on Page and Screen*. Dallas: Benbella Books, 2011.
McCloud, Scott. *Understanding Comics: The Invisible Art*. New York: HarperPerennial, 1994.
McCray, Rebecca. "When Battered Women Are Punished with Prison." *Take Part*, September 24, 2015. http://www.takepart.com/article/2015/09/24/battered-women-prison.
McEwan, Melissa. "Rape Culture 101." *Shakesville*, October 9, 2009. http://www.shakesville.com/2009/10/rape-culture-101.html.
McGlotten, Shaka, and Steve Jones, eds. *Zombies and Sexuality: Essays on Desire and the Living Dead*. Jefferson, NC: McFarland, 2014.
McKay, James, and Helen Johnson. "Pornographic Eroticism and Sexual Grotesquerie in Representations of African American Sportswomen." *Social Identities: Journal for the Study of Race, Nation and Culture* 14, no. 4 (2008): 491–504.
Mexal, Stephen J. "Darwin's Anachronisms: Liberalism and Conservative Temporality in *The Son of the Wolf*." In *The Oxford Handbook of Jack London*, edited by Jay Williams, 259–76. New York: Oxford University Press, 2017.
Miles, Kevin Thomas. "Body Badges: Race and Sex." In Zack, *Race/Sex: Their Sameness, Difference and Interplay*, 131–43. Abingdon-on-Thames: Routledge.
Miller, Cynthia J., and A. Bowdoin van Riper, eds. *Undead in the West: Vampires, Zombies, Mummies, and Ghosts on the Cinematic Frontier*. Lanham, MD: Scarecrow Press, 2012.
Moers, Ellen. *Literary Women*. Oxford: Oxford University Press, 1985.
Moreman, Christopher M., and Corey James Rushton, eds. *Zombies Are Us: Essays on The Humanity of the Walking Dead*. Jefferson, NC: McFarland, 2011.
Morton, Timothy. *Dark Ecology: For a Logic of Future Coexistence*. New York: Columbia University Press, 2016.
Mosher, Donald L., and Mark Sirkin. "Measuring a Macho Personality Constellation." *Journal of Research in Personality* 18, no. 2 (June 1984): 150–63.
Moyer, Justin Wm. "'The Walking Dead' Finale Recap: Black Man Survives." *The Washington Post*, March 30, 2015. https://www.washingtonpost.com/news/morning-mix/wp/2015/03/30/walking-dead-lets-black-man-live-despite-history-of-killing-african-american-males/.

Mulvey, Sarah Jane. "The Zen of Daryl: A New Masculinity within AMC's *The Walking Dead*." Honor's thesis, Bridgewater State University, 2015.
Murphy, Kelly J. "Why 'The Walking Dead' Zombie Apocalypse Is Like Faith and Rooted in a Hope for Humanity." *The Washington Post*, March 29, 2015. https://www.washingtonpost.com/news/acts-of-faith/wp/2015/03/29/why-the-walking-dead-zombie-apocalypse-is-like-faith-and-rooted-in-a-hope-for-humanity/?utm_term=.aee2c64b5193.
Nama, Adilifu. *Black Space: Imagining Race in Science Fiction Film*. Austin: University of Texas Press, 2008.
Nerd HQ. "A Conversation with the Cast of *The Walking Dead*." YouTube Video, 47:43. July 26, 2014. https://www.youtube.com/watch?v=v0y1rZXthmI.
Nurse, Angus. "Asserting Law and Order Over the Mindless." In Keetley, *"We're All Infected": Essays on AMC's* The Walking Dead *and the Fate of the Human*, 68–79. Jefferson, NC: McFarland.
O'Hehir, Andrew. "Trump, Sanders and Tribalism: Why the Donald's Dark Allure Goes Deeper Than Racism and Xenophobia." *Salon*, September 12, 2015. https://www.salon.com/2015/09/12/trump_sanders_and_tribalism_why_the_donalds_dark_allure_goes_deeper_than_racism_and_xenophobia/.
Okihiro, Gary Y. *Margins and Mainstreams: Asians in American History and Culture*. Seattle: University of Washington Press, 1994.
Pierce, Leonard. "The Walking Dead: Days Gone Bye." *A.V. Club*, October 31, 2010. http://www.avclub.com/tvclub/the-walking-dead-days-gone-bye-46865.
Plous, S., and Tyrone Williams. "Racial Stereotypes from the Days of American Slavery: A Continuing Legacy." *Journal of Applied Social Psychology*, 25 no. 9 (1995): 795–817.
Pokornowski, Steven. "Burying the Living with the Dead: Security, Survival and the Sanction of Violence." In Keetley, *"We're All Infected": Essays on AMC's* The Walking Dead *and the Fate of the Human*, 41–55. Jefferson, NC: McFarland.
Punter, David, and Glennis Byron. *The Gothic*. Oxford: Blackwell, 2004.
Pye, Danee, and Peter O'Sullivan. "Dead Man's Party." In Yuen, The Walking Dead *and Philosophy: Hungry for More*, 107–16. Chicago: Open Court.
Radcliffe, Ann. *The Mysteries of Udolpho*. Oxford: Oxford University Press, 1998.
_____. *The Romance of the Forest*. Oxford: Oxford University Press, 1988.
Rees, Shelley S. "Frontier Values Meet Big-City Zombies: The Old West in AMC's *The Walking Dead*." In Miller and van Riper, *Undead in the West: Vampires, Zombies, Mummies, and Ghosts on the Cinematic Frontier*, 80–94. Lanham, MD: Scarecrow Press.
"Rick Grimes." *AMC Network Entertainment*. January 22, 2018. http://www.amc.com/shows/the-walking-dead/cast-crew/rick-grimes.
Ropeik, David. "How Tribalism Overrules Reason and Makes Risky Times More Dangerous." *Big Think*, [n.d.]. http://bigthink.com/risk-reason-and-reality/how-tribalism-overrules-reason-and-makes-risky-times-more-dangerous.
Ross, Dalton. "'The Walking Dead': Robert Kirkman Explains Why Glenn Had to Die." *Entertainment Weekly*, October 28, 2016. http://ew.com/article/2016/10/28/walking-dead-glenn-steven-yeun-robert-kirkman/.
_____. "'Walking Dead' Star Steven Yeun Describes a 'Hardened' Glenn in Season 5." *Entertainment Weekly*, September 23, 2014. http://www.ew.com/article/2014/09/23/walking-dead-steven-yeun-glenn-season-5.
Ross, Dalton, Jonathon Dornbush, Christian Holub, Dylan Kickham, and Danielle Zhu. "WE SEE Dead People." *Entertainment Weekly*, no. 1403/1404 (2016): 58–63.
Rushton, Cory James, and Christopher M. Moreman. "Introduction—They're Us: Zombies, Humans/Humans, Zombies." In Moreman and Rushton, *Zombies Are Us: Essays on the Humanity of* The Walking Dead, Kindle File. Jefferson, NC: McFarland.
Ryan, Erin Gloria. "*The Walking Dead* Is Spreading Icky Morning-After Pill Myths." *Jezebel*, November 21, 2011. http://jezebel.com/5861592/the-walking-dead-is-spreading-icky-morning-after-pill-myths.
St. John, Allen. "The Most Watched Hour Ever: Why 'The Walking Dead' Season Finale Will Break a Ratings Record." *Forbes*, March 20, 2014. http://www.forbes.com/sites/allen

stjohn/2014/03/30/the-most-watched-hour-ever-why-the-walking-dead-season-finale-will-break-a-ratings-record/.
Salter, Anastasia, and Bridget Blodgett. "Hypermasculinity & Dickwolves: The Contentious Role of Women in the New Gaming Public." *Journal of Broadcasting & Electronic Media* 56, no. 3 (2012): 401–16.
Saria, Oliver. "Into the Deep End with *The Walking Dead*'s Steven Yeun." *Kore Asian Media*, October 15, 2012. http://kore.am/october-cover-story-into-the-deep-end-with-the-walking-deads-steven-yeun/.
Scarlet, Janina. "The Walking Traumatized." In Langley, The Walking Dead *Psychology: Psych of the Living Dead*, 182–91. New York: Sterling, 2015.
Scheff, Thomas J. "Hypermasculinity and Violence as a Social System." *Universitas* 2, no. 2 (2006). https://universitas.uni.edu/archive/fall06/pdf/art_scheff.pdf.
Schweitzer, Dahlia. *Going Viral: Zombies, Viruses, and the End of the World*. New Brunswick, NJ: Rutgers University Press, 2018.
Schwindt, Oriana. "'The Walking Dead' Season 7 Premiere Ratings: Huge, but Not a Record." *Variety*, October 25, 2016. http://variety.com/2016/tv/news/the-walking-dead-season-7-premiere-ratings-1201899174/.
Sepinwall, Alan. "'The Walking Dead'—'Pretty Much Dead Already': Opening the Barn Door." *Hitfix*, November 27, 2011. http://www.hitfix.com/blogs/whats-alan-watching/posts/the-walking-dead-pretty-much-dead-already-opening-the-barn-door.
Shelley, Mary. *Frankenstein*. Oxford: Oxford University Press, 1980.
Shildrick, Margrit. *Embodying the Monster: Encounters with the Vulnerable Self*. London: Sage, 2002.
Simmons, Dan. *Ilium*. New York: HarperTorch, 2005.
Simpson, Philip L., "Sects and Violence: The Allegory of Sectarian Conflict in AMC's Zombie Apocalypse." In Simpson and Mallard, The Walking Dead *Live!: Essays on the Television Show*, 165–88. Abingdon-on-Thames: Routledge.
———. "The Zombie Apocalypse Is Upon Us! Homeland Insecurity." In Keetley, *"We're All Infected": Essays on AMC's* The Walking Dead *and the Fate of the Human*, 28–40.
Simpson, Philip L., and Marcus Mallard, eds. The Walking Dead *Live! Essays on the Television Show*. Lanham, MD: Rowman and Littlefield, 2016.
Singer, Peter. *The Expanding Circle: Ethics, Evolution, and Moral Progress*. Princeton, NJ: Princeton University Press, 2011.
"So That Was the Worst Episode of *The Walking Dead*." *Angry Asian Man*, October 24, 2016. http://blog.angryasianman.com/2016/10/so-that-was-worst-episode-of-walking.html.
Soles, Carter. "Sympathy for the Devil: The Cannibalistic Hillbilly in 1970s Rural Slasher Films." In *Ecocinema: Theory and Practice*, edited by Stephen Rust, Salma Monani, and Sean Cubitt, 233–50. Abingdon-on-Thames: Routledge, 2013.
Springer, Kimberly. "Divas, Evil Black Bitches, and Bitter Black Women: African American Women in Postfeminist and Post-Civil-Rights Popular Culture." In *Interrogating Postfeminism: Gender and the Politics of Popular Culture*, edited by Yvonne Tasker and Diane Negra, 249–76. Durham: Duke University Press, 2007.
Squires, Catherine R. *The Post-Racial Mystique: Media and Race in the Twenty-First Century*. New York: New York University Press, 2014.
Stabile, Carol A. "'Sweetheart, This Ain't Gender Studies': Sexism and Superheroes." *Communication and Critical/Cultural Studies* 6, no. 1 (2009): 86–92.
Staton, David. "Mad Hatters: The Bad Dads of AMC." In *Television and the Self: Knowledge, Identity, and Media Representation*, edited by Kathleen M. Ryan and Deborah A. Macey, 85–96. Lanham, MD: Lexington Books, 2013.
Steiger, Kay. "No Clean Slate: Unshakable Race and Gender Politics in *The Walking Dead*." In Lowder, *Triumph of* The Walking Dead, 99–114. Dallas: Benbella Books.
Sterba, James P. "Racism and Sexism: The Common Ground." In Zack, *Race/Sex: Their Sameness, Difference and Interplay*, 61–71. Abingdon-on-Thames: Routledge.
Sugg, Katherine. "*The Walking Dead*: Late Liberalism and Masculine Subjection in Apocalypse Fictions." *Journal of American Studies* 49, no. 4 (October 12, 2015): 793–811.
Svehla, Gary J., and Susan Svehla. Introduction. *Bitches, Bimbos and Virgins: Women in the*

Horror Film, edited by Gary J. Svehla and Susan Svehla, 3–12. New York: Midnight Marquee Press, 1996.

Tenga, Angela, and Jonathan Bassett. "'You kill or you die, or you die and you kill': Meaning and Violence in AMC's *The Walking Dead*." *The Journal of Popular Culture* 49, no. 6 (2016): 1280–1300.

Tesler, Michael. *Post-Racial or Most-Racial?: Race and Politics in the Obama Era*. Chicago: University of Chicago Press, 2016.

Thomas-Hunt, Melissa C., and Katherine W. Phillips. "When What You Know Is Not Enough: Expertise and Gender Dynamics in Task Groups." *Personality and Social Psychology Bulletin* 30, no. 12 (December 2004): 1585–98.

Tothill, Darryl. "Valkyries Rising." *The Walking Dead: The Official Magazine* 12 (Spring 2015): 42–47.

Trujillo, Nick. "Hegemonic Masculinity on the Mound: Media Representations of Nolan Ryan and American Sports Culture." *Critical Studies in Media Communication* 8, no. 3 (1991): 290–308.

Valenti, Jessica. *Full Frontal Feminism: A Young Woman's Guide to Why Feminism Matters*. Berkeley, CA: Seal Press, 2007.

———. "Why Do Women Love The Walking Dead? It Might Be the Lack of Rape Scenes." *The Guardian*, June 12, 2014. https://www.theguardian.com/commentisfree/2014/jun/12/women-love-walking-dead-rape-scenes.

Vossen, Emma. "Laid to Rest: Romance, End of the World Sexuality and Apocalyptic Anticipation in Robert Kirkman's *The Walking Dead*." In McGlotten and Jones, *Zombies and Sexuality: Essays on Desire and the Living Dead*, 88–105. Jefferson, NC: McFarland.

"'Walking Dead' Star Steven Yeun on Resisting Asian Stereotypes." *Backstage*, October 13, 2012. https://www.backstage.com/interview/walking-dead-star-steven-yeun-resisting-asian-stereotypes/.

Wampler, Scott. "The Walking Dead Recap: Pretty Much Dead Already." *Collider*, November 27, 2011. http://collider.com/the-walking-dead-recap-pretty-much-dead-already/.

Warner, Kristen J. "The Racial Logic of *Grey's Anatomy*: Shonda Rhimes and Her 'Post-Civil Rights, Post-Feminist' Series." *Television and New Media* 16, no. 7 (2015): 631–47.

Wayne, Michael L. "Ambivalent Anti-Heroes and Racist Rednecks on Basic Cable: Post-Race Ideology and White Masculinities on FX." *The Journal of Popular Television* 2, no. 2 (2014): 205–25.

"Who Is Glenn? The Walking Dead." *AMC Network Entertainment*, January 22, 2018. http://www.amc.com/shows/the-walking-dead/video-extras/season-01/episode-01/who-is-glenn-the-walking-dead.

Williams, Linda. "Melodrama Revised." In *Refiguring American Film Genres: Theory and History*, edited by Nick Browne, 42–88. Berkeley: University of California Press, 1998.

Wilson, Natalie. "Re-Composing Zombie Politics: Evolved Zombies and Female Survivors/Saviors." Paper presented at Southwest Popular Culture Association Conference, Albuquerque, NM, February 12–15, 2015.

Yuen, Wayne, ed. *The Ultimate Walking Dead and Philosophy: Hungry for More*. Chicago: Open Court, 2016.

———. *The Walking Dead and Philosophy: Zombie Apocalypse Now*. Chicago: Open Court, 2012.

Young, P. Ivan. "Walking Tall or Walking Dead? The American Cowboy in the Zombie Apocalypse." In Keetley, *"We're All Infected": Essays on AMC's The Walking Dead and the Fate of the Human*, 56–67.

Zack, Naomi, ed. *Race/Sex: Their Sameness, Difference, and Interplay*. Abingdon-on-Thames: Routledge, 1997.

Zevallos, Zuleyka. "The Walking Dead: Gender, Race and Sexuality." *Medium*, April 2, 2015. https://medium.com/@OtherSociology/the-walking-dead-gender-race-sexuality-486dcd40341a#.g83t8ys27.

"Zombies! NOC 'Em Dead with Angry Asian Man," *The Nerds of Color*, October 18, 2013. https://thenerdsofcolor.org/2013/10/18/hard-noc-life-noc-em-dead/.

About the Contributors

Brooke **Bennett** is a second-year MA student in cinema and media studies at the University of Southern California. Her research interests include feminist media studies, television studies, gender studies, new media, video games, representational issues and horror film and television.

Tiffany A. **Christian** is an English professor at Skagit Valley College in Mount Vernon, Washington. She holds a Ph.D. in American studies from Washington State University. She also holds an MFA in creative writing from Chapman University.

Dustin **Dunaway** is the chair of the English and Communication Department at Pueblo Community College in Colorado. His research interests include language, media and power, and their effects on the social structures of America. His publications include scholarly essays on Joss Whedon.

Elizabeth **Erwin** received her MLIS from the University of Pittsburgh. She is a writer, librarian and aca-fan and research interests include American horror, serialized storytelling, LGBTQ+ media representation and digital literacy. She has presented her research at various conferences and is planning a series of video essays on the experiences of female horror fans.

Helen K. **Ho** is an assistant professor of communication studies at Saint Mary's College in Indiana where she teaches courses in media studies, film studies, and gender and women's studies. Her research interests include race and gender in popular culture with a focus on Asian American masculinities as represented throughout the American mediascape.

Elexus **Jionde** holds a bachelor's degree in history from Ohio State University. She is the owner of Intelexual Media, an online learning platform that creates videos and essays about racism and history. In addition to speaking engagements and news appearances, she has published two books: *The A–Z Guide to Black Oppression* and *Angry Black Girl*.

Dawn **Keetley** is a professor of English at Lehigh University in Pennsylvania. She is the editor of *We're All Infected*, coeditor of *Plant Horror*, and coeditor of *The Ecogothic in Nineteenth-Century American Literature*. She writes regularly for Horror Homeroom.com, a horror website she cocreated.

About the Contributors

Deborah **Kennedy** is a professor of English at Saint Mary's University in Halifax, Nova Scotia, Canada. She specializes in literature of the 18th century and the Romantic period. She is the author of *Helen Maria Williams and the Age of Revolution* and *Poetic Sisters*, which was selected as a Choice Outstanding Academic Title.

Kom **Kunyosying** earned his Ph.D. in English from the University of Oregon. He teaches writing at Nashua Community College in New Hampshire. He has published articles on the rise of geek culture for *Jump Cut* and on metonymy and ecology in Charles Burns's *Black Hole* for *Interdisciplinary Studies in Literature and Environment*.

Catherine **Pugh** is an independent scholar who completed her Ph.D. at the University of Essex in the UK. Her research interests are cinematic insanity and real-life mental illness in regard to the body and external landscapes, which she explored in her dissertation, "Unhuman Borderlands."

Carter **Soles** is an associate professor of film studies at the College at Brockport (SUNY). His research interests include ecomedia studies, gender and identity studies, and film genre studies. His work includes a chapter on the cannibalistic hillbilly in 1970s slasher films and on environmental apocalyptic themes in 1950s horror films.

Natalie **Wilson** teaches women's, gender, and sexuality studies at Cal State San Marcos in California. She is the author of *Seduced by Twilight* and coeditor of *Theorizing Twilight*. Her published work can also be found in *The Norton Anthology of Cultural Studies*, *Feminist Media Studies*, and the *International Journal of Sexuality and Gender Studies*.

Emily **Zarka** received her Ph.D. in British Romantic literature from Arizona State University, where she has taught literature, writing, and film and media. Her research focuses on the undead and gender and sexuality in Gothic works, as well as representations of the female corpse in scientific and fictional texts. She has also contributed to the Frankenstein Bicentennial Project.

John R. **Ziegler** is an assistant professor of English at Bronx Community College (CUNY) in New York. His research interests include popular and material cultures of the 16th/17th and 20th/21st centuries. He has contributed to *The Encyclopedia of the Zombie* and published articles in *Medieval and Renaissance Drama in England*, among others.

Index

"A" (season four) 36–37, 47, 89
Aaron 51, 95, 121
Abraham (Abe) 33, 37, 40, 56, 61, 62, 101, 127
Abrams, Simon 78
abuse 83, 87, 93, 102, 103, 159; *see also* domestic violence
"After" (season four) 88, 89
Alexander, Michelle 27
Alexandria: Carol and 87, 98, 99; Daryl and 95, 99, 103, 104; diversity and 161; Maggie and 91; as matriarchy 40; Michonne and 121; Rick and 99; tribalism and 159; whiteness and 56
Aliens (film) 73, 98
"Alone" (season four) 34, 35, 101, 115
"Always Accountable" (season six) 104
Amy (Andrea's sister) 80, 81–82, 144, 145
Andre (Michonne's son) 89, 112
Andrea Dulanto: Dale and 144, 145, 151*n*11; death of 83; Ed and 131–132; fans memes and 69; gender roles and 2, 6, 66, 79; Glenn and 58; Governor and 18, 69, 82–83; Lori and 82, 90; Maggie and 90; Michonne and 2, 82; motherhood and marriage and 6, 79, 80, 81–83, 85; power and 17–18, 19, 80; rape culture and 139; rescuers of 90, 112; sexuality and 2; survival and 82; Tyreese and 151*n*11; violence and 18
androgyny 79, 83, 84, 88
Angry Asian Man 55, 59
animalistic behavior 94–95, 151
animals 35, 39, 95
Annette (Hershel's wife) 108, 109, 110
"Arrow on the Doorpost" (season three) 112
Asian Americans 4, 5, 37–38, 57–61, 123; *see also* Glenn Rhee
audiences: catharsis and 7–8; hyperreal hillbilly and 32, 41; Michonne and 127; multiculturalism and 38; protagonists and 31; psychopathic killers and 37; Rick and 47; stereotypes in comics and 38; white male leaders and 45; widowed, single father and 47; *see also* fans and memes
Axel 111

Balaji, Murali 57
Baldwin, Martina 45, 57
Barkman, Ashley 2, 78
beauty 7, 107–117, 115, 116, 117
Bechdel test 78, 92*n*3
Berry, Lorraine 162*n*4
"Beside the Dying Fire" (season two) 26, 39, 106*n*14
Beth Greene (Hershel's daughter): Carol and 98; clothing and 114; Daryl and 17, 35, 96, 100–102, 103, 104, 107, 112, 113–115, 116, 117; death 35, 58, 117; emotions and 98, 114; femininity and 6–7, 107–117, 109–111, 112, 114–117; gothic novels and 107–108; Hershel and 108; introduced 107, 108, 109; kidnapped 115–116; masculinity and 116–117; motherhood and 84; music and 107, 112, 115, 116, 117; rape culture and 139; sexuality and 35; "Slabtown" and 137–138; suicidal 109, 147, 152*nn*25,28; survival and 109, 116–117; violence and 51, 109, 117; writing and 112, 115
"Better Angels" (season two) 146, 151*n*21
The Birds (film) 152*n*25
Birth of a Nation (film) 25
Bishop, Kyle 126–127
Black Lives Matter 40
"Black Man Problem" 2, 157, 162*n*9
black women, liberated 7, 127–128
Blink, Megan 93, 96
"Bloodletting" (season two) 23, 57, 157
Bob 34, 48, 50, 63*n*13
Braindead (film) 85
Brayton, Sean 48
Breaking Bad (TV show) 41
Brexit 159
The Brood (film) 85
Buchbinder, David 16
Burial Ground: Nights of Terror (film) 79

Campbell, Joseph 9*n*6
Canavan, Gerry 56–57
cannibalism 12, 63*n*13, 75, 86–87, 142
Caravaggio painting 116

185

Carl Grimes: banishment 84–85; Beth and 110, 117; Carol and 98; as the Child 145; childhood naivety and 82; death 162n12; emotions and 19, 98; Jessie and 150; Judith and 110; Lori and 68–69, 81, 82, 109, 110; masculinity/leadership and 19; Michonne and 89; power currency and 18–19; protective paternalism and 47; rape threats and 36–37, 47; Rick and 46, 47, 64n17, 85, 127, 146, 147, 162; Shane and 15, 18, 69, 80, 146; survival and 18

Carol Peletier: Andrea and 83; Beth and 116; Cherokee Rose and 96; Daryl and 87, 100, 101–105; death 123, 152n37; emotions and 93; fans and memes and 5, 73–76; femininity of, burning away 6, 97–100, 101, 102, 105; fire and 104; gender roles and 5, 6; leadership and 98–99; Lori and 109, 128n17, 144–145, 151nn1,14; Maggie and 91; masculinity and 73–76, 83–84, 86–88, 98–99, 101, 102, 105, 111; Merle and 103; Michonne and 124; motherhood and marriage and 6, 8, 75–76, 79–80, 81, 83–85, 86–88, 97–98, 111; Paula and 99; queered 128n17, 143–145, 151n11; race/violence and 73; Rick and 87, 93, 128n17, 151n11; sexuality and 100; suicidal 124, 145; survival and 54, 74–75, 76, 83–84, 85, 86–87; T-Dog and 29, 63n13; tribalism and 159, 161; violence and 73, 74, 83, 84, 85, 86, 87, 88, 99, 104, 111, 159

Carrie (film) 85
Castle of Otranto (Walpole) 108
"Cell" (season seven) 160
Centers for Disease Control (CDC) 84, 86–87, 94
Chaney, Jen 15
Charlie Chan 57–58
"Cherokee Rose" (season two) 58, 60, 96, 100, 147
the Child 8, 82, 142–143, 144, 145, 146, 147, 148, 149, 150, 152n25; *see also* reproductive futurism
The Children (film) 79
"Chupacabra" (season two) 17, 88, 96, 97, 103, 157
city-revenge sub-genre of horror 95
"Claimed" (season four) 88, 161
the Claimers and Joe 36–37, 96–97, 106n14, 159–160, 162
class 16, 24, 43, 56, 113, 114, 132; *see also* hyperreal hillbilly; identity politics
"Clear" (season three) 112
clothing 113–114, 116, 121
Clover, Carol J. 37, 95
"Coda" (season five) 35, 40, 58, 116
Cohen, Jeffrey Jerome 150, 152n37
Collins, Sean 160
Colombe, Audrey 38; *see also* magical negro
colorblindness 43, 48, 50, 65
comics: black characters and 3, 27, 38; family and 8, 149, 151n1; female characters and 67; gender roles and 7, 66; Glenn and 37–38, 62; Hershel's undead and 149; identity politics and 119–127; issue 3 41; issue 7 38; Lori and 41, 145; masculinity and 38; Michonne and 39, 70, 120, 123, 128n1; Morgan and 22; people of color and 4; queers and 8, 123–124, 151nn11,12,13,18; reissue 41; Rick and 37–38, 123, 145, 146; sexuality and 120, 122–127; Shane's death and 146; stereotypes and 38; violence and sexuality and 119–120; *see also* Kirkman, Robert

Connell, R.W. 4, 43, 56
"Consumed" (season five) 98, 104–105
Cronan, William 66

Dale: Andrea and 17, 144, 145, 151n11; Daryl and 33; Glenn and 60, 61; Rick and 56, 152n25; T-Dog and 23, 57, 157
Darabont, Frank 23–24, 25, 27
Daryl Dixon: Alexandria and 95, 99, 103, 104; Beth and 17, 35, 96, 100–102, 103, 104, 107, 112, 113–115, 116, 117; Carol and 87, 100, 101–105; character arc of 96, 103, 113; the Child and 147; emotions and 17, 35, 58, 93, 95, 96–97, 100, 102, 103, 110; fans and 72; fire and 104; Glenn and 33, 38, 41, 62, 63; as hyperreal hillbilly 4, 9n6, 33–35, 39; identity politics and 96–97, 157; Judith and 110; Latino men and 45; leadership and 98–99; masculinity and 4, 16–17, 75; masculinity of, burning away 6, 94–97, 101–102, 105, 115; Merle and 16–17, 34, 88, 96, 103, 106n14, 157; Michonne's masculinity compared 72–73; personal history and 39; racism and 32, 34, 41, 106n14; Rick and 37, 46, 158; romantic hero narrative and 100–101; sexuality and 35, 100; survival and 4, 35, 37, 93, 104; T-Dog and 22; tribalism and 159–160; as victim-hero 34–35; violence and 16–17, 94, 96, 104; whiteness and 4, 32–33, 56; *see also* gender roles, burning away of
David 104
Dawn Lerner 56, 116–117
"The Day Will Come When You Won't Be" (season seven) 33, 53n45, 62, 95, 101, 106n14
"Days Gone Bye" (season one) 13, 46, 55, 58, 80, 111, 145
Deanna 49, 56, 95
death 48, 51, 54, 58, 115, 117, 143, 148, 152n25; *see also* Ed Peletier *and other dead characters*
delusions and hallucinations 88–89, 96, 122, 157
Denise 58, 124
Die Hard (film) 14
Dirty Harry (film) 40
"The Distance" (season five) 61
diversity 31, 48, 54, 107, 117, 161
Doane, Ashley 48
Dr. Edwards 116
domestic violence 97, 139; *see also* abuse

Index   187

Donna 144
Duane, Anna Mae 147–148
Duane Jones 46
Duck Dynasty (TV show) 31
Duvernay, Eva 27
Dwight 97, 102, 104, 140

"East" (season six) 61, 99, 103
Eastbound and Down (TV show) 31
Eastman 39
ebony saint character archetypes 22, 24, 25
Ed Peletier (Carol's husband) 83, 84, 93, 97, 103–104, 105
Edelman, Lee 8, 142–143, 144, 145, 148, 152nn23,25
"18 Miles Out" (season two) 15, 17, 82, 109, 146, 152n28
emotions (feelings) 13, 33, 149; *see also* Daryl Dixon *and other characters*
Entertainment Weekly 48
equality 4; *see also* feminism and postfeminism; postracism
Esposito, Jennifer 48
Eugene 40, 121
expertise currency 12, 13, 17–18, 20n21; *see also* leadership; survival, protection and safety
exploitation 7, 127
Ezekiel 39, 102, 124, 161

family: Beth and 115; Carol and 103; comics and 8, 149, 151n1; Daryl and 103, 115; Governor and 149–150, 152nn41,43; "The Grove" and 101; heteronormative sexuality and 8; Lori and Rick and 143–147, 150, 151n11; morality and 49; power and 120; queers and 2, 8, 142–143, 145–149; sexuality and 151n11; tribalism and 158; zombies and 149; *see also* fatherhood; motherhood and marriage
fans and memes: Asian masculinity and 54–55, 62, 63; gender roles and 5, 70; masculinity and 5, 16–17, 67, 68–76; motherhood and marriage and 68–69, 80–81; overviews of memes 68, 76, 77nn8–9; race and 2; Rick's leadership and 15–16; sexism and 69; sheriff trope and 33; violence and 17, 62; *see also* audiences; Michonne *and other characters*
fascism 160
Father Gabriel 121
fatherhood 44–45, 46–47, 145, 146; *see also* family
female characters: diversity 107, 117; independence and 6; masculinity and 5, 17–18, 65–76, 82, 125–126; nonviolence and 6–7; protective paternalism and 46–47; sexualization and 67; survivor to season seven 54; white dominance and 56–57; *see also* femininity; gender roles; Lori Grimes *and other female characters*; motherhood and marriage; sexism; sexuality

femininity: devalued 67, 122–125; examples 16, 17–18; "female in distress" trope and 5–6; heroism and 6, 7; leadership and 50; male characters and 13, 37, 38, 40, 47, 50, 55, 56, 61; masculinity and 43–47; racial 58; *see also* Beth Greene *and other characters*; female characters; gender roles; motherhood and marriage; sexuality; vulnerability and weakness
feminism and postfeminism 14, 44–45, 78, 88, 130, 155; *see also* antifeminism; equality
films *see* Hollywood; horror and horror films
Final Girl (film) 36, 37
fire 6, 94, 96, 100, 101, 103–105, 115, 159
"First Time Again" (season six) 61
"flowers" memes 74–75
Fong, Ken 59
food 1, 148, 159, 160
"Forget" (season five) 95
"Four Walls and a Roof" (season five) 40
Frankenstein (Shelley) 112
friendship 2, 13, 24, 25, 29, 60, 82, 89; *see also* gender roles, burning away of

Gareth 50, 56, 75
Garland, Tammy 66
Gencarella, Stephen Olbrys 160
gender roles: comics and 7, 66; defined 128n16; exploitation and 7; fans and memes and 77n8; interdependence 43; popular media on 2; post-race discourses and 45; power and 128n27; power currencies and 20n21; race and 52, 71, 119–127; real world and 19; simpler times and 66; social exchange theory and 18; survival and 76, 79, 89; tribalism *versus* 159; violence and 67; *see also* androgyny; femininity; gender roles, burning away of; identity politics; masculinity; sexuality; vulnerability and weakness
gender roles, burning away of: abuse and 93; Carol's femininity and 6, 94, 97–100, 101, 102, 105; Daryl's masculinity and 6, 94–97, 101–102; gendered narratives and 6, 100–102; horror tropes and 93; overview 93–94; phoenixes and 6, 94, 103–105
Glenn Rhee: abortion pills and 147; Asian stereotypes and 4, 37–38, 40, 41; becoming 54–63; Daryl and 33, 38, 41, 62, 63; death 33, 39–40, 53n45, 55, 58, 62–63, 91, 97, 101; emotions and 61; fans and 54–55, 62, 63; Governor and 38, 121; leadership and 38, 57, 60–61; Maggie and 38, 90, 91, 112, 152n25; marginalized 33, 58, 60; masculinity and 4–5, 40, 50, 51, 55, 59, 60–63; race and 4, 5, 90; Rick compared 46, 53n45, 58, 60; sexuality and 60; survival and 61; violence and 50; watch of 102; zombies and 149
globalization 158–159, 162n13
Goldman, Eric 26

The Good Son (film) 85
Gorman 138
gothic influences 107–108, 109, 111–113, 115
the Governor (Philip Blake): Andrea and 18, 69, 82–83; attack on prison of 121–122; Carol and 98; the Child and 148; Daryl and 103; death 150; family and 149–150, 152nn41,43; hopelessness and 28; Maggie and 38, 90; masculinity and 5, 75, 126; Merle and 34; Michonne and 2, 7, 39, 70, 120, 121, 125–127, 149; power and 50; protective paternalism/leadership and 59; queered 40; rape by 7, 120, 125–127; Rick and 55, 59, 120, 121; sexuality and 18, 38, 90, 149; Tyreese and 51; violence and 111; whiteness and 56; zombies and 8, 149, 152n41; *see also* Woodbury
Grace (film) 85
Grady Memorial Hospital and "Slabtown" (season five) 40, 56, 115–117, 131, 137–138
Granshaw, Lisa 125
Graves, Abby 2
The Green Mile (film) 23–24
Greene, Joshua 161
Gregory 56, 59, 159, 161
Grizzell, Trevor 149
"The Grove" (season four) 74, 86, 101
Gurr, Barbara 11
"Guts" (season one) 1, 16, 22, 38, 48, 60, 65, 157

Halloween (film) 36
hallucinations and delusions 88–89, 96, 122, 157
Hamad, Hannah 45
Handlen, Zack 26
Hannabach, Cathy 120, 123
Harkins, Anthony 31
Harris, Geraldine 44
Hawaii Five-O (TV show) 57
"Hearts Still Beating" (season seven) 102
Heath 123, 124, 125
Here Comes Honey Boo Boo (TV show) 31, 41n8
"Here's Not Here" (season six) 39
Hershel Greene: Beth and 108, 110, 115; Carol and 74, 97–98; the Child and 147; Daryl and 17, 115; family and 8, 149; fans and memes and 74; Glenn and 61; introduced 108–109; Lori and 109; Maggie and 90; Michonne and 88; protective paternalism and 46, 58; walkers and 15; whiteness and 56; zombies and 149
Hershel's farm 19, 94, 108
heteronormative sexuality 2, 8, 123, 143, 144, 151n11, 157; *see also* the Child; family; queers
Hetterly, Jonathan 96
hillbilly *see* hyperreal hillbilly
The Hills Have Eyes (film) 37
Hilltop Colony 56, 91, 127, 159, 161; *see also* Gregory

Hitchcock, Alfred 36, 152n25
Ho, Helen K. 50
Hollywood 23–24, 24–25, 27, 29; *see also* specific films
"Home" (season three) 34, 90–91, 96
hooks, bell 125
horror and horror films 85–86, 88, 92, 92n5, 93, 108; *see also* melodrama; *Night of the Living Dead* and other films
"Hostiles and Calamities" (season seven) 95
"Hounded" (season three) 38, 104
"How It's Gotta Be" (season eight) 102
Huckvale, David 108
Hughey, Matthew 23–24
The Hunger Games (film) 31
hunter/gatherer/provider norms 78, 94
hypermasculinity: Abe and 40; characterized 13; defense 2; defined 67; fans and 67; female characters and 5, 6; Michonne and 70, 71; as power currency 11–19; survival and 13–14; Tyreese and 38; value 12; violence and 3; *see also* hyperreal hillbilly; leadership; power currencies
hyperreal hillbilly: Daryl as 4, 9n6, 33–35, 39; marginalization and 31–32, 41n8; Merle as 34–35, 41, 49; racism and 32, 34, 41; Rick as 33, 36–37; suffering and 3–4; whiteness and 32–33, 38; *see also* rednecks

"I Ain't a Judas" (season three) 111
identity politics: comics and 119–127; Daryl and 96–97, 157; expertise currency and 18; masculinity and 43; overviews 1–8, 51–52; pre-apocalyptic 16; tribalism *versus* 156–157, 158; *see also* class; gender roles; race and characters of color; sexuality; tribalism
Indiana Jones and the Temple of Doom (film) 37–38, 60, 64n21
"Indifference" (season four) 84–85, 97, 106n14
individualism 66, 132n16, 162n8
"Infected" (season four) 72, 104
"Inmates" (season four) 101, 113
insanity and mental instability 23, 25, 85, 86, 121–122, 127–128, 143, 145, 147; *see also* hallucinations and delusions
"Isolation" (season four) 74

Jacqui 22, 48, 132
Jadis 161
James, Paul 158, 159
Jeffords, Susan 36
Jessie Anderson (Pete's wife; Sam's mother) 49, 83, 87–88, 124–125, 139, 150
Jimmy 109
Joan 116
Joe and the Claimers 36–37, 96–97, 106n14, 159–160, 162
John McClane (*Diehard*) 14
Johnson, Helen 77n11
Joseph, Ralina L. 45

"JSS" (season six) 99, 104
"Judge, Jury, Executioner" (season two) 26
Judith Grimes (Lori's daughter): Beth and 110, 111, 112; Carol and 75–76, 84, 86, 98, 99; as the Child 146; Daryl and 102; death of (in comics) 121–122, 150; "The Grove" and 101; Lizzie and 74, 86; Michonne and 72; Rick and 46, 47, 162n12; Tyreese and 86

Karen 104
Katerberg, William 66
Kearns, Megan 2
Keetley, Dawn 48
"Killer Within" (season three) 26, 63n13, 109
King, Stephen 11, 12
"The King, the Widow, and Rick" (season eight) 102
Kingdom 102, 161
Kirkman, Robert 2, 23, 36, 40, 63
Kistler, Alan 100
Kremmel, Laura 103–104
Kuniak, Stephen 93, 96
Kushner, Jared 156

landscapes 77n9, 96, 108, 111; see also wilderness
"Last Day on Earth" (season six) 62, 103, 161
laundry scene ("Tell It to the Frogs") 41, 78, 97
Lavin, Melissa 120
leadership: emotions and 17; femininity and 50, 117; gender and 66, 80; masculinity and 68; race and 2, 57; racialized masculinity and 5; violence and 3; white masculinity and 36, 45, 46, 56, 58; see also paternalism and patriarchy; power; Rick Grimes and other characters
Lee, Spike 23
Lewis, Matthew 108
LGBTQ people 31; see also queers
Lilly 150
Lincoln, Andrew 65, 67
Lizzie 51, 74, 75–76, 85, 86, 97, 98, 101, 104
London, Jack 161, 162
The Lone Ranger (TV show) 39
Lori Grimes: Andrea and 82, 90; Beth and 109, 110; Carl and 13, 18, 19, 69, 81, 82; Carol and 109, 128n17, 143, 144–145, 151nn11,14; character arc of 79, 80; death 81, 84, 109–110, 121–122, 150; fans and 68, 76, 80–81; fans and memes and 5, 69–70; femininity and 5, 6, 68–70, 82; feminism and 41; gender roles expectation and 17–18; motherhood and marriage and 6, 76, 80–81, 85, 109, 111, 152n22; power currencies and 17–18, 19; pregnancy and 98, 145, 146, 147, 152n25; queers and 143–144, 143–147, 144, 145; Rick and 46, 47, 69, 82, 121–122, 124, 145–146, 147, 152nn22,25; sexuality and 15, 69, 82; Shane and 15, 69, 80, 82, 109, 124, 145–146, 151n18
Lotz, Amanda 4, 44

Lowe, Brian 120
Luke Cage 40

Mad Max 11
Mad Men 41
"Made to Suffer" (season three) 149
Maggie Greene (Beth's sister): abortion pills and 147, 149; Beth and 112, 117; character arc of 89–90; feminized 40; Glenn and 55, 57, 58, 60, 61, 91, 152n25; Hilltop leader and 159; introduced 108; Judith and 110; leadership and 127, 161; Lori and 109; masculinity/survival and 90, 91–92; Michonne and 121, 124; motherhood and marriage and 6, 90–92; race and 90; Sasha and 117; sexuality and 38, 90–91; singing 107; T-Dog and 23; tribalism and 159; violence and 159; Woodbury and 61; zombies and 149
magical negro 3, 4, 21, 22, 24, 27, 28, 29, 38–39
Magna 127
male characters. see Daryl Dixon *and other male characters*; femininity; masculinity; sexuality
Martin 51
masculinity: alternatives to 4–5, 6, 49–50, 51–52, 59; emotions and 13; fans and memes and 5, 16–17, 67, 68–76; fascism and 160; female characters and 5, 17–18, 65–76, 82, 125–126; "female in distress" trope and 5–6; leadership and 16, 36, 58; marginalized 94; neo- 17; Old West iconography and 66; overviews 2, 4, 43–47, 56, 63n8; power currencies and 12, 14; punishment and 50–51; race and 3–5, 44, 45, 46, 50; racism and stereotypes and 4, 38, 125; rape culture and 7–8; social exchange theory and 3; suffering and 3–4, 40, 41; survival and 6, 13–14, 67; value 66–67, 122–126; violence and 3, 12–13, 47–52; whiteness and 56–58; see also Daryl Dixon *and other characters*; fatherhood; gender roles; hunter/gatherer/provider norms; leadership; misogyny; paternalism and patriarchy; power; romantic hero narrative; survival, protection and safety; violence
matriarchy 40; see also paternalism and patriarchy
McCarthy, Mark 45, 57
McCloud, Scott 38
McKay, James 77n11
melodrama 4, 32, 33, 34, 35–36, 40, 41
memes see fans and memes
Merle Dixon: Carol and 103; Daryl and 16–17, 34, 88, 96, 103, 106n14, 157; death 34; evil and 28; Glenn compared 38; as hyper-real hillbilly 34–35, 41; masculinity and 16–17; racism and 1, 41, 48–49, 157; Rick compared 37; sexism and 157; T-Dog and 22; violence and 91

Index

Messerschmidt, James W. 4, 43
Meyer, Stephanie 36
Michonne: Andrea and 2, 18, 82; androgyny and 88; dream sequence and 88–89; emotions and 121–122; fans and memes and 5, 70–73, 76, 120; femininity and 6, 72, 73; gender roles and 2, 7; Governor and 70, 121, 125–126, 149; Joe's gang and 36–37; leadership and 18, 121; Maggie and 91, 124; as magical negro 39; masculinity and 4, 70, 71, 72–73, 75, 122, 123, 126, 127–128; motherhood and marriage and 72, 81, 88–90, 89–90, 147; in *Playboy* magazine 119, 121; power economy and 19; protective paternalism and 49–50; queerness and 2, 123–124; race and stereotypes and 26, 27, 28, 70–71, 125, 127–128; rape and 7, 120, 125–127; Rick and 119–127; sexualized heroics 119–127; survival, protection and safety and 71, 72, 120; violence and 70, 88, 89, 126–127; *see also* race and characters of color
"Michonne Special" (comic) 128n1
Mika 51, 85, 86, 98, 101, 104
Miles, Kevin Thomas 120–121
Milton Mamet 40, 112
mirroring 6, 29, 93, 101–105
misogyny 13, 127, 135
money 3; *see also* social exchange theory
The Monk (Lewis) 108
the monster and monstrosities 79, 149–150, 152n37
"Monsters" (season eight) 102
moonshiner's cabin 96, 104, 114–115
Moore, Tony 23
Morales 102
morality and value systems: Beth and 107; the Child and 147; Dale and 17; Daryl and 4, 16–17, 34, 113; excuses and 142; family and 49; fans and memes and 77n9; gender and 44; Governor and 121; Michonne and 121, 124, 127; Old West iconography and 66; post-apocalyptic narratives and 11, 19; race and 45; Rick and 14, 22, 47–50, 59, 147; sexuality and 124–125; tribalism and 161; victim-heroes and 32; zombies and 149
Moreman, Christopher M. 148
Morgan Jones: Carol and 161; comics and 22, 29; as magical negro 38–39; masculinity and 4; Michonne and 124, 125; protective paternalism and 46; Rick and 27, 46, 54; writing and 112
Morton, Timothy 158
Mosher, Donald L. 13, 16
motherhood and marriage: child as disruption and 81, 86; as destructive 78–79, 87–88; fans and memes and 68–69, 80–81; horror and 85–86; laundry scene and 78; marginalized 47; passivity and 89–90, 91–92; polyamorous 8, 128n17, 143, 150; subversive depictions 6, 78–79; *see also* Carol Peletier *and other characters*; family; matriarchy

Moy, Matthew 57
multiculturalism 38, 48
Mulvey, Sarah 16
music 7, 107, 108, 109, 111, 112, 115, 116, 117, 149
The Mysteries of Udolpho (Radcliffe) 108

Natania 56
Native Americans 94
nature 94–96; *see also* wilderness
"Nebraska" (season two) 37, 103, 109
Negan *see* the Saviors and Negan
neoliberalism 132n16, 162n8
Nerds of Color (website) 59, 162n9
"New Best Friends" (season seven) 95, 104
The New Jim Crow (Alexander) 27
"The Next World" (season six) 103
Nicholas 61
Night of the Living Dead (film) 36, 79
9/11 155
No Future (Edelman) 8, 142–143, 144, 145, 148, 152nn23,25
"No Sanctuary" (season five) 86–87, 104
"No Way Out" (season six) 61, 89, 99, 104
Noah 104, 116
nonviolence 6–7, 51
Norris, Chuck 70
"Not Tomorrow Yet" (season six) 9, 97, 159, 160–161

Obama, Barack 155–156
Oceanside 56
Officer Gorman 116
Officer Shepherd 117
O'Hehir, Andrew 156
Okihiro, Gary 57–58
Old West (frontier) and sheriff iconography 18, 23, 36, 39, 66, 67, 69, 94; *see also* Rick Grimes
The Omen (film) 85
Orphan (film) 85
Oscar 63n13
the other (outsider) (exclusion) 13, 16, 38, 48, 120, 124, 127–128, 148, 149
Owen 56

passivity 89–90, 91–92, 94; *see also* vulnerability and weakness
paternalism and patriarchy: Andrea and 82; Carol and 84; the Child and 148; comics and 127; dismantling 120; Dixons and 34; fatherhood and 44–45; Glenn and 61, 63; Governor and 59; Hershel and 46, 58; hillbilly trope and 32; masculinity and 45–47; Michonne and 128; queers and 143; real world and 14, 125; Rick and 46–47, 49–50, 51, 58–59; survival and 76, 79; television and 44; violence and 4, 7–8, 49–50; white 162n4; *see also* fatherhood; heteronormative sexuality; leadership; matriarchy; power; survival, protection and safety
patriarchy *see* paternalism and patriarchy

Patricia 110
Paula 99
Penny (the Governor's niece) 149
Percy 116
personal currency 12, 18
Pete Anderson (Jessie's husband; Sam's father) 49, 50, 137, 139–140
Phillips, Katherine W. 20n21
Phillips, Nickie 66
phoenixes 6, 94, 103–105, 115
Pierce, Leonard 13
place 158–159, 160
Playboy magazine 119, 121
Poitier, Sidney 21, 25
politics *see* real world
polyamorous marriage 8, 128n17, 143, 150
polygamy 128n17
postfeminism 43–47
postmasculinism 44, 45
post-9/11 tribalism 155
Post-Racial or Most-Racial: Race and Politics in the Obama Era (Tesler) 155, 156
postracism 45, 48, 49, 50, 155–156
power: Andrea and 83; gender and 127, 128n27; Lori and 80; Maggie's masculinity and 90; race and 128n27; sexuality and 125; stereotypes and 56; struggles for 120; violence and 126; wives and motherhood and 81; *see also* fire; leadership; masculinity; paternalism and patriarchy; power currencies; survival, protection and safety
power currencies 11–19, 20n21; *see also* social exchange theory
pre-apocalypse and "simpler times" 41, 65, 66, 89, 99
pregnancy and birth 81, 90, 91–92, 98, 109, 147, 151n18, 152n25
"Pretty Much Dead Already" (season two) 15 the prison 75, 107; fire and 94; Governor's attack on 111; leadership and 98–99; Lori's pregnancy and 81
protective paternalism. *see* paternalism and patriarchy; survival, protection and safety
Psycho (film) 36

queers: comics and 8, 123–124, 151nn11,12,13,18; family and 2, 8, 142–143, 145–149; hyperreal hillbilly and 2, 4, 31, 33; negated 145; real world and 150–151; rejection 143–144; zombies and 8, 148–151, 152nn23,37; *see also* Carol Peletier *and other queered characters*; LGBTQ people

race and characters of color: comics and 3, 27, 38; femininity and 58; feminized masculinity and 50; gender and 52, 71; gender and sexuality and 52, 71, 119–127; "Guts" and 1; hyperreal hillbillies and 41; leadership and 2, 57; masculinity and 3–5, 44, 45, 46, 50; post-apocalypse 16; power and 56, 128n27; protective paternalism and 46; season five and 48; seasons four through eight and 162n4; sexuality and gender and 52, 71, 119–127; sheriff trope and 46; simulated 31; stereotypes and 37; suffering and 71; support for whites and 45, 48, 57, 58, 60; survivors to season seven 54; tribalism and 161–162; violence and 67, 128n27; visual representation and 128n16; white characters compared 48–49; *see also* Asian Americans; "Black Man Problem"; black women, liberated; colorblindness; diversity; ebony saint character archetypes; identity politics; magical negro; masculinity; postracism; racism and stereotypes; Tyreese *and other characters of color*; whiteness

racism and stereotypes: aversive racism 24, 27–28; black women and 77n11, 120; Hollywood (race) and 23–24; hyperreal hillbilly and 32, 34, 41; masculinity and 4, 38, 125; people of color and 37; postracism 45, 48, 49, 50, 155–156; power and 56; rape and 125; "Strong Black Woman" 70–71; T-Dog and 1, 21–24, 27–29, 34, 157; "Tell It to the Frogs" and 78; Tyreese and 40; *see also* Asian Americans; class; colorblindness; hyperreal hillbilly; identity politics; magical negro; sexism; "Strong Black Woman" stereotype; T-Dog *and other characters*

Radcliffe, Ann 107, 108, 112
Rambo 73
rape 7–8, 36–37, 47, 61, 96, 116, 120, 125–127
real world: cannibal and zombie films and 12; horror and 92; hyperreal hillbilly and 41, 41n8; paternalism and patriarchy and 14, 125; patriarchy and 125; place and 158; power currencies and 11–12, 19; queers and 150–151; race and 24, 155–156, 162; race and assault and 128n27; sexual hegemony and 123; tribalism and 156–157, 158–159; victim-heroes and 40; women/clothing and 114; *see also* globalization; racism and stereotypes

rednecks 95, 96, 97; *see also* hyperreal hillbilly
Reedus, Norman 33
Rees, Shelly S. 94, 96
religion, Christianity and faith 11, 99, 103, 110, 111, 117, 144
"Remember" (season five) 98, 99
reproductive futurism 8, 142–143, 144, 145, 146, 147, 148, 150; *see also* the Child
Rick Grimes: Alexandria and 99; Beth and 116; Carl and 85, 127, 146, 147; Carol and 84, 87, 98, 99, 128n17, 143, 151n11; the Child and 150; Daryl and 96, 158, 160; emotions and 13, 14, 17, 121–122; fans and memes and 15–16, 33, 69; Glenn and 37–38, 40, 53n45, 58, 63; Governor and 55, 59, 120, 121; Greene family and 108; gun 102; as hyperreal hillbilly 33, 36–37; Jessie and 124–125, 150; Joe's rape threat and 36–37; Judith and 110; Latino men and 45; leadership and 15–

16, 17, 33, 40, 47–48, 51, 55, 59, 84–85, 98; Lori and 69, 80, 82, 109, 121–122, 124, 145–146, 147, 152nn22,25; masculinity and 4–5, 13–14, 15, 40, 45–47, 49, 50, 51, 55, 100; Michonne and 89, 119–127, 120, 161, 162; neoliberalism and 162n8; Old West/sheriff iconography and 14, 33, 45–46, 55, 56, 58, 60, 66, 94; people of color and 38, 50; postracism and 48; power economy and 19; pro-gun stance and 40; protective paternalism and 49–50, 51, 58–59; queers and 151, 151n12; race and stereotypes and 1, 4, 16, 22, 38, 48–49, 50; Saviors and Negan and 63, 102, 120, 159; sexist memes and 69; sexuality and 7, 49, 124; sexualized heroics 119–127; Shane and 15, 120, 145–146, 151n21; Sophia and 149; survival, protection and safety and 15, 120; tribalism and 158, 161–162; Tyreese and 40, 46, 51; violence and 14, 40, 47, 49–50, 55, 64n17, 126, 127, 142, 159

Rohmer, Sax 57
Romance of the Forest (Radcliffe) 112
romantic hero narrative 100–101
romantic love 151n11
Romero, George A. 36
Rosita 40, 101
Rushton, Cory James 148

Sam (Jessie's son) 87–88, 97, 99, 150
"Same Boat" (season six) 91, 99, 104, 159, 160–161
San Juan, Billy 100
Sanctuary 160
Sasha (Tyreese's sister) 64n13, 117
"Save the Last One" (season two) 100
the Saviors and Negan: burned 104; Daryl and 95, 97, 101, 102, 104, 106n14; fire and 104; Maggie and Carol and 91; murdered 142; political economy and 19, 55; Rick and 55, 56, 63, 102, 120, 159; tribalism and 160; tyranny and 59; violence and 62
"Say the Word" (season three) 110
"Say Yes" (season seven) 161
Scarlet Janina 105
the Scavengers 161
Schweitzer, Dahlia 162n13
science fiction 27–28, 48, 66
Scream 2 (film) 85
seasons: one 57, 87, 111; two 57, 60, 94–95, 100, 102, 108–109; before three 162n4; three 18, 55, 75; before four 162n9; four 36, 47, 55, 85, 98, 100–101; four through 8 155, 157, 162; five 47, 49–51, 56, 98–99, 155; six 48, 55, 56, 61, 99, 100, 103, 155; seven 33, 53n45, 54, 55, 62, 88, 91, 155; eight 102, 155, 162n12; *see also* "Days Gone Bye" *and other episodes*
"Secrets" (season two) 25–26, 147, 149
sectarianism 162n1
"Seed" (season three) 107, 109
Selected Short Stories of Jack London 161, 162

"Self Help" (season five) 40
Sepinwall, Alan 15–16
sexism 2, 69, 77n11, 78, 92, 161; *see also* antifeminism; rape
sexuality: Asian male stereotypes and 37, 58; black stereotypes and 24, 25; damsel saved and 100; data about 128n16; defined 128n16; diverse 161; expertise currency and 18; family and 151n11; gender and race and 119–127; heteronormative 2, 8, 123, 143, 144, 151n11, 157; masculinity and 13, 14; sinthomo- 145, 148, 152n25; survival and protection and 17, 49, 123, 124; violence and 7–8, 119–120; zombies and 148; *see also* family; identity politics; queers; rape; Shane *and other characters*
Shane: Andrea and 18, 69; Carl and 18, 80, 146; deaths 146, 152n23; emotions and 133; evil and 28; fans and memes and 69; Lori and 15, 69, 80, 82, 109, 124, 145–146, 151n18; marginalized 146; masculinity and 13–14, 15; misogyny of 13; power economy and 19; Rick and 36, 120, 145–146, 151n21; sexuality and 15, 69, 82; whiteness and 56
The Shawshank Redemption (film) 23
Shelley, Mary 112
Shildrick, Margrit 150
Short Round 37–38, 41, 60, 64n21
"Sick" (season three) 26
"Sing Me a Song" (season seven) 104
Singer, Peter 158
Singleton, IronE 26
sinthomosexuality 145, 148, 152n25
Sirkin, Mark 13, 16
"Slabtown" (season five) and Grady Memorial Hospital 40, 56, 115–117, 131, 137–138
social commentary *see* real world
social exchange theory 3, 12, 18; *see also* power currencies
Soles, Carter 37
Sophia (Carol's daughter): Carol and 75, 80, 96, 98, 111; Daryl and 17, 100, 103, 147; death 15–16, 84, 97, 149; disappearance 96
Springer, Kimberly 71
Squires, Catherine R. 48, 155–156
"Start to Finish" (season six) 99
Steiger, Kay 78
Sterba, James 120
"Still" (season four) 96, 101, 113, 114; victim-heroes and 34–35
Stowe, Harriet Beecher 24
"Strangers" (season five) 63n13, 106n14
"Strong Black Woman" stereotype 70–71
suffering 3–4, 6, 34–35, 40, 41, 71; *see also* victim-heroes
Sugg, Katherine 66, 120, 132n16, 162n8
"The Suicide King" (season three) 28, 106n14, 135
survival, protection and safety: female characters and 6, 79; gender roles and 76, 79, 89; heterosexuality and 2; masculinity and 6, 13–14, 45, 67; motherhood and marriage

and 6, 81, 89; Old West iconography and 66; patriarchal gender hierarchies and 76, 79; power currencies and 12; sexuality and 17, 123, 124; tribalism and 160–161; white characters and 45, 48; *see also* Carol Peletier *and other characters*; paternalism and patriarchy; power
Swamp People (TV show) 41n8

T-Dog (Theodore Douglas): Carol and 29, 63n13; Dale and 157; Daryl and 16, 22, 38; faith and 110; fans and memes and 21, 26; Latino men and 45; magical negro and 3, 4, 21, 22, 24, 27, 28, 29; masculinity and 3; Merle and 16, 38, 41; as minority 57; protection and 22, 24, 26–27, 28–29; racism and stereotypes and 1, 21–25, 27–29, 34, 157; seasons one to three and 22, 23, 25–26; Tyreese and 38; violence and 22
The Talking Dead 54
Talladega Nights (film) 31
Tara 40, 102
television 3, 4, 44, 92; *see also The Lone Ranger* and other TV shows
"Tell It to the Frogs" (season one): Carol's motherhood and marriage and 97; fatherhood and 145; gender roles and 41, 78, 82; Glenn and 58; hyperreal hillbilly and 33–34, 36; masculinity and 16; patriarchy and 131–133; Rick and 36; violence and 16
Terminus 19, 29, 40, 50, 86–87, 98, 104; *see also* Gareth
Tesler, Michael 155, 156
The Texas Chain Saw Massacre (film) 34, 35, 37
"Thank You" (season six) 54
"Them" (season five) 34–35, 104, 117
13th (film) 27
"30 Days Without an Accident" (season four) 91, 112
"This Sorrowful Life" (season three) 34, 103
Thomas-Hunt, Melissa C. 20n21
Tobin 97, 99
"Too Far Gone" (season four) 98
Toy Story (film) 33
trauma 100, 104, 105, 115; *see also* abuse
tribalism: fascism *versus* 160; globalism *versus* 158–159; non-tribal communities 159–160; place and 158–159, 160; race and 161–162; real world and 156–157, 158–159; Rick and 158, 161–162; sexuality and 161; violence and 160–161; *see also* sectarianism
Trujillo, Nick 56, 63n8
Trump, Donald 40, 156, 159
"Try" (season five) 49
Tucker and Dale vs. Evil (film) 31
"Twice as Far" (season six) 58, 106n14
Two Broke Girls (TV show) 57
Tyreese: Andrea and 151n11; Carol and 86; death 39–40, 51, 117; feminine traits 86; "The Grove" and 74, 101; Maggie and 124; masculinity and 4, 38, 50–51; Michonne

and 124; motherhood and 86; prison and 64n13; race and stereotypes and 4, 27, 28; Rick compared 46, 51; as victim-hero 34; violence and 50–51

Uncle Tom's Cabin (Stowe) 24
"Us" (season four) 36, 40, 96, 106n14, 160
utilitarianism 12
utopianism 1, 65, 157, 162, 162n8

"Vatos" (season one) 22, 45
victim-heroes 31, 32, 34–35, 40, 74, 79, 108, 116, 117; *see also* suffering
violence and aggression: Claimers and 97; class and 114; fans and 17, 62; fatherhood and 46; gender and 67; gothic and 108; leaders and 36; magical negro and 38–39; masculinity and 3, 12–13, 47–52; Old West iconography and 66, 67; paternalism and 4, 7–8, 49–50; power currencies and 16; sexuality and 7–8, 119–120; social exchange theory and 3; tribalism and 160–161; vulnerability *versus* 67, 74; zombies and 148; *see also* domestic violence; fascism; fire; Michonne *and other characters*; punishment; rape
Vollum, Scott 66
Vossen, Emma 123, 143
vulnerability and weakness: aggression *versus* 67, 74; Beth and 115; Carol and 83, 87, 99, 101; civilization and 56; Daryl and 96; Glenn and 61; Maggie and 91; Michonne and 70–71; nonhuman savages and 115; protective paternalism and 46; *see also* emotions (feelings); passivity

Waits, Tom 111
walkers 15, 35, 37, 103–104, 109
The Walking Dead Magazine 125
Walpole, Horace 108
Wampler, Scott 15
Wayne, Michael L. 44–45
weakness *see* vulnerability and weakness
"The Well" (season seven) 106n14
"What Happened" (season five) 50, 117
"What Lies Ahead" (season two) 38, 97
"When the Dead Come Knocking" (season three) 38, 60–61, 110, 131, 135
whiteness: characters of color compared 48–49; civilization and 37; Glenn and 62–63; hyperreal hillbilly and 32–33, 38; leadership and 58; magical negro and 27; marginalized males and 31–32; masculinity and 56–58; patriarchy and 162n4; sexuality and 123
Wicked Little Things (film) 79
wilderness 6, 66, 76, 95, 96, 156
"Wildfire" (season one) 103, 146
Williams, Linda 32, 34
Williams, Serena 77n11
Williams, Venus 77n11
Winter's Bone (film) 31

Wolves 56, 99
Woodbury 18, 19, 40, 56, 61, 82, 111, 112, 126; *see also* the Governor
working-class southern whites 31
writing 111–113, 115

Yeun, Steven 54, 55, 59, 60
Young, P. Ivan 94
Yu, Phil 59

Zach 112
zombies: black 57; children 79, 80; clothing and 113; colorblindness and 48; emotion and 149; motherhood and 79; queers and 8, 148–151, 152*nn*23,37; whiteness and 56–57; *see also* Sophia *and other zombies*